Occupying
PRIVILEGE

ONVERSATIONS ON LOVE, RACE & LIBERATION

BY JLOVE CALDERÓN

Top row, left to right:

Pedro Noguera, Sonia Sanchez, Jeff Chang, Ariel Luckey, Talib Kweli, Margery Freeman, Jeff Hitchcock

Second row from top, left to right:

April R. Silver, Perry Greene, Inga Muscio, Eddie Ellis, Sofia Quintero, Tim Wise, Arnette Ball

Third row from top, left to right:

Jonny 5, Marcella Runell Hall, Jared Ball, Peggy McIntosh, Baba Israel, Chelsea Gregory, Richard Chavolla

Bottom row, left to right:

Z! Gonwa Haukeness, M1, Danny Hoch, Esther Armah, Chris Crass, DJ Kuttin Kandi, Héctor Calderón

Please note: Not all contributors are pictured.

❧ *Love-N-Liberation Press* ❧

Library of Congress Catalog-in-Publication Data

Calderón, Jennifer.
Occupying privilege: conversations on love, race, & liberation /
Jennifer Calderón.
Includes index.
TX 7-553-592   2012
ISBN-13: 978-0-6156-3933-8
ISBN-10:   0-6156-3933-X

Cover Design & Layout: Nikki Orzel

Praise for Occupying Privilege

"JLove Calderón addresses the often-ignored reality of "white privilege" and all that comes with it. If we are going to progress into an age of true equality and fairness everyone must examine how we can aspire to become a post-racial society."

   -*Russell Simmons*

"*Occupying Privilege* is a necessary weapon in the war against unearned privilege and unmerited suffering. This volume—which brings together some of the most brilliant, committed, and principled cultural workers on the planet—provides us with the tools for thinking, struggling, and loving our way into new forms of freedom, justice and healing. This book is an instant classic!"

   -*Marc Lamont Hill*, author of *The Classroom and the Cell: Conversations on Black Life in America.*

"In *Occupying Privilege*, JLove weaves together a multi-genre journey of political memoir, anthology, history lesson, and 'how to' for the radical yet necessary vision of global liberation for all people. Get it, spread it, do it."

   -*Richard Nash*, ex-Publisher, Soft Skull Press

"JLove radiantly intertwines personal journeys of struggle, power, privilege, transformation, and agency— crafting a powerful, inspiring, useful, and healing message situated in social justice, love, and liberation. *Occupying Privilege* is a much needed and insightful dialogue by some of today's most courageous, authentic, creative, and influential voices."

   -*Michael Benitez Jr.*, social justice educator, activist, scholar

"When privilege is a way of life it can become over looked. Occupying Privilege enables white men and women to peer into a lens through which they never thought to look. By having these honest conversations, we will become a better nation."

   -*Michael Skolnik*, Editor-In-Chief of GlobalGrind.com

"In this timely anthology, JLove has brought together some of the greatest thinkers of our generation to tackle one of the most vital and often overlooked topics of the day."

   -*Ben Synder,* writer, producer

"Original, fresh, and inspiring; a useful tool in the fight against racial injustice."

   -*Eddie Moore, Jr.* Founder/Program Director of The White Privilege Conference

When you Occupy Privilege you'll discover:

- ❖ A deeper look at issues, such as the media, education, and the criminal justice system, through the lens of race and privilege— knowledge is power!

- ❖ The stories and struggles of people of color, their own relationships to privilege, and how they are undoing it one poem, flow, rhyme, letter, beat, and day at a time. Here, the personal is political.

- ❖ How not to drown in the guilt of the history of whiteness in America. You are not alone in this work!

Buy this book, support a movement! 100% of the proceeds from the first year of sales go to these six non-profit organizations fighting for racial justice and liberation.

Rebel Diaz Arts Collective: A Hip-Hop community center in the South Bronx, NY that provides a safe space for cultural exchanges through performances, educational workshops, and multi-media training.
www.rdacbx.org (Bronx, NYC)

Groundwork: A white anti-racist collective dismantling white supremacy to achieve racial justice in our communities.
www.groundworkmadison.wordpress.com (Madison, WI)

The Alliance of White Anti-Racists Everywhere(AWARE-LA): is an alliance of white anti-racist people working together to challenge racism and work for racial justice in transformative alliance with people of color. We take collective action to build white anti-racist and multiracial alliances to challenge the white supremacist system and all systems of oppression.
www.awarela.org (Los Angeles, CA)

The People's Institute for Survival and Beyond: An organization that focuses on understanding what racism is, where it comes from, how it functions, why it persists and how it can be undone.
www.pisab.org (New Orleans, LA)

El Puente: New York's most comprehensive Latino arts and cultural center inspiring and nurturing leadership for peace and justice.
www.elpuente.us (Brooklyn, NYC)

Catalyst: A center for political education and movement building. Committed to anti-racist work with mostly white sections of left/radical social movements with the goal of deepening anti-racist commitment in white communities and building multiracial left movements for liberation.
www.collectiveliberation.org (San Francisco, CA)

Other Titles by JLove:

We Got Issues!
A Young Woman's Guide to a Bold, Courageous, and Empowered Life

By Rha Goddess and JLove Calderón
Published by New World Library, 2005

That White Girl

By JLove
Published by Atria (a division of Simon and Schuster), 2007

Conscious Women Rock the Page:
Using Hip-Hop Fiction to Incite Social Change

by Black Artemis, E-Fierce, JLove and Marcella
Published by Sister Outsider Entertainment, 2008

Love, Race and Liberation; 'Til the White Day is Done

Edited by JLove Calderón and Marcella Runell Hall
Published by Love-N-Liberation Press, 2010

Table of Contents

In Loving Memory

Kibibi Dillon

Trayvon Martin

Foreword

❧ *It's Bigger than Privilege* ❧

By *Jonny 5 (of the Flobots)*

There's a conversation I've witnessed a few different times in a few different places.

The first person in the conversation has been the same person each time, Dr. Vincent Harding, a man whom I consider to be a mentor. He plays this role not just for me, but for many others, numbering probably in the hundreds. He was a friend and associate of Martin Luther King Jr. and a historian and thinker of the southern freedom movement. Today, at age 75, he continues to be involved in movement building, in preserving the histories of elders, in encouraging and lifting up the work of young people, and in building bridges among all of us.

The second person in the conversation has been different on each occasion. Like me, person number two has been white, but he or she is usually much older. These various second people in the conversation are always individuals who have dedicated their lives to combatting racism. They are progressive white people who in both word and deed have committed themselves to a lifetime of trying to make things right.

The conversation goes something like this. In a public discussion, the progressive white friend uses the phrase "White Privilege." My mentor, in response, begins by recognizing the importance of open disagreement among friends. He then refers to the phrase and asks:

"Why is it a privilege to oppress people?"

❖ ❖ ❖

When I first met Dr. Harding, I was an attending an Ivy League college. I was also a white rapper.

At the time I made a point of calling what I did "rap" and not "Hip-Hop," because I had virtually nothing in common with the creators of Hip-Hop. I did not come up organically from the culture, not even the local culture in Denver, where I grew up. I couldn't claim to have taken my inspiration from the classics. (My first tape had been Young M.C.) All I knew was that from the second I started writing rhymes, I loved it. More than anything else I was doing, writing rhymes was a way for me to process my world on a daily basis and have it make sense.

But in the post-Ice, pre-Em era, I felt that I had some explaining to do, and the first person I had to convince was myself. Was it really okay for me to perform this art form I had not helped create?

Yes, I decided. It had to be, because there was no way I was going to give it up. In exchange for what it gave me, though, I had to find a way to give back. So I made a promise to myself that I would listen carefully to the lyrics, to the stories and messages in the music. I would tune in to the Black CNN not for the thrill of the curse words but to learn about the struggles faced by those who had created this music. I would identify the wrongs, and I would do my best to right them. I would become an activist.

What kind of activist? I didn't know. But, in the late 90s on my college campus I learned quickly that being an activist meant immersing myself in the theory of identity, oppression, and privilege. So I dove into the swirl of forums, dialogues, panels, and conversations taking place on campus, joining a multiracial cast of other students trying to make sense of things.

The framework of privilege provided a language that I had long been missing. My high school had been nearly half people of color, and yet the honors classes, by senior year, were nearly entirely white. My frustration with this situation had prompted me to sign up for African-American Studies and join the school's Pan-African Club. I had selected as my senior quote a sentence from a book called "For Whites Only" by Robert Terry, which I'd come across rummaging through the "Black Studies" section of our neighborhood's posh but beloved bookstore. "Racial unrest has its root causes in white attitudes and white institutions…the time has come to attack the causes of the racial crisis, not its victims."

Now I had the words of academics to affirm that my inklings were correct. Rather than being the one weirdo with the super-serious senior quote, I was surrounded by other people who recognized the same realities. That felt good. But there was something else about our collective application of the theory that did not feel good.

I noticed it first in myself. The ability to analyze and critique the privileges associated with my many identities had developed into a desire to prove that I was "not like them." In order to prove this, I found myself closing myself to perspectives of other white people who were not yet "enlightened" like I was, lest my openness be mistaken for agreement. I sought approval from people who I believed to be experiencing "real" oppression. (Who else was qualified to tell me if I was doing a good job?) I later realized that the very folks I was looking to for approval were themselves playing a similar game, jockeying for authentic status, hoping no one would call them out on their private school education, their white parent, or any other marker of privilege.

As we sought to transform theory into action, the divisions deepened. The actions served as props for us to declare who we would and wouldn't talk to. We turned our backs on each other and ourselves. We'd been given tools to dismantle injustice, but we'd used them to dismantle trust.

In retrospect, it is obvious that we were asking for too much from theory.

When I met Dr. Harding, he did not talk to me about theory. He shared stories of real people. He demonstrated a deep knowledge of unknown figures who made history. He spoke from seven decades of experience. And he conveyed something that was almost entirely new to me.

Wisdom.

The questions that I had been asking on campus—what to do, who to talk to, how to be—were not questions best approached through theory. They needed a deeper sort of guidance, communicated best not through explaining, but through modeling.

Dr. Harding had what it took to provide this guidance, to model what it means to orient oneself towards liberation while rooting oneself fully in compassion. He had nothing to prove to me and no interest in demonstrating he was "not like" anyone. Perhaps these tendencies had been present in him before at some earlier time in his life, but if so, there was no longer any trace of them.

From our first conversations, his respect and encouragement for me made it clear that he saw relationships as valuable investments and that he placed great hope in developing the potential of young people, such as myself. As I was able to spend more time with him, something changed in my sense of identity, something that allowed me to escape what I believe King was referring to when he spoke of "the paralysis of analysis." In effect, I decided to spend less energy examining my privilege and more energy dismantling white supremacy.

❖ ❖ ❖

So why talk about privilege?

In this book you will find plenty of reasons. In my story, the language and theoretical framework of privilege was the scaffolding I climbed in order to take my first step.

But for me, there was a crucial next step. Identifying myself as a holder of privilege was not enough. I needed to transform myself into a seeker of liberation. And, I think the crux of this paradigm shift is contained in Dr. Harding's initial question.

"Why is it a privilege to oppress others?"

I have thought a lot about what he was saying. Surely, he wasn't denying the existence of a system in which white people receive preferential treatment. I think, instead, he was rejecting the idea that these advantages or, rather, that these *benefits* or, rather, (it's hard to come up with a word that doesn't have a positive connotation) that these injustices constitute something desirable. He is objecting to the idea that being white is a privilege.

Let's think this through for a second.

It's one thing to declare that my liberation is tied up in someone else's, that no one is free while others are oppressed. That is the beautiful symbiotic interdependence of MLK's dream and legacy, the root assumption that oppressing others does not feel good, nor does it lead to anything good. It's easy for us today to see that segregated seating is not a privilege, because it would keep us all apart from our friends!

But what happens when my skin color gets me a job interview? Or my "white" speech patterns make a potential landlord more comfortable on the phone? Or my Anglo last name insulates me from "random" searches at the airport? Can we really say that a white person getting a taxi first while others are passed by is not receiving a privilege? That they are not, in fact, more free? Consider the extent to which the ebb and flow of our daily lives consists of a myriad mundane interactions with strangers and how their unexamined biases, fears, and prejudices can impact our progress, achievements, and mood. If the invisible knapsack (more about this from Peggy McIntosh on page 29) gets me further in my journey—isn't that a privilege? If I end up with more money, nicer housing, and arrive at my destination first, how can that be anything but "privilege"?

To declare these unearned advantages anything but a privilege seems almost anachronistic.

But what would it mean to try? I don't mean just to reject the privileges themselves, but to reject even the idea that they represent privilege.

It would mean appealing to another reality altogether. It would mean living a life that transcends "getting ahead." It would mean evaluating ourselves on more than our material success. It would mean valuing more than our daily progress, achievements, or even our mood.

It would mean assessing resources, like loans, housing, employment, police protection, and public policies not just by whether they work for you but by whether they work for everyone.

It would mean a set of things that are easy to say but very difficult to do.

Why is it a privilege to oppress others?

Because the world we live in is compartmentalized, individualized, and competitive, and because we're told that's the way it has to be.

But another world is possible, one that is interdependent, communal, and cooperative. Building it up is hard work, maybe even impossible, but it is what my mentor has called on me to do.

If we're going to be successful, we will have to learn to transcend white privilege.

But first, we're going to have to talk about it.

"Identifying myself as a holder of privilege was not enough. I needed to transform myself into a seeker of liberation."

Introduction

My deepest desire is that every human being has the opportunity to reach his or her highest potential. White supremacy, interwoven into the fabric of American culture, institutions, society, and the mindsets of citizens, does not allow this to happen. I believe we have the ability to collectively eradicate this inequality.

To that end, this book brings together an eclectic group of people who have been influential in the public conversation about race, privilege, and justice. You'll find voices from the black, white, Native American, Latino, and Asian communities; you'll hear from rappers, academics, playwrights, poets, queer folk, straight folk, gender fluid folk, black nationalists, white Jews, working class, working poor, middle-class, educated, and everyday people who care about doing the right thing. I've collected their ideas, their words, and their artistry so that you, whoever you are, picking up this book, might walk along this path of liberation and justice for all a little more steadily than I have.

Maybe you'll stumble a little less; maybe you'll find joy a little more. Whatever the case, I hope that what you find in the pages that follow inspires you to have the courage to act so that all may be free.

To Truth, Love, Freedom, and Liberation for all people and the planet.

JLove

Chapter 1

❦ *What's the Big Deal, Anyway?* ❦

I never truly understood racism until I was a freshman in college.

I knew that prejudice, stereotypes, and hate existed. I was certainly aware that a lot of people didn't like it when I dated black guys. I had friends told by guidance counselors to get a GED instead of a high school diploma and saw my crew consistently targeted by cops. All of that was apparent. But, I didn't comprehend the systems, ideologies, and policies discriminating against, targeting, and oppressing people of color while simultaneously giving white people unfair and unearned advantages—white people like me.

When it was time to pick a college, I was desperate to leave my hometown. Good girl gone bad had ended up with too many rivals and my best friend and my boyfriend locked up. If I stayed, there was no place to go but down. Survival depended on the ability to re-invent myself, so California became my new home.

I was completely out of my element when I arrived on the huge, almost entirely white campus. My roomie's one goal was to become a Little Sister of the most popular white fraternity on campus. Rock music bounced off the walls of my dorm. What could we possibly talk about? This may sound weird coming from a white girl, but there were some fundamental cultural-relatedness issues that were difficult for me.

Now, there's nothing wrong with white people. Some of my best friends are white. But I was raised multiculturally, influenced by both white communities and communities of color, and, more specifically, Hip-Hop culture. It wasn't that I didn't get along with most of the white folks I was surrounded by; it's that we were into different things. For no other reason than to have more diversity, I signed up for African-American studies classes. I wish I could say it happened differently.

Mind you, there were white kids into Hip-Hop with whom I did kick it, and they were my salvation. (Of course, there was a little drama, that "white on white" hate that happens to those who feel the need to be the coolest white kid on the block.) For the most part, however, I ran with a multicultural crew that ranged from gang-bangers gone college and graffiti artists gone political muralists to just straight up Hip-Hop lovers. My crew became my sanity, but what happened during my classes changed my life.

Never before had I seen, heard, read about, and discussed the staggering magnitude of white supremacy's impact. I knew the story, but the atrocities revisited in detail caused physical and emotional pain so deep that a profound despair remains locked in my body to this day. I walked around depressed for several semesters, got drunk, smoked weed, did Ecstasy when I had enough money, and mourned. I mourned my ignorance and the ignorance of most white people. I mourned those who died because of racism. I mourned for our country. Afraid to move forward, apologizing myself into invisibility, I was trapped in the paralysis of analysis. I tried so hard to be different, as if present-day consciousness could erase the past. It was all I was equipped to do at that point.

Who was I helping in acting like a victim? Who benefited from me being small? In internalizing white peoples' collective sins, did I change racism by hating myself for being white? I think you know the answer. It took time to pull myself out. That time was spent acknowledging the role of my people in the history of oppression. I can't take it back. I can only learn from it, yes?

And, imagine, I am the privileged one.

❖❖❖

Before Inga, there weren't many smart white female role models of my generation actively interrupting racism, let alone doing it well. (Not to say there weren't smart white girls out there doin' it, I just didn't have the awareness of that community yet.) Her style attracted me immediately. She wrote powerful stories that brought home the devastating impact of racism with unparalleled wit, and she became someone I could count on to speak with a bold, unwavering voice. What was different about Inga was that she was effective at getting her message across in white communities in ways I never experienced. Her accessible language, ease with herself, general friendliness—all those characteristics let people in and me in. She tells the plain ol' truth without a hidden agenda, allowing an opening for white people to engage in a different way. If we can agree that racism exists without triggering blame, shame, or guilt, maybe we can break this system down a bit more quickly.

She gives it to you like it is, no sugar or cherry on top. But it still tastes good if you let yourself appreciate the information. Welcome to Inga.

⧉ Can I Post-Racistly Touch Your Hair? ⧉

By *Inga Muscio*

The day after Obama became president-elect, the wife came home from work and threw her bag on the floor. Hyperventilating.

"Dang, what's wrong with you?" I said.

"I don't know if I can deal with white people for the next four years," she said. "I think I might go crazy."

The wife is trailer trash (as she says) from the Florida Panhandle. She understands the failings, psychology, and duplicities of white folks pretty good. Hailing from such hearty, racist (complete with mammy collection) stock, she sees the mainstream passive-aggressive, namby-pamby, normative, racist shit coming from at least forty acres and a mule away.

She went on to tell the tale of her boss's arrival at work that morning.

"She comes in wearing a brown suit, brown shoes, brown purse. She even had brown eyeshadow and a brown clip in her hair. I really didn't think anything of it until she announces: 'I'm wearing all brown today in honor of Obama!'"

"Yeah that's normal," I said. "Black folks all wore ivory cashmere when Bush stole two elections."

No one was in any mood for my jokes, but this news was so appalling, I couldn't stop myself. Part of my survival strategy in this violently racist society involves inappropriate humor. In this case, the wisecracks lined up like 2nd graders in the hot lunch line.

"Did she bring everybody watermelon and fried chicken for lunch? Did she sign off on all her emails with 'I have a dream'?"

"This shit is not funny," the wife hollered, sending the hot lunch line scattering. "White people are going to spend the next four years pretending like racism is so over."

One last 2nd grader popped into the cafeteria:

"Yeah, I mean, when you get right down to the nitty-gritty of things, it's hardly really even been a problem at all. Shouldn't take much more than the appearance of a black president to fix it all."

"I'm gonna claw my fucking face off," she said. "This is gonna be out of control."

I understood "this" to mean white normative racism. In my second book, *Autobiography of a Blue-Eyed Devil: My Life and Times in a Racist Imperialist Society*, I defined white normative racism thusly:

> White normativity is a debilitating and widespread condition/ affliction where the assumption of whiteness and the overall goodness of whiteness is, uh, normal. Not unlike cancer or poverty, white normativity manifests in fractalized, endless scenarios. Racism, hate groups, legal and illegal lynching, tokenism, and economic, sexual, and legal slavery all exist within white normativity. It gives these forms of oppression an environment in which to thrive. White normativity itself, however, is generally an innocuous, day-to-day, moment-by-moment assumption that whiteness is the accepted standard of worth for everyone on the planet.

Yes, a black president sure changed America for good: "It's called post-racism! Strike up the band, we've seen the light! We get it! How dare you call me racist! Don't you see my fist bump?" White folks collectively screamed as we watched the new president festivities on television, where white commentators were wondering aloud what would "happen" to Michelle Obama's hair if it rained during the inaugural parade. "Will her hair keep its shape? Does it even get wet?"

This may seem trifling. What does it matter if some white news commentators are curious about Michelle Obama's hair? Does something so insignificant really mean someone is racist? Isn't it just an innocent question?

This hair fascination thing is fascinating.

Ask any black person and he or she will tell you that they don't appreciate white people freaking out about their hair (that is, when it wasn't life-endangering to do so). And yet, white folks will not relent on this. We will not let it go, we will not listen, and we will not shut the fuck up about black people's hair.

I haven't noticed a cultural phenomena where people of color are perpetually "innocently fascinated" with white people's hair, which leads me to believe that this is not an innate human curiosity. It is, in fact, a pesky minion within the vastly populated ranks of the dreaded Unexamined Learned Behaviors.

A black person has never asked me if they could touch my hair, whereas I have witnessed and/or heard of this cultural phenomena happening to many black folks—especially children. I can't count the number of times I have cringed in the grocery store, overhearing white women discuss a toddler's hair. "Ooo! Those poofball ponytails are just so cute! I have to squeeze them!!!"

I know if I went to Japan or Kenya, my hair and skin might be of note. I get otherness. I experienced otherness every day when I had a job, delivering milk. I loaded my van, cruising through busy crowds of people at the Pike Place Market in Seattle. Certain tourists found this activity to be picturesque and took photos and videos of me with my hand truck and whatnot. This bothered me, but not enough to say anything other than, "Please get out of my way." It's merely annoying to be viewed as nothing more than a backdrop for someone's breathtakingly exotic vacation. But when people had their kids pose near me while I was carting a hand truck loaded with five cases of milk in glass bottles, I raised a serious ruckus. It's one thing to refuse to see people as living, breathing entities leading complex lives, and it's quite another to actively not see someone to the point of imperiling your child's life.

So, I understand going to some relatively homogeneous culture where people might marvel at my hair. The U.S., however, is kinda known for not being homogeneous. Lotsa people live here. Black folks have lived here for 500 years. One of the first things almost any black person will say if you ask them what annoys the fuck out of them is this: "White people wanting to touch my hair." If you are a news commentator, how can you not know this? You have to actively not see in order to be a grown-up person wondering what Michelle Obama's hair will do in the rain. That is why these small, insignificant things are, indeed, racist. They reside within an unconsidered racist consciousness that most white folks inherit in this society. In recognizing this legacy one sees quite clearly that Michelle Obama's hair in the rain is not abnormal, whereas wondering about it on national television or touching a child's hair in the grocery store is.

In a considered consciousness, where learned behaviors are unearthed and found to be patently absurd, the desire to comment on Michelle Obama's hair or to squeeze a toddler's ponytails is completely absent.

The unexamined learned behaviors that many whites "innocently" espouse around black people's hair represent one of millions of interchangeable cultural constructs.

The thing with unexamined learned behaviors is they can easily be replaced with healthier behaviors. Learned behaviors are interchangeable, mix-and-matchable, just like clean panties.

Pathological abnormalities and the attendant unexamined learned behaviors of white normativity lead a white woman to make a fashion statement by wearing brown to "honor" Obama. And, she'd likely suffer honest-to-god befuddlement if she had the opportunity to witness the horror and anger her idea inspired in others. This particular woman did not have this opportunity, because the wife knew good and well that her boss would only be confused. Plus, as everyone who does apprehend the nature of the dominant culture knows, there's a good chance your pay check will stop when you go up against this shit.

It is one of those of Catch-22s.

No matter how articulately you lay it out about exactly why it is morbidly offensive to honor Obama by wearing brown, for instance, the confused person will remain confused, and all of your efforts will be a total waste of time. You will become the topic of conversation. You will be named as the problem. You will be called "uptight," "touchy," or "overly sensitive." In days gone past if you were white you might have been called a "nigger-lover," and if you were not white you might have lost your life or freedom.

This change can be viewed as "progress" if one is willing to overlook the fact that community shunning is the end result no matter what the term du jour is.

Revered scholar Neely Fuller once said, "If you don't understand White

Supremacy (racism), what it is and how it works, then everything else you think you know will only confuse you."

While millions of white folks are committed to—if not champing at the bit for—a "post-racism" time, few seem willing to see our own racism, how it operates inside our hearts, and the difficult work that is required in order to uproot it.

There are many kinds of racism and hatreds, and whites are not the only folks who choose to engage with the world in this way. However, and this is a big however, white folks, whether consciously or not, inherit a life in the dominant culture, and if that is not reckoned with white racism will continue as it has for the past 500 years in the Americas.

I know we're not lazy.

Folks know how to put in the work.

And, I know we're not cowards, at least not when we're facing off with external monsters. It's the internal monsters we don't have a lot of inclination, much less skills, to contend with.

What seems to be going on with whites folks is we've found a kind of comfort in understanding racism to involve crosses burning on the lawn, not being allowed to sit at the lunch counter, and including the word "nigger" in one's lexicon. It's difficult to see the breadth of racism in our culture when one is best served by not seeing it.

This is a choice, and in that choice is the only "benefit" of white privilege. One has the luxury of actively not seeing, meanwhile cashing in on, the white supremacist racism that surrounds us.

It seems not to matter how well one lays out the history and contemporary reality of white normative and supremacist racism. If folks aren't willing to look inside our hearts to try to see how the legacy of racism has infiltrated our lives, we just won't see it.

Instead, we're confused.

Or worse, defensive.

I have spoken about racism at hundreds of colleges across America. I spoke recently on the above-mentioned subject of white people's abnormal fixation on black folks' hair. I thought this was a pretty clear example, and certainly many of the white students seemed to think about it. Nevertheless, one young man felt like it was a good idea to tell me about a white friend of his who had adopted four black children. One day, he went by to visit, and the woman told him to touch the hair of one of the toddlers. He saw nothing wrong with this.

"So," I said, "you wouldn't mind being raised by someone who invites her friends to objectify you?"

No, no, no, he explained to me, there was no objectification! She was just giving him the opportunity to have a different experience! It was not racist at all!

Why should a child, any child, who is at the mercy of an adult for sustenance, caring, and love, be the object of someone else's opportunity?

Keeping with the theme of racial ignorance, what if a white kid was being raised by a black woman and she invited all her friends over to watch him dance? "Yeah, we're having a party and the main event is watching how badly white people dance, even when they're only nine! This is quite a learning opportunity for y'all!"

I laid out this scenario for the student, and he thought it would be cruel if a black woman were to do this. Yet he stood by his claim that the invitation to touch a child's hair was well-intentioned. To help me understand this, he cited Lewis and Clark. Evidently, one of the indigenous people was on an expedition to "rub the paint off" of a black man traveling with them.

Here's a word of wisdom for white college students: If we are having a discussion about racism, do not cite Lewis and Clark.

It will shatter your world.

I understand this young man wanted to negate my words because they did not fit in with the historical narrative he had come to understand throughout his life. My points about white folks touching black folk's hair stuck in his craw. If it was not okay to other-ize the hair of a black child, then what his friend did was wrong. But in order for that to be wrong, a lot of other things must also be wrong. He could trace his friend's action towards the child in her care all the way back to Lewis and Clark, and if all of that was wrong, where did it leave this young man?

Well, for starters, in a netherworld of confusion, a lá Neely Fuller.

Does this mean that all of the studying he did for his sixth grade history test was in vain? Does this mean his senior year report on Reconstruction was a hugely tedious indoctrinational exercise? Does this mean his high school teacher who excoriated Custer's murderers was biased?

Why, yes.

Yes, on all of the above.

When discussing history—things that involve founding, discovering, allegiances, and exploring—it is a great idea to first delve deeply into indigenous, Asian-American, and black narratives. Irish, Jewish, and Italian immigrants have great perspectives too. Most of us growing up here are taught a generic, freedom-lovin' white man's perspective on history—flag sewin' and constitution-signin' revolutionaries. Sure, they were revolutionaries. How hard is it to revolt against people an ocean away? Okay, it was hard. It sucked. But, so did the need for an underground railroad.

When I was a kid, I wanted to know how the Underground Railroad operated. How, exactly, did Harriet Tubman do it? I wanted every single detail, every nuance, every character involved. I wanted the same volume of information that was afforded to me about the Revolutionary War. I did not have that because the Underground Railroad doesn't go with the generic "white man" narrative. But it had to be stuck in there because Harriet Tubman (and many other folks) are simply impossible to ignore. Mentioning a black hero or two is fine, but that's where whites draw the line and get back to the real story of our nation's founding 'n continuation. Most of the texts we study for historical facts and exams were written by like-minded white men, who went to college for many years in order to get this particular story straight.

Let's say John Wayne Gacy—the Chicago rapist and serial killer responsible for the deaths of at least thirty-three teenage boys—lived 300 years ago. Let's say he orchestrated a huge uprising against the British, along with all the other crimes he committed. His act of heroism would outshine his many acts of depravity. If the story of American Independence could not be told without including John Wayne Gacy's uprising, then he would be included and lauded in history, and all of his other crimes would be ignored. Sad but true.

Okay, now just apply that thinking to Christopher Columbus, Andrew Jackson, Henry Ford, William Randolph Hearst, and many, many more men of history who were single-handedly responsible for crimes against humanity. Prescott Bush (father of one president, grandfather of another) stole Geronimo's earthly remains (they remain at Yale to this day) and went on to fund Nazi dreams in Germany, so throw in Prescott Bush and all his issues.

We think of John Wayne Gacy as a bad man, and yet he was responsible for far fewer deaths than most "heroes" of the history we've been taught to revere. Rape, sexual torture, enslavement, and senseless murder were active pastimes in the founding of our nation. (And they're still pretty popular today, too.) But for the most part, we don't read too much about those things in our standard history books…Hmmm.

Citing Lewis and Clark's expedition in order to rationalize present-day micro-atrocities is a dearly beloved mechanism that is frequently employed to depict racism as justifiable.

This mechanism can be represented as a work of art:

The word "shit" is formed on a surface—such as a piece of cardboard, plywood, or marble—using actual fecal matter as the medium in which to spell out the word. It is a tactile representation of itself. This image flashes into my mind whenever someone does stuff, like cite Lewis and Clark to justify a white woman objectifying a black child, so it's sometimes fun to be me.

Here, in no particular order, are five Shit Cites Shit historical justifications, along with my No Shit interpretations, based on years of studying the history of my country from as many perspectives as I can find:

1. Shit: Reconstruction's failure was due to black folks being, well, not exactly lazy, just mildly incompetent. I mean, they tried and all. It just didn't work out for them.

No shit: After the Northern Mechanized Industrialists vs. Southern Plantation Slavers War, also known as the Civil War, black folks were only relatively safe while the National Guard hung around. As soon as the federal government removed the National Guard from southern states, whites set to work destroying every black community and government in existence. It was an organically occurring movement within the collective consciousness of whites. Over the next decade or so, black communities were systematically destroyed. The KKK got their uniform down, and whites hunted black leaders, lynched innocent young men, destroyed entire communities, and sabotaged every effort and stellar achievement of entire populations (see below). In this time, from 1878 to 1898, Ida B. Wells recorded 1.4 lynchings a day, for a total of 10,000 of these crimes against humanity. She met with President McKinley and told him about it, but he cared about as much as G.W. Bush cared about the men being held in Guantanamo.

And Ida B. Wells probably knew that, but she went and told him about it anyway.

2. Shit: There were "race riots" in Tulsa, Oklahoma (1921); New Orleans, Louisiana (1866); Wilmington North Carolina (1898); and pretty much every other black community that came into being during the relatively short period of Reconstruction.

No shit: "Race riot" is a term of comfort that whites use. It actually means whites massacring blacks. What generally happened was a married white woman was on the verge of getting outed for fucking the milkman, so she unimaginatively accused a black man of raping her. Or, someone tells the sheriff a young man whistled at her. Or some white man just made the story up, using his sexually molested daughter as evidence. In almost every case of whites destroying black communities, white women were somehow being avenged. (It's funny how we come in handy at certain times.) In the case of Tulsa, whites fire-bombed the black community…Using airplanes. This was after they deputized each other and murdered every black person they could hunt down. Every time you hear the term "race riot," watch the movie Rosewood.

Some communities, such as the Faubourg Treme in New Orleans, have been destroyed by laws and freeway construction, cleaving through the main local commerce street. South Central Los Angeles was destroyed when Ronald Reagan closed all of the local factories and crack cocaine made its debut. Property taxes snuffed Harlem. White folks have become much less violent and much more imaginative when it comes to destroying black communities.

I guess we call this progress too.

3. Shit: The indigenous people were savage heathen bastards who ate each other's babies.

No shit: Adolf Hitler has nothing on Manifest Destiny's holocaust. Hitler only had four or five years to kill Catholics, artists, homos, black folks, Nazi-resisters, Romani, and Jews. Whites in the Americas have, willy-nilly, spent the past 500 years killing native people.

4. Shit: The indigenous people weren't making use of the land.

No shit: Well maybe, if we asked nicely, their descendents might be willing to teach us a thing or two because we've sure made use of the land. Our livestock and farming practices disease our food and parch the earth. Entire species have been wiped out. The birds are suffering migratory devastation due to man-made climate changes, and the bees don't get on much past their toddler years these days. Bats are having a tough time of it, too. We have definitely used the land in a way the indigenous people did not. In the 100+ short years since the industrial revolution we have sucked almost every last resource out of the earth.

Meanwhile, indigenous folks managed to live here for over 10,000 years without pushing any other species into extinction, blowing up mountains, or annihilating entire eco-systems to grab a buck.

5. Shit: The slaves came from black Africans who sold them. We were just buying something that was for sale.

Related shit: The only reason the military makes video games is because there's a demand. Kids want the military to make videos. "We in the military would have never thought of this idea except kids kept bugging us to make a video game that indoctrinates them into soldier-dom."

That is also why *Grand Theft Auto* exists. Kids just naturally love to pretend to spray bullets and slaughter folks.

Also: "We here in Hollywood produce hilariously racist or vengefully, often sexually, violent movies because that's what people want."

We are all just selling something people want to buy.

"Columbine? We and the gun industry have nothing to do with that. Those were a few bad apples, like at Abu Ghraib."

No shit: The indoctrinational practices of this predator-consumer mentality have been handed down from generation to generation, long before slaving ships landed on African shores; since before a king in England decided he could "buy" land that did not belong to him. How can you "buy" something that belongs to itself? Maybe the Romans are the ones who started viewing the earth and everyone on it as items on shelves to be carefully considered as potential commodities before purchasing. All this is palmed off as normal, so our own predator-consumerism is therefore difficult to discern. But it is there, causing confusion, and keeping this social disease called racism alive in our hearts.

Racism has a "post" after a generation or so manages to re-educate ourself and re-write our histories, knowing where we come from and using that knowledge to decide where we'll go. For this life, it is about every individual facing this ugliness inside of ourselves and in the world, one day at a time.

> *"While millions of white folks are committed to—if not champing at the bit for—a "post-racism" time, few seem willing to see our own racism, how it operates inside our hearts, and the difficult work that is required in order to uproot it."*

❧ Bringing It Home:
White Privilege and Universalizing White Experience ❧
By *Chris Crass*

A Citizen of the White Nation: "Where are all the Black people?"

My family was on vacation, and we had just passed through the Canadian border. I was a little kid; it was the first time I'd been to another country. Looking at all the people at the border check-point, I asked my parents, "Where are all the Black people?" With a confused look, my parents asked me what I was talking about. I assumed that, because we were going to another country, everyone there would be Black because to me at the time the United States was a white country.

In other words, in my little kid's mind, if America was a white country, my "not-America" would be "not-white." Logical enough. The idea that the United States is a society for white people was not a conscious thought explicitly taught to me. I was raised by liberal parents, committed to a pluralistic, multicultural antiracism—beliefs that were very important during my childhood. Most of my friends in elementary school at that time were Latino/a. So why would I assume the United States is a white nation?

I grew up believing that white people were responsible for all of the good things in life, not because I chose to believe this, but because that's just the way it was. On television, in newspapers, in the textbooks in my classes, the posters around school—everywhere I looked—I saw white people occupying positions of respectability and power. According to my history lessons, White people founded this nation, and, over time, white people let other people come into their country, which was really nice of them. It was kind of like letting people stay at your house when they don't have a place of their own. Everything I studied in school reinforced this idea of a white nation. It was white people who invented everything, governed, and wrote the literature, poetry, and drama that gave meaning to life.

There were people of color in my life. My third grade teacher was Black, and most of the kids at school I played with were Mexican, but they didn't have histories, cultures, nations, and stories, so they were white people with different-colored skin. Again, it wasn't that I consciously wondered if there was an African-American historical experience and decided there wasn't. The question never entered my mind because I assumed white history was everyone's history. My common sense understanding of the world was based on the same white supremacy that is the basis for the United States.

The common sense worldview of the U.S. is best represented by the contradictions of Thomas Jefferson, the passionate defender of liberty and freedom. The slave owner who defended State's rights to rule on the question of slavery and resisted attempts to put a time-table on the institution's end. The crusader for democratic government in which everyday people held power at the local level. A leading advocate of the position that African people are genetically inferior to Europeans and incapable of self-governance. A white man who secretly had children with an African woman he owned as a slave and never released, even as others like George Washington released slaves they owned. A founding father who made it clear that this was a nation for white citizens and denounced race mixing. Thomas Jefferson, from a position of political, economic, and cultural power over the vast majority of everyday Americans, maintained these contradictions through profound self-delusion and denial. He remains one of the most popular political figures in U.S. history, and his words, more than those of anyone else, have come to define both the liberatory possibilities and the institutionalized injustice the of the United States.[1]

My common sense understanding of the U.S. was shaped by systemic and collective self-delusion and denial by white people about the reality of this country's history. Additionally, I had a deep belief in democracy and liberty for all people and believed that the U.S. was fully committed to these principles.

I went through life thinking that my experience as a white person with gender and class privilege was the universal experience of all people. This is an important aspect of white supremacy: internalizing white superiority by making oneself normal and everyone else other, outsider, different. It creates a common sense understanding of the world that rationalizes injustice. If all people experience reality as white people do and if there are disproportionate numbers of people of color living in poverty, that can only mean that those people have themselves to blame—because we all have the same opportunities. What does it mean that we all have the same opportunities? It means there's only today. And if you don't like where you are today, well, hey, that has nothing to do with me. Your history (such as it is and if it's even worth considering) has nothing to do with me.

Growing up with this completely unacknowledged mindset, it became logical to reduce historic and institutional economic conditions to "Mexicans are lazy," "Black people are criminals," and "White people work hard." The underlying logic of racist social policy was socialized into me without the need of anyone speaking a word directly about it. And, if anyone brought up the history of white supremacy, the chorus of responses from white authority figures was either, "We can't keep living in the past," or, "Clinging to the past is what is keeping you from succeeding today." My lack of historical understanding led me to agree with those sentiments, because it wasn't that big of a deal to begin with. Everyone had it hard, and you either pull yourself up or blame others for your failure.

As I became politically active in high school, a T-shirt that I used to wear can best summarize my understanding of racism: "Love sees no color." I tried not to see people as Black, Latino/a, Asian American; they were all just people, or so I said to myself.

A colorblind worldview combined with the unconscious (and pervasive) habit of universalizing white experience meant that I still thought everyone was white, just with differently colored skin, but now I would also try to not see their colors at all. To me, "difference" meant a physical characteristic (skin color) that ignorant, prejudiced people still thought signified that some people are better than others. Colorblind meant everyone can be just as good (economically, politically, and culturally) as everyone else, and if they're not, well now, that's their fault.

So rather than explore questions such as why so many Black people are in the prison system, I thought my commitment to antiracism began and ended with not seeing Black people as Black. So it could be reasoned that the only white people who explicitly talked about Black people, including why so many were in prison, were right-wing and often unabashedly racist. People of color who talked about race were told to move on with their lives. So, I believed that the antiracist choice to make was to stop talking about race and to move toward a better future, leaving the past in the past.

At the core of the colorblindness framework is the idea that we are all individuals who have personalities, ambitions, fears, and hopes, but no histories. Yet, it is the history that helps us understand that, while we are all individuals, we are also parts of groups that have different levels of economic, political, and social power in this society. Being colorblind meant that I believed I was furthering the goals of the Civil Rights movement by not seeing groups. Universalizing white experience meant that I did not have a historical grounding to understand the many different histories that shape U.S. history. I was left operating from the perspective that my history *is* history.

How did this universalizing white experience play out in my life? History was taught to me as an abstract past that didn't relate to me or the world today. Without a historical understanding of white supremacy and with a near total absence of people of color-led resistance struggle, I thought of racism only in terms of individual behavior. I knew who Martin Luther King, Jr. was, and, from what I learned of him in school it seemed like he wanted me to move on from the past and be colorblind too.

Racism, to me, was therefore something experienced and expressed only by individuals. For example, there was a short-lived gang at my school whose name announced they were against Gays, Blacks, and Asians. Obviously, the gang members were racist. That was clear to me and to pretty much everyone. I didn't notice that white people wrote every assigned book that I read in four years of English class. I didn't think about the fact that Latino/as who spoke English as a second language, about one third of my school's population, were in under-funded programs and marginalized in school functions and media (including both the underground newspaper and the official newspaper I worked on).

Post-Racial White Supremacy: "We don't think of you as Mexican."

The first real challenge to my understanding of racism in my life came during high school from people of color. My friend Tim Santos is Latino, but I tried not to think of him like that. He was just a person, like me. But the colorblind framework wasn't working for me. It felt like a lie. I wanted to talk about race, but the white people who did talk about it were racists. Tim, who rarely talked about race either, wanted to talk about it as well. We had a long conversation one day, during which he expressed how hard it was to spend his entire life trying to fit in. He was a sophomore, a couple of years younger than me, and struggling with his own understanding of race and white supremacy. He talked about how in elementary school his white friends would say, "We don't think of you as Mexican," or, "You're not like those Mexicans, you're one of us." He told me about how hard he tried to be "one of us" and how much shame and guilt he felt for being Mexican. While he knew more about Mexican history than I did, he didn't have much historical understanding either. What he said hit me on a gut level; it was a major revelation about race. I didn't know what it meant exactly, but his statement helped me understand how race was not just someone's skin color but how one connected to history and power. As he talked about his struggle to understand himself through family, culture, and history, I began to wonder what it meant to be white.

Searching for Direction: "These people are your leaders too."

I first met Terence Priester at a party at his house when I was 18. My group of friends was mostly in high school with some like Terence, a couple of years into college. In addition to our interests in tequila and making out, we were mostly social justice left, feminist, pro-queer liberation, progressive people. With a social group of over 50 people, a core of over a dozen of us organized anti-war protests and distributed radical literature, and we called ourselves the United Anarchist Front. While we protested economic and political inequality, we didn't know how to think about race.
This was about to change, and Terence was at the center of that change.

There was a poster in Terence's living room that caught my attention the first time I was at his place. In fact, it was the first time I had ever been in a Black person's home. The poster read "Celebrating African-American History." I studied that poster, looking at the faces of all twelve leaders featured. I recognized two of them, Martin Luther King, Jr. and Malcolm X. I had heard part of Martin Luther King's "I have a Dream Speech" and knew he was a leader of the Civil Rights movement, but that was it. While King wanted everyone to get along, my understanding was that Malcolm X hated white people and called them "devils."

"Who are all these people?" I asked. Terence gave me summaries of the main contributions of Harriet Tubman, Marcus Garvey, Martin Delany, Frederick Douglas, W.E.B. Du Bois, Mary McLeod Bethune, Langston Hughes, Elijah Muhammad, Adam Clayton Powell, Jr., and Sojourner Truth. He used all these historical reference points that I only vaguely knew about: the Underground Railroad, Reconstruction, the Abolitionists, and Women's Suffragists. But he also talked about Black Nationalism and millions of working class Black people in the Garveyite movement and the tensions between different positions in the Black liberation struggle. I had never heard of any of this before. Furthermore, I'd never heard a Black person explain history and politics before.

At this point, I knew that colorblindness was a failed framework, but I didn't know what to replace it with. I knew that the people on this poster were important, and I set out to memorize their names. I asked Terence at several subsequent parties to tell me their names and backgrounds again.

After the third time he was frustrated and said to me, "You need to learn about these people and not just because you want to know who leaders in the Black community are, but because these people are your leaders, too."

It was a profound moment. He pushed me to realize not only that I had a lot to learn but that there were sources of knowledge I had not known existed. He was telling me that there was a radical democratic tradition of struggle in this country that had a history I could learn from. Furthermore, that history and these leaders put forward visions, strategies, and tactics that could help me understand the society we live in and imagine the word I wanted to live in. From then on, when I looked at the faces of those leaders, I felt a connection to them. I felt that somehow, in order to help understand who I am, I needed to learn who they were.

Burning the Illusions: The Rodney King verdict

A few months later, on April 29th, 1992, the "not guilty" verdict was announced in the Rodney King police brutality case. I had just finished reading W.E.B. Du Bois's *The Souls of Black Folk* that morning (the first book I read knowing it was written by a person of color). In it, Du Bois wrote about the double consciousness of Black people and a lived experience of not being fully a part of this country. As I sat in front the television listening to the news, anger, rage, and sadness boiled over in me, and, while it felt absolutely right to feel this way, I couldn't put any words to it other than "this is so fucked up." I wanted to join the growing rally at the Parker Center Police Station in Los Angeles where thousands were gathering to protest the verdict, but I didn't have a ride.[2]

Over the next six days a massive uprising and riot took place. Hundreds of thousands of people took to the streets. Around the country protests and riots against the racist verdict took place in several dozen cities, including Seattle, Chicago, Las Vegas, Madison, Oakland, San Francisco, and Atlanta.

The night of the verdict, as Los Angeles was ablaze, a group of friends gathered at my parents' house to watch the news and to support each other. Terence came over. He explained that in order for him to be with us as white people, we needed to understand what this verdict meant for him.

He told us about being stopped by the police on his high school campus. He had been searched and forced to prove that he went to the school. (He was one of the few people of color that did.) He told us about other experiences with the police and about people assuming he's a criminal or dangerous. Or people telling him "you're not like other Black people." He told us about his day-to-day reality dealing with white supremacy in this country. He explained how this verdict impacted every Black person and how it demonstrated to Black people that they would never have justice in this country. It was deeply painful and powerful.

What also proved painful, as well as disempowering, was my inability to challenge the overwhelmingly racist response to the riots in my mostly white classrooms at school. My high school teachers were not offering a systemic analysis of the economy and history of state repression against the Black community. As white people talked about Black people acting like irrational animals, I could feel how powerful the white supremacist "common sense" was. The white, middle-class experience as universal made everything I said in response to them sound crazy, like I was making up fantastic stories about de-industrialization, unemployment, and corporations moving to other parts of the country and other countries entirely for cheap labor, leaving poverty in the cities. Mostly, I was consumed by the realization of how much race matters and how much it shapes the society we live in. A big part of universalizing white experience is the reality that white people don't have to think about race and generally don't think about it, unless it is to notice what people of color are doing. White people are, therefore, without a race—above it all.

Shortly after the L.A. riots, Terence gave me *Simple's Uncle Sam*, a book of short stories about a Black working class family by Langston Hughes. In his inscription he quoted Martin Luther King, Jr.: "If you can't fly, run. If you can't run, walk. If you can't walk, crawl. But by all means, keep moving." Terence encouraged me to study Black history and the history of other people of color. He helped me understand that I needed to take responsibility for

> **During L.A. Riots:**
>
> Over **3,600** fires set
>
> **1,100** buildings burned down
>
> Over **50** people died
>
> Over **2,000** were injured
>
> Over **10,000** were arrested
>
> **Forces Deployed:**
>
> **5,000** LAPD
>
> **1,000** Sheriff's Deputies
>
> **950** County Marshals
>
> **2,300** Highway Patrolmen
>
> **9,975** National Guard
>
> **3,500** Army and Marines with armored vehicles
>
> **1,000** Federal Marshals, FBI agents, Border Patrol SWAT[3]

this learning, and that, while he was helping me, it was not his job to educate me about white supremacy.

This was an important lesson. It is not the responsibility of people of color to educate white people. If and when people of color help white people it should be on terms set by people of color. Given this reality, it's important for white people to remember that people of color did not set the terms of white supremacy. This means it's a challenging dynamic and usually a risk for people of color to talk with white people about white supremacy. In the end, white people need to take on this work as their own.

Throughout struggles for justice, people of color have and will continue to provide white people with insights, analysis, lessons, leadership, and strategy. One of the ways that white people can act responsibly when building these multiracial alliances is to develop their own leadership so that they can work with other white people to challenge white supremacy, help pass on the lessons from struggles in communities of color, and work to build movements for economic, racial, and gender justice.

Choosing Sides: "I'm not responsible for what happened in the past."

Another way that the dynamic of universalizing white experience plays out is that we'll be able to hear something from a white person that we might resist or dismiss if it was said by a person of color. This is also one of the reasons I believe white people working with other white people against white supremacy is a key strategy in the overall struggle against white supremacy.

Months after the Rodney King verdict, I met up with Terence at a bar. He was there with some of his co-workers, two white guys. They were drinking shots and telling jokes. One of the white guys brought the verdict up. Terence said the verdict was racist, and this was met with, "Come on, that was a long time ago, let's move on." But the other white guy asked Terence to explain himself. Terence presented a summary of U.S. history with a focus on the genocide of indigenous people and slavery. He followed that up with some examples of institutionalized racism today. The white co-worker came back with, "Look, I'm not responsible for what happened in the past, but what I am responsible for is what happens now, and we have equal opportunity, and, yeah, things aren't perfect, but it doesn't help anyone to keep talking about the legacy of slavery." When Terence persisted, he was told,

"You see everything as about race. You're not neutral."

I had that nervous feeling in my body, knowing that I needed to jump in. I was really scared to say anything, but I took the plunge and basically made the same points that Terence did, adding in occasional comments about why this was important to me as a white person. The response was incredible. "Well, I can see what you're saying with that," one of the co-workers granted me. "That's exactly what I told you ten minutes ago," Terence said, exasperated. "Yeah," the co-worker shrugged, "but I just think that you see racism everywhere, whereas this guy is more neutral." Universalizing white experience means that white people remain the standard, the objective observers, and the impartial and rational norm.

Universalizing white experience plays a significant role in how white privilege impacts activism. Laura Close and Nisha Anand, antiracist activists in the global justice movement, describe this as white activists internalizing the belief that their ways of doing activism are the right, best, and normal ways to do it. The challenge for white activists is finding ways to actively undermine white supremacist common sense, to learn about the histories of people of color and working class people, and to rethink what is normal, best, and the right way. We can play a strategic role bringing antiracism into white communities. We have a responsibility and an opportunity to break the stranglehold of white supremacy on the consciousness of white people.

Since my high school experiences more than twenty years ago, I have worked with tens of thousands of white people with a commitment to building broad-based grassroots movements for racial, economic, and gender justice. Whether it's while leading trainings, working with organizations, helping build alliances, or developing new leaders, I often think back to Tim, Terence, the Rodney King Verdict, my high school group of activists, and my own process of coming to race consciousness. White people are presented with the options of colorblind denial, racist resentment, or antiracist guilt. When Terence encouraged me to see Ella Baker, Harriet Tubman, Malcolm X, and W.E.B. Du Bois as my leaders, he was also encouraging me to understand how my own liberation was connected to the Black Freedom struggle.

He was presenting me with another option. He didn't want me to come to antiracist consciousness and hate myself while working on behalf of other people's liberation. He helped me to understand that not only can we look honestly and deeply at one another and our histories and to see how racism and race have shaped our society and who we are, but that in seeing the pains, divisions, and limits of racism and race, we can see what lays beyond it. We can see the liberation struggles against racism of our communities and of our shared people advancing a vision of dignity, equality, and freedom for all people. This is the option of collective liberation, and it has guided me in all that I do. I don't look back on my experiences and cringe for my shortcomings and mistakes. I look back with gratitude for those who shared their lives with me and challenged me. I look back with tenderness for my teenage self and say thank you for staying present in those moments when I could have retreated and missed learning moments by saying, "no, no, no, that's not what I meant, I'm not racist," trying hard to not let anyone see that in fact I had fear in my heart, not understanding.

I bring this gratitude and tenderness to my work in white communities and see antiracist organizing as consisting of opportunity after opportunity to move white people to open their hearts and minds to collective liberation struggle. To move white people to work against white supremacy and its brutal lies, and join with the Ella Bakers, Harriet Tubmans, Malcolm Xs, and W.E.B. Du Bois' of today to win and create racial, economic, and gender justice.

---

[1] These liberatory possibilities include a democratic revolution against feudalism with working people winning a Bill of Rights; the separation of church and state with humans put in command of political life; and a belief in the capacity of ordinary people to self-govern. While Jefferson and the founding fathers intended for a very small sector of the people to be involved in a republican government, these ideas nevertheless opened themselves to revolutionary interpretations and struggles. They represent an advance in the Western democratic tradition.

[2] My best friend since Cub Scouts, who also became a radical and was part of the United Anarchist Front, went to the protest and described the incredible power of a multiracial, majority Black march going through downtown Los Angeles smashing corporate offices, the L.A. Times office and moving past small businesses leaving them undisturbed.

[3] Statistics from http://en.wikipedia.org/wiki/1992_Los_Angeles_riots.

*"Universalizing white experience meant that I did not have a historical grounding to understand the many different histories that shape U.S. history. I was left operating from the perspective that my history **is** history."*

❖ ❖ ❖

A Love Letter

This is to all my Indigenous sisters and brothers that come from all over the world; my sisters and brothers who have relations, nations, and monumental achievements that precede the European conquests, enslavements, forced laboring; my sisters and brothers who hold memory in their blood, cultural ties and spiritual connections to lands before they were called the Americas, Africa, or the Pacific Rim.

We wake up each day facing a world that ignores or undervalues our most essential beliefs and actions, but we prevail. We must walk within physical spaces and environments that have been irreconcilably altered. We must often communicate in ways that do not express love, community, cooperation, sharing, respect, and the cyclical nature of the universe just to display what is considered strength and confidence and efficiency and progress. Oh progress, Western progress, that which has brought us to where we are today. Let's really think about its impact on relationships and intimacy and human equity and emotional fulfillment.

We are tempted and forced every moment to consume ideas, images, things, that represent no real connection to our souls, our intellectual history, our eternal bond to our ancestors. In educational institutions we must learn layer upon layer of knowledge and information. First we learn the formal curriculum, then we devise a way to integrate the wisdom of our elders into this curriculum so as to keep our sanity, and then we analytically filter out the racist codes and assumptions imbedded in each and every lesson. In this way we continue to stay close to one another, flourish, learn, resist. When we're young we often sit in classes that are only us and then if we go on to college, we are often the only one. And then after we leave our formal schooling we dress as we should, talk as we should, operate under the proper worldviews as we should, acknowledge, endure and sometimes even perpetuate the frequently indifferent or hostile timber of the hierarchy as we should.

And, of course, this just isn't quite enough. We still have eyes and attention avert to others lighter complexioned than ourselves, speaking with that exceedingly comfortable Euro-centric perspective that only comes when it is, in fact, your identity, or exhibiting a dozen other subtle traits that make those in power feel good about themselves. Conversely, in other situations, all eyes are upon us, curiously, judgmentally, romantically, as if we speak for an entire population, a population that has been colonized and must explain itself over and over or, then again, may get just one chance. And yes, we do know how to unravel and articulate the mysteries of our oppression if anyone truly cares to listen, but what we know as well is how to demand our liberation, our equality, and our happiness.

So to all my sisters and brothers who keep explaining, who keep demanding, who keep resisting, and who keep flourishing, my love goes to you. The world will continue to change, and we'll continue to change the world, so as to reflect our lives as we truly wish to lead them.

Richard Chavolla

In case you forgot...

What is White Privilege?

In her "Challenging White Supremacy Workshop," Sharon Martinas defines white privilege as "a historically based, institutionally perpetuated system of…preferential prejudice for and treatment of white people based solely on their skin color and/or ancestral origin from Europe." This preferential treatment of white people exists on an individual and institutional level in every aspect of our society.

Say what?

Simply put, white privilege refers to the unearned benefits and advantages that white people have just because of the color of our skin.

What is White Supremacy?

Renowned author and activist Elizabeth Martinez defines white supremacy as: "a historically based, institutionally perpetuated system of exploitation and oppression of continents, nations, and peoples of color by white peoples and nations of the European continent for the purpose of maintaining and defending a system of wealth, power, and privilege."

Say What?

Racism=Prejudice + Power

Ethnocentrism - Everyone else's culture pretty much sucks in comparison to yours. Why? Because you think your culture is the center of the universe, so you judge according to that. You know that white dude on the block that is always yellin' at the brown and black people who walk by to "go back to your own damn country"? He is practicing ethnocentrism.

Hegemony - A really big word for "take over the world."

Xenophobia - Fear or hatred of the strange or foreign. Remember that dude above? He is xenophobic.

Anti-Semitism - Discrimination against or prejudice or hostility toward Jews. (Why you hatin' on their yarmulkes?)

Discrimination - Treating someone better or worse because of what they look like or stand for. Example: People think it's cool to chop an imaginary tomahawk as they cheer on teams like the Atlanta Braves or Washington Redskins. Who cares that it's mocking Native American tribes? Yeah, that's discrimination.

Chapter 2

❧ *The Darker Side of Privilege:*
*How Racism F**ks White People, Too* ❧

Over time, talking white privilege to white people got frustrating. Especially when after having explained unearned benefits, the response was, "Why would I give that up?" I changed tactics and moved away from the moral argument to a more personal one: Our people have caused the most widespread damage in all of United States history with reaches far beyond our own borders and shores.

Our collective unconscious holds every one of the dirty deeds committed as the oppressor. I call this white people's soul wound. The wound may be hard to find, but ignore it forever and it will gorge on your spirit and shrivel you up. In other words, it's fuckin' you and me up, too, white dude.

In my early days as an activist I did not educate with compassion, no matter how many tears, dumbfounded looks, and anxiety attacks come back at me in return. If people of color deal with racism every single minute of every single day, I reasoned, white people in pain is just what the doctor ordered.

Years of this strategy left me without a cadre. In fact, my tough love left many disempowered—including me. Eventually, I realized that if I was truly attempting to help eradicate racism, I had to figure out how we white folks have been negatively impacted by it. We have been taught for so long that racism hurts only people of color, but, as it turns out, that's not right at all. Until we dig deep though, it is difficult to be in healthy action against it.

I took a self-inventory in order to see racism's impact on my life and discovered some ugly truths. Here are just a few of them:

- Loss of relationships due to historical distrust of white people and the stress that race can place on friendships and intimate partnerships.

- Dimming my light and not fully shining for fear of shutting out opportunities for people of color.

❖ Lack of confidence in my abilities. I know that although I have worked my ass off I will always question that all of my gains lead back to the unearned advantages due to my skin color. All of my gains? Some of my gains? Most of my gains? See how it works? I really don't know what I've gotten because I've "deserved" it and what I've gotten because I'm white.

What about you? Can you identify what racism has cost you in your life? Activist Paul Kivel has done some incredible work on this issue in his book *Uprooting Racism; How White People Can Work for Racial Justice*, which gives an extensive list of how racism hurts white people.

What I found particularly accurate is:

Our feelings of guilt, shame, embarrassment, or inadequacy about racism and about our response to it lower our self-esteem. Because racism makes a mockery of our ideals of democracy, justice, and equality, it leads us to be cynical and pessimistic about human integrity and about our future, producing apathy, blame, despair, self-destructive behavior and acts of violence, especially among our young people. (Kivel, page 37)

What to do with this information? The first step: Acknowledge: Stare racism in the face, and fully acknowledge the role it has played in your life.

Next step: Healing: Create a healing process. The slow and steady practice of reviewing, reliving, releasing, and moving forward is a good way to start. It is important to take a moment to pause here and say to my white readers that while there's no doubt that racism hurts white people, we can never ever compare our pain and struggle to that of communities of color, which have been and continue to be horrifically devastated and dehumanized.

Last step: Action: Do something where the hurtful experiences are transformed into a passion for justice so deep that your very essence screams through fear of the unknown and puts you on the frontlines in the fight for equality. Some examples beyond just going to a workshop or conference (which are good places to start, but not stay): Get involved in a local campaign; organize with like-minded people on an issue that matters; speak up and speak out on local community concerns.

It is in action that we will be most helpful as allies to communities of color in the struggle for liberation of *all* people and the planet. And that, my friend, is revolutionary.

❧ *Knapsack 2012* ❧

By *Peggy McIntosh*

I was born in Brooklyn, New York, with a view from Brooklyn Heights to the skyscrapers of Wall Street. JLove's title for this book, drawing on "Occupy Wall Street," reminded me that I was raised not to Occupy lower Manhattan but to admire those handsome towers. Wall Street was in my prudent, cultivated, upper class, white female psyche, and perhaps to an extent I was in Wall Street's psyche, as a type of desirable female dependent, for stock brokers had to think they were helping someone besides themselves and the world. Perhaps I stood in for "America's families."

So what does it mean for me now, to "Occupy Wall Street"? Go outside the buildings; sit down; camp out, make noise, work with others to demand a new balance of power to replace the systems in which the rich get richer and aspire to take over the world.

When I published my first White Privilege article in 1988 (reprinted here) I had stopped admiring the towers of the university and was Occupying Knowledge—protesting the versions of reality academic institutions had given me to justify their power and make me protect mine. Of course, the towers were now academic rather than financial. White men controlled formal Knowledge and would not cede male power. But I, with the other fledgling Occupiers coming out of the big towers into encampments of antiwar movements, the Civil Rights movement, and Women's Studies, had some white enclaves, and did this not mean that we had made some little Wall Streets of our own? My list of 46 examples (26 are reprinted here) that, for me, answered that question has now traveled far, and the method of consciously limited autobiographical testimony that framed the list is helping to re-form learning and knowing in many fields. I am very gratified to be part of this history.

But most of the world outside of the academy still has not heard of and cannot think in terms of privilege systems. How can we "Occupy Privilege" if it is still invisible to most people? This matters enormously. Many good-hearted people think they are working against racism when they are still in denial about white privilege. I envision a hypothetical horizontal line of social justice, below which individuals or groups, through no fault of their own, are pushed down, neglected, punished, exploited, hated, enslaved, deprived, and may be victims of war, murder, or genocide. Above the hypothetical line of social justice I envision an area of privilege in which groups or individuals, through no virtue of their own, are pushed up, elevated, encouraged, believed in, rewarded, empowered, advanced, lauded, kept safe, and considered as models of success. Almost no one in the United States outside of the academy grants that this area of privilege above the hypothetical line of social justice exists and prevents equity. So policy makers attempt to fix deficits while ignoring their causes—the dominating holds of privilege. I believe that people cannot solve problems of inequity below the line without seeing systemic privilege above the line that causes the suffering. To address oppression without addressing privilege simply protects and increases the privilege of the already privileged. The time has indeed come to name privilege and then to Occupy it, camping out, protesting, making a noise, weakening its authority, learning to redistribute its unearned assets.

One reason that Occupiers have been criticized for not having a clear agenda (and I am not very concerned about this) is that so much of what the Occupiers resist is invisible to almost everybody, including themselves: systemic unearned power. We were taught not to realize it or talk about it. But over the long term, Occupiers will need to

> "How can we 'Occupy Privilege' if it is still invisible to most people?"

learn about the nuances of the ways in which power accumulates in all sectors of social life and works structurally. I think very great specificity of language will be needed to protest privilege over the long run. We will need to become scholars of our own situations and of all institutional dynamics at the minutest level. If Occupiers cannot explain privilege systems we will not be able to educate the press, the other media, and the institutions of U.S. culture about the ways it frames what people do.

My 1988 paper ended with the question: *Having seen unearned power, would I use it to share power?* For me, choosing to do so has been a transformative journey. My life changed dramatically once I used my privilege to weaken privilege systems. Occupying and protesting privilege was far better than dwelling unconsciously within it. My little Wall Street had nothing to give me in terms of a meaningful life as a dependent of powerful investors.

Ironically, I have arrived at a new financial metaphor for thinking about my relation to privilege. I have not traded in the metaphor of the invisible knapsack and never will do so. But, many people who came to understand that they had white privilege were asking me, "What can I do about it?" I suggested that we see white privilege or any other kind of privilege as a bank account that we did not ask for but that we can spend down to weaken privilege systems. Because arbitrarily awarded privilege will keep refilling such bank accounts, we will never go bankrupt spending down our bank accounts of unearned advantage. So now I came back to a financial metaphor—banking. As the field of privilege studies grows, some of us will have our bank accounts refilled to an unusual degree because we become prominent in the field. Then mini-Wall Streets will be rebuilt if we decide to live within our fame, rather than moving outside of the buildings into the encampments of the Occupiers, and to continue to occupy privilege in protest against it in all of its forms.

I attribute the blindness to privilege systems of the United States to the stranglehold which five key myths have on its dominant cultural life. All of the myths reinforce the habit of seeing individually, rather than systemically, and all reinforce privilege systems. If you cannot see systemically you cannot see privilege in its overarching and interwoven structural forms. The first myth is meritocracy: the idea that the unit of society is the individual, and whatever a person ends up with must be what he or she individually wanted, worked for, earned, and deserved. The second myth is that of monoculture: the United States is one big unified society, and if it is not working for you there is something wrong with you or with your behavior. The third myth is that of manifest destiny: God had a plan for the control and ownership of the land that is now the continental United States, and He designated those who should rightly control it and any lands they felt they should colonize elsewhere. The fourth myth is that of white racelessness: White people are normal, and other people have the misfortune of having race. If they will assimilate as individuals into normalcy, they may be able to overcome their "race problems." The final myth is that of white moral superiority: White people run things because they are so competent at it, aren't they? Under this myth, it is seen as natural for white people to run the world.

Since all of these myths are intertwined in a culture not accustomed to thinking of itself as deluded and not accustomed to thinking in terms of being misled, it will be a work of many decades to persuade people in the United States that they have indeed been missing out on major understanding of how we have been used to keep power in the hands of those who already have most of it. This work will require a lot of discipline. At present, the words "power" and "privilege" are often used loosely to mean more or less the same thing. Privilege is carelessly assumed by many people to be consciously held. Emotions of blame, shame, guilt, and reproach take over discussion and interfere with a more historical understanding that we as individuals were born into power systems we did not invent. Since all of education including "higher" education prepared us not to notice, let alone think deeply about, the operations of privilege in and around us, major homework is now required if we are to Occupy Privilege. We need to study ourselves and all of the institutional frames of reference and rewards we were made to assume as we grew up. One privilege of dominance is to think that dominant people deserve to think well of ourselves and our ancestors. Studying privilege challenges such a sense of deservedness. Our task ahead is to be more tough-minded and less sentimental. We need to live our lives with better awareness of how everything is political, and everything political has been disguised to keep even the powerful compliant or senseless. We can despair, but we may better use our energy to recognize, resist, and Occupy privilege systems that keep us from making a world that fosters the decent survival of all.

"To address oppression without addressing privilege simply protects and increases the privilege of the already privileged."

✎ *White Privilege: Unpacking The Invisible Knapsack* ✎

By *Peggy McIntosh - Copyright 1989*[1]

I think whites are carefully taught not to recognize white privilege, as males are taught not to recognize male privilege. So I have begun in an untutored way to ask what it is like to have white privilege. I have come to see white privilege as an invisible package of unearned assets that I can count on cashing in each day but about which I was "meant" to remain oblivious. White privilege is like an invisible weightless knapsack of special provisions, maps, passports, codebooks, visas, clothes, tools, and blank checks.

Through work to bring materials from Women's Studies into the rest of the curriculum, I have often noticed men's unwillingness to grant that they are over-privileged, even though they may grant that women are disadvantaged.

They may say they will work to improve women's status, in the society, the university, or the curriculum, but they can't or won't support the idea of lessening men's. Denials which amount to taboos surround the subject of advantages which men gain from women's disadvantages. These denials protect male privilege from being fully acknowledged, lessened, or ended.

Thinking through unacknowledged male privilege as a phenomenon, I realized that, since hierarchies in our society are interlocking, there was most likely a phenomenon of white privilege that was similarly denied and protected. As a white person, I realized I had been taught about racism as something that puts others at a disadvantage but had been taught not to see one of its corollary aspects, white privilege, which puts me at an advantage. Describing white privilege makes one newly accountable. As we in Women's Studies work to reveal male privilege and ask men to give up some of their power, so one who writes about white privilege must ask, "Having described it, what will I do to lessen or end it?"

After I realized the extent to which men work from a base of unacknowledged privilege, I understood that much of their oppressiveness was unconscious. Then I remembered the frequent charges from women of color that white women whom they encounter are oppressive.

I began to understand why we are justly seen as oppressive, even when we don't see ourselves that way. I began to count the ways in which I enjoy unearned skin privilege and have been conditioned into oblivion about its existence.

My schooling gave me no training in seeing myself as an oppressor, as an unfairly advantaged person, or as a participant in a damaged culture. I was taught to see myself as an individual whose moral state depended on her individual moral will. My schooling followed the pattern my colleague Elizabeth Minnich has pointed out: whites are taught to think of their lives as morally neutral, normative, and average, and also ideal, so that when we work to benefit others, this is seen as work which will allow "them" to be more like "us."

I decided to try to work on myself at least by identifying some of the daily effects of white privilege in my life. I have chosen those conditions which I think in my case attach somewhat more to skin-color privilege than to class, religion, ethnic status, or geographic location, though of course all these other factors are intricately intertwined. As far as I can see, my African-American co-workers, friends, and acquaintances with whom I come into daily or frequent contact in this particular time, place, and line of work cannot count on most of these conditions.

1. I can if I wish arrange to be in the company of people of my race most of the time.

2. If I should need to move, I can be pretty sure of renting or purchasing housing in an area which I can afford and in which I would want to live.

3. I can be pretty sure that my neighbors in such a location will be neutral or pleasant to me.

4. I can go shopping alone most of the time, pretty well assured that I will not be followed or harassed.

5. I can turn on the television or open to the front page of the paper and see people of my race widely represented.

6. When I am told about our national heritage or about "civilization," I am shown that people of my color made it what it is.

7. I can be sure that my children will be given curricular materials that testify to the existence of their race.

8. If want to, I can be pretty sure of finding a publisher for this piece on white privilege.

9. I can go into a music shop and count on finding the music of my race represented, into a supermarket and find the staple foods that fit with my cultural traditions, into a hairdresser's shop and find someone who can cut my hair.

10. Whether I use checks, credit cards, or cash, I can count on my skin color not to work against the appearance of financial reliability.

11. I can arrange to protect my children most of the time from people who might not like them.

12. I can swear, or dress in second-hand clothes, or not answer letters, without having people attribute these choices to the bad morals, the poverty, or the illiteracy of my race.

13. I can speak in public to a powerful male group without putting my race on trial.

14. I can do well in a challenging situation without being called a credit to my race.

15. I am never asked to speak for all the people of my racial group.

16. I can remain oblivious of the language and customs of people of color who constitute the world's majority without feeling in my culture any penalty for such oblivion.

17. I can criticize our government and talk about how much I fear its policies and behavior without being seen as a cultural outsider.

18. I can be pretty sure that if I ask to talk to "the person in charge," I will be facing a person of my race.

19. If a traffic cop pulls me over or if the IRS audits my tax return, I can be sure I haven't been singled out because of my race.

20. I can easily buy posters, postcards, picture books, greeting cards, dolls, toys, and children's magazines featuring people of my race.

21. I can go home from most meetings of organizations I belong to feeling somewhat tied in, rather than isolated, out-of-place, outnumbered, unheard, held at a distance, or feared.

22. I can take a job with an affirmative action employer without having co-workers on the job suspect that I got it because of race.

23. I can choose public accommodations without fearing that people of my race cannot get in or will be mistreated in the places I have chosen.

24. I can be sure that if I need legal or medical help, my race will not work against me.

25. If my day, week, or year is going badly, I need not ask of each negative episode or situation whether it has racial overtones.

26. I can choose blemish cover or bandages in "flesh" color and have them more less match my skin.

I repeatedly forgot each of the realizations on this list until I wrote it down. For me, white privilege has turned out to be an elusive and fugitive subject. The pressure to avoid it is great, for in facing it I must give up the myth of meritocracy. If these things are true, this is not such a free country; one's life is not what one makes it; many doors open for certain people through no virtues of their own.

In unpacking this invisible knapsack of white privilege, I have listed conditions of daily experience that I once took for granted. Nor, did I think of any of these prerequisites as bad for the holder. I now think that we need a more finely differentiated taxonomy of privilege, for some of these varieties are only what one would want for everyone in a just society, and others give license to be ignorant, oblivious, arrogant, and destructive.

I see a pattern running through the matrix of white privilege, a pattern of assumptions that were passed on to me as a white person. There was one main piece of cultural turf; it was my own turf, and I was among those who could control the turf. My skin color was an asset for any move I was educated to want to make. I could think of myself as belonging in major ways and of making social systems work for me. I could freely disparage, fear, neglect, or be oblivious to anything outside of the dominant cultural forms. Being of the main culture, I could also criticize it fairly freely.

In proportion as my racial group was being made confident, comfortable, and oblivious, other groups were likely being made unconfident, uncomfortable, and alienated. Whiteness protected me from many kinds of hostility, distress, and violence, which I was being subtly trained to visit, in turn, upon people of color.

For this reason, the word "privilege" now seems to me misleading. We usually think of privilege as being a favored state, whether earned or conferred by birth or luck. Yet some of the conditions I have described here work systematically to overempower certain groups. Such privilege simply confers dominance because of one's race or sex.

I want, then, to distinguish between earned strength and unearned power conferred systemically. Power from unearned privilege can look like strength when it is in fact permission to escape or to dominate. But not all of the privileges on my list are inevitably damaging. Some, like the expectation that neighbors will be decent to you, or that your race will not count against you in court, should be the norm in a just society. Others, like the privilege to ignore less powerful people, distort the humanity of the holders as well as the ignored groups.

We might at least start by distinguishing between positive advantages, which we can work to spread, and negative types of advantage, which unless rejected will always reinforce our present hierarchies. For example, the feeling that one belongs within the human circle, as Native Americans say, should not be seen as privilege for a few. Ideally it is an unearned entitlement. At present, since only a few have it, it is an unearned advantage for them. This paper results from a process of coming to see that some of the power that I originally saw as attendant on being a human being in the United States consisted in unearned advantage and conferred dominance.

I have met very few men who are truly distressed about systemic, unearned male advantage and conferred dominance. And, so one question for me and others like me is whether we will be like them or whether we will get truly distressed, even outraged, about unearned race advantage and conferred dominance, and, if so, what will we do to lessen them. In any case, we need to do more work in identifying how they actually affect our daily lives. Many, perhaps most, of our white students in the U.S. think that racism doesn't affect them because they are not people of color; they do not see "whiteness" as a racial identity. In addition, since race and sex are not the only advantaging systems at work, we need similarly to examine the daily experience of having age advantage, or ethnic advantage, or physical ability, or advantage related to nationality, religion, or sexual orientation.

Difficulties and dangers surrounding the task of finding parallels are many. Since racism, sexism, and heterosexism are not the same, the advantages associated with them should not be seen as the same. In addition, it is hard to disentangle aspects of unearned advantage which rest more on social class, economic class, race, religion, sex, and ethnic identity than on other factors. Still, all of the oppressions are interlocking, as the Combahee River Collective Statement of 1977 continues to remind us eloquently.

One factor seems clear about all of the interlocking oppressions. They take both active forms, which we can see, and embedded forms, which as a member of the dominant group one is taught not to see. In my class and place, I did not see myself as a racist because I was taught to recognize racism only in individual acts of meanness by members of my group, never in invisible systems conferring unsought racial dominance on my group from birth.

Disapproving of the systems won't be enough to change them. I was taught to think that racism could end if white individuals changed their attitudes. But, a "white" skin in the United States opens many doors for whites, whether or not we approve of the way dominance has been conferred on us. Individual acts can palliate, but cannot end, these problems.

To redesign social systems, we need first to acknowledge their colossal unseen dimensions. The silences and denials surrounding privilege are the key political tool here. They keep the thinking about equality or equity incomplete, protecting unearned advantage and conferred dominance by making these taboo subjects. Most talk by whites about equal opportunity seems to me now to be about equal opportunity to try to get into a position of dominance while denying that systems of dominance exist.

It seems to me that obliviousness about white advantage, like obliviousness about male advantage, is kept strongly inculturated in the United States so as to maintain the myth of meritocracy—the myth that democratic choice is equally available to all. Keeping most people unaware that freedom of confident action is there for just a small number of people props up those in power and serves to keep power in the hands of the same groups that have most of it already.

Although systemic change takes many decades, there are pressing questions for me and I imagine for some others like me if we raise our daily consciousness on the perquisites of being light-skinned. What will we do with such knowledge? As we know from watching men, it is an open question whether we will choose to use unearned advantage to weaken hidden systems of advantage and whether we will use any of our arbitrarily awarded power to try to reconstruct power systems on a broader base.

❧ *White Privilege = White Obama Supporters…HUH?* ❧

An Interview with *Danny Hoch conducted by JLove Calderón*

Actor Danny Hoch and I are similar in our histories: White kids who loved Hip-Hop culture, ran with a multi-racial community, and were steeped in radical politics. However, we are exact opposites when it comes to strategy. Most of the time we straight up disagree not on the what, but on the how. That's made for lively discussions, whether at a late-night post party or over early morning pancakes with special coffee that he whipped up.

Danny uses his artistic ability to challenge the most controversial issues of the day and gets standing ovations time after time from huge audiences globally. In his work, he often opens up about the complex issues, such as gentrification and race, of which he finds himself in the middle of it all. He brings us face to face with issues we do not like to talk about, and he doesn't leave himself out of it. He is honest, courageous, and brilliant. His popularity, especially with white audiences, gives me hope.

Danny: Most of the time, when you hear white privilege, we think of rich people, and we think of people who run institutions... But when I think of white privilege what's really on my mind today is…white Obama supporters. Particularly, white Obama supporters who left where they were from in the United States and moved to California, Illinois, and New York. I feel that no matter how progressive we white folks think we are, and no matter what kind of work we do—even if we're teachers and we're activists or community organizers—we are still unaware of our own white privilege in our everyday lives because we have identified the enemy as older rich white people. And therefore, the words "white privilege" cannot possibly apply to us because we're well-intentioned. But what white privilege has afforded us to do is to blindly leave our white community and go to a big city and displace African-Americans and displace immigrants and displace the children of immigrants and the grandchildren of immigrants and displace the great-grandchildren of immigrants and not think that we are responsible because we think that we are victims, too. And that is a symptom of white privilege. We are not aware of our economic footprint.

JLove: What do you mean by economic footprint?

Danny: …Collectively, our white lower-class economic footprint, or our middle-class economic footprint—our Democrat economic footprint—is shockingly powerful. And that means the money we spend collectively when we move in and gentrify a neighborhood displaces people. And erases people. And, we're not aware of it. And, if we're aware of it we justify it. White privilege is when the Latino immigrant and resident and citizen community of a neighborhood have been asking for a school for 35 years and been asking for a hospital for 40 years and been asking for a traffic light at an intersection where 5 different children got killed over 25 years and nothing happens… and then a whole bunch of progressive white folks move into a neighborhood and ask for a bike lane and within 2 weeks and they get it. That's white privilege. So the white folks want to say, "But a bike lane is good. We need a bike lane so there's less accidents." Yeah, that's right. But what we're denying when we celebrate the bike lane and we celebrate the new green spaces and we celebrate the options of health food stores is the disenfranchisement and the displacement and the erasure of the people that were there before us. Which, to me, makes us pilgrims. It makes us either pilgrims or missionaries. Now, we certainly don't want to identify as conquistadors and we probably don't want to identify as missionaries. And we probably don't want to identify as pilgrims, either. But that's what we are…

The reason why those white folks are pilgrims is because the excuse is always the same. It's, "I couldn't stay in suburban Kentucky and be a filmmaker." "I couldn't stay in rural Washington and help people." "I couldn't stay in Texas with the fundamentalists." "I couldn't stay at home, in Wisconsin, where everybody's ignorant." And what white folks would rather do is go to a big city where they can be anonymous and where they don't have to be responsible to their community. They don't even have to be responsible to themselves. It's kinda like a vacation, if you will. They may not think that they're on vacation, but that's kinda what it is. Because they don't have to be responsible to themselves, or their family, or their community. They can just leave that behind. And they're ignoring and denying the fact that if they did stay home in Wisconsin, in Kentucky, in Washington, and Massachusetts, and Texas…there would be less competition for funding to do all the good progressive things that they want to do…Because the problem is, when you leave your white community at home bereft of any thought-provoking culture and activism, then your community grows up and becomes soldiers and senators and congressmen and even presidents. And they wind up making policy for us in New York and Los Angeles and San Francisco. And then you complain that the right wing is fucked up, but the right wing is there because you left. That's why the right wing is there. So you're a hypocrite to sit in New York City with your Obama button at your Obama party and your Obama rally voting for Obama in New York State when Obama is already gonna get elected here without you. But it's not glamorous to go to Colorado and try to get your community to vote for Obama. It's not glamorous to stay in Wisconsin and get your white community to vote for Obama. As a matter of fact, it's dangerous.

JLove: And why is it dangerous?

Danny: Working with your community no matter where you are, no matter what your background is, is dangerous. Because you really have to face who you are and who you're a product of. And some of these people you're a product of may be fundamentalists, or people you don't like, or people you deeply disagree with. And these are the people who, theoretically, you would be embracing and who would be embracing you. But, white privilege affords you the ability to leave. If you are black, you can't really do that. Because your community is more important. If you're Latino, you can't really do that. I'm not saying it doesn't happen. It does happen. But your community is more important. If you're Native American, you can't really do that because your community is more important. So I'm not saying that it happens across the board that every non-white stays at home. I'm just saying you're not afforded the privilege that you are if you're white to abandon your community. So what happens? You move to a big city, and after 5 years in New York or 10 years in Chicago or 15 years in San Francisco you feel entitled again because it's in our DNA as white folks. And I'm gonna tell you why it's in our DNA, ok?

You feel entitled because after 5 or 10 or 15 years of struggling in a big city that you're not from, you feel that you have struggled because you had roaches in your apartment. Because you had a fight with your landlord. Because you got mugged. Because you lived through a cold winter. Because you were stuck on a subway with a million people and someone groped you. You feel like you struggled. But, really, what you've done for yourself is you have simulated struggle. You have lived a simulated struggle because the real struggle would have been to stay at home in your white community and work with your community and be a teacher there. Or be a voter registration person there. Or be an activist or an artist there. But you haven't really struggled in the city. You have simulated struggle. And we like to simulate struggle as white folks. We love it.

JLove: It's a choice to stay or leave?

Danny: There's an element of choice. But also—it's sexy. It's part of our objectification and our exotification of people of color. We want to feel like we were black. We want to feel like we're Latino. We want to feel like we struggled and overcame things. But we don't actually want to be black. We don't actually want to be kicked out of our apartment or get arrested by the cops or get sodomized in prison or get sentenced to a Rockefeller Drug law. But we want to feel like we did because it affirms our sense of entitlement that we ignore. Why is it in our DNA? It's in our DNA to feel comfortable going to a place that's not ours and setting up shop and simulating struggle because centuries and centuries and centuries of our leaders have told us that it's okay. So it doesn't matter what our politics are: it's part of us. The same way for centuries and centuries and centuries black folks were told they were inferior. So even if you're a college professor and you're black, you have been programmed to think—because of slavery and because of colonialism—that you are inferior. Of course, you can educate yourself out of that, and if you're white you can educate yourself out of thinking that you're entitled. But it's still your instinct. So it's in your DNA. People on the left refuse to believe that. White folks on the left refuse to believe that. Because we don't want to be blamed for white privilege because, clearly, it's the Bush regime and the Cheney regime and, you know, McCain and Palin that are the oppressors of society and it's not us. But it is.

JLove: I don't know if you remember or not, but I moved from Colorado when I was 17 years old. I didn't know any of this shit. I was like, "I need to get the hell out of here." And now listening to you the idea comes up, like, what would it actually be like if I moved back? It's been a long journey, I have roots here now. But maybe you're right. What you're saying makes absolute sense to me. But what now?'

Danny: Sure. Well, it's interesting what your questions are, even just there… "Does that mean I should move back home?" or "What does that mean?" There's a writer named Adrianne Piper, and she talks about something called white people's fatigue, which means that we just want an answer, a quick fix answer that absolves us of our participation in racism. In other words, "So what does that mean? Should I NOT vote for Obama? What should I do? Just TELL me what to do! I don't actually want to do the work, I just want to know what to do. Tell me what to do so I'm not guilty." Because white folks are tired at having the finger pointed at us. Where do we go from here? We displace more people. We continue to affirm our entitlement as white progressives. We feel great, and we pat ourselves on the back because we elected a black president, and, therefore, we're all revolutionaries. We continue to do our good work on the left. And we continue to destroy other people's lives while helping some.

JLove: Should I go get the razor out now?

Danny: J, we can't help it…A whole bunch of progressive white folks, maybe one of them in this room, would like to think that that's not true. That, "There's an end to this. We can stop racism." Look, we can all continue to do our work. And, a lot of that work is good work. Dana Kaplan is in Louisiana doing amazing work in the Juvenile Justice Project… The work you're doing, the work I'm doing, right? It's great work. And we're effective with that work. I'm not saying that we're not effective, and I'm not saying that work doesn't lead to good things. But that work also makes us feel good because we feel that, if we're doing that work, well, then we're not entitled. And if we're doing that work, then we don't have to worry about white privilege. And I'm just saying that it's simultaneous. So when I sit here and I indict us as white folks—as progressive white folks—I'm not saying that we're fucked up and we should all go away. White people get defensive because that's part of our white privilege DNA. It's to feel that we are the victim here. We are being attacked. We don't want to think that if we're doing good, progressive work that has proven to be effective, that we are part of the problem. And if you tell us that we're part of the problem while we're part of the solution, then we become indignant. As us white folks know how to do very well. Malcolm X said, "If you're not part of the solution, you're part of the problem." And I feel that at the same time that I agree with that, right now the majority of progressive white folks—if not all of us—are part of the solution and part of the problem at the same time. Which is why people of color get so frustrated with us.

JLove: Well, do you believe that will ever change? You keep referring to DNA, and it feels very lasting, like, this is who we are, and it's not going to change.

Danny: Not during our lifetime. But look, we have centuries and centuries of colonialism to work through. So it's not going to happen in 100 years. It didn't happen in 400 years, you know? You know when people ask me at the end of my show, "What's the solution to gentrification?" I say, "That's like saying, 'What's the solution to colonialism?'" Because what we're talking about here, as white privilege or racism or entitlement, is all colonialism. That's all it is. So we may think that we're advanced somehow in our thinking because you're interviewing me and typing it in your wireless laptop, a black man is the president of the United States, which used to be a former colony of another empire. But what happens in everyday reality around the world and in our lives is no different from colonialism as it went down in the 1500s. So...the solution would be for, like...I don't know. There is no solution. The solution is that we keep doing the work that we're doing mindfully? I don't know. The solution is that we blow people up and take their wealth and distribute it equally? That's not gonna happen.

JLove: You know, I have to say…you're really negative, dude. (Both laugh) And you're clear about the issues but it just seems like you're nihilistic about the possibility of change.

Danny: No, I think we're making change. And, as we make change we also run over people in the street. So I'm not nihilistic. I'm realistic. I know that as we make change, we inevitably run over some people in the street at the same time. And I'm going to make this analogy for you. The analogy is, the U.S. going into Iraq. Now, of course, progressive white folks will get mad with that analogy because we don't want to think of ourselves as down with that policy. Right? Because it came from an oil baron and his oil baron friends. But let's talk about the soldiers. Right? Not the people who made the policy. The soldiers were told they were going to liberate this country from oppression. So, that's what they're thinking as they're going in, and that's what progressive white people think. We think that we're going to liberate the world from oppression. But because the soldiers are unaware of their power and their colonial privilege, they ride around in Humvees, and they can't see—literally, they cannot see—the children that they've run over in the street while they're driving in their Humvees liberating the country. And we, as progressive white folks, who are liberating the world from oppression, which is a noble cause that either we were told that we were doing, or we told ourselves that we are doing, we cannot see the people that we are running over in the street because we are sitting in a Humvee, and the people we are supposedly trying to liberate are on the street. So I'm not nihilistic, but realistic, when I say we run over people while we do good work. Or, while we think we're doing good work.

JLove: You've talked a lot about progressive whites. What would you say to politically conservative or middle of the road white people who maybe are angry about things like affirmative action, who feel like black people are taking our jobs and immigrants are taking over? What do you say to those folks?

Danny: I say that the reason that you feel that way is because of white liberals. (Laughs) Because in white liberal politics there's no room for working class white people. Working class white people don't exist.

JLove: The work that we're doing is primarily aimed at white people—our community. How do we have the conversation of white privilege when the stance from some people is, like, "I have no white privilege. It doesn't exist for me." How do we engage?

Danny: With great difficulty. That's how we engage. The way people are going to engage when they read what the fuck I just said. With great difficulty. The Ku Klux Klan exists because of Northern white liberalism. Because when there was the drive for abolition and the Civil War happened, the progressive whites in the North, who felt like, "Hey, yay! We're going to liberate black folks!"—even though it was really about economy and not about the liberation of black folks—left all these poor white folks with no place in the conversation. So what are you going to do when you have no place in the conversation? You're going to go to extremism.

JLove: I just wanna keep that conversation happening.

Danny: Ok. Let's talk about that specifically. You don't want to alienate white people. JLove, my producers have told me they don't want me to alienate white people in my show, because white people can't stand to feel alienated. It would do the white left some good to know what it's like to feel alienated. (Both laugh) But, we can't stand it. There was an old white woman who came up to me after a show of Jails, Hospitals, and Hip-Hop where there were a majority of young folks— particularly young folks of color— in the audience. She said, "I love your show. I learned so much about racism. I learned so much about Hip-Hop, and I learned so much about things going on in society. But, I felt alienated for the first time ever sitting in the theatre, and it didn't feel good." And I said, "Congratulations." And I hugged her, and said, "That's what those young people feel like every time they're dragged to a theatre and you are the majority. And that's white privilege." Why do white folks have to feel good about what we're doing all the fucking time? Is it illegal for white progressive folks to feel alienated? Why do we have to feel included? Why do we have to feel like shit is about us? Why do we, as white progressive activists and artists, have to feel celebrated all the time? What would happen if we all sat there together alienated and thought about it for a little bit? Huh? What would happen? Would we turn into Klan members? I don't think so. But we're not allowed to feel alienated. It's too painful. This is what folks of color do every day for a living!

JLove: Obviously, the white community is not monolithic. People are in different places. The majority of white people who come to my workshops are mostly dealing with white guilt and shame, like I was doing when I started this work. When I first found out about how fucked up white people were I wanted to kill myself. You know? I couldn't believe I never knew about the injustice. And then, just the burden of being white, and truly understanding that we're responsible! My ancestors, my family-

Danny: I hope you put that in the book. That's really important what you just said.

JLove: So, I'm dealing with people who are suffering from guilt, and it manifests itself in different ways. For me it turned into self-hatred because I hated being white. In my experience when white people have been educated in a way where they finally understand and learn about white supremacy, there's a phase where you feel extremely shitty about yourself for being white. When I think of those people my goal is to get us to a place where we can accept our whiteness and be okay with it, and actually celebrate it. I think it's absolutely essential to support white people in the process of moving out of guilt and shame.

Danny: The majority of white folks I meet on the left, their layers of entitlement are so deep that white guilt is not gonna do it for them, embracing them is not gonna do it either. What my response is: I am so sorry if I made you feel uncomfortable. I apologize, God forbid, you feel uncomfortable in the theater in one night, when every cultural event in this city is made to make you feel comfortable. Now you can write my show off and everything that is in it, because white people like our analysis of white privilege in a way that affirms us, but not in a way that implicates us. Because it is inconvenient to be implicated. And, it would seem contradictory, especially if we are working for justice, but what we are doing is contradictory; everybody is contradictory. White privilege is a collective of housing advocates who aren't from here. They don't see the irony that we would not need any housing advocates if they hadn't moved here.

JLove: Is anybody doing anything right?

Danny: The key to understanding white privilege is to know that while you are doing good, you are doing bad. Once you think that you are doing just all good, there's a problem, because someone is getting run over because of something you are doing, because you are sitting in a Humvee. If you get out of the Humvee, your presence as a white person on the street in a community of people of color leads to the police showing up to protect you. And you spend money, and you change the economy of the community. Nobody used to pay four dollars for an espresso; now they do. Even people of color cater to you, because of colonization. Every action you take because of your whiteness is going to dispossess people of color. Sorry if that contributes to white guilt, but welcome to the club.

✎ *Sonia Sanchez: Full Circle* ✎

An Interview with *Sonia Sanchez conducted by April R. Silver*

April: You've traveled all over the world and have met so many different kinds of people. There's wisdom in those relationships, and you have an analysis that could really elevate the conversation about race. In your work, how have you, over the years, addressed issues facing both white people and people of color on the issue of race?

Sonia: My dear sister, one of the things that my generation had to answer is the question of what does it mean to be human even after having your ancestors enslaved, even after segregation, even after being turned down for a million jobs when people said you didn't qualify or you were overqualified? How do you approach this whole thing of humanity; can you actually keep any supposed hatred at bay? A lot of people give up doing any kind of struggle against racism. They say "You hate me? Okay. I'll hate you back." My generation had to say "no," there's another way we can do this.

People didn't really talk about slavery, racism, discrimination, segregation, you know. It was a one-liner some place in the history books. There might be a picture of some guy with a watermelon or someone working out in the cotton fields. I think what we'd begun to do in the 1960s was to begin this conversation with the country about race, racism, and what it means to be human. What it means to be a black man and a black woman. Obama talking about change was a conversation that we had in the 60s, a conversation that had begun in the 20s, before the Harlem Renaissance.

There has been in my head a constant conversation in this place called America. How do we change the status quo, change from something that, in a sense, infects this whole country? How do we do something beyond putting a Band-Aid on it? We said we're gonna do surgery, we're gonna massage that heart, and we're gonna *deal*.

April: Not too long ago, me, you, and Kevin Powell had gone to dinner in New York. We talked about many things, including race, and you recalled this interesting dynamic, a number of scenarios and conversations where some white people today desire to be punished for what their ancestors did to our ancestors; they want to hear us, black people, call them these names and be hurtful to them. I suppose that this is an attempt to release some of the guilt, I guess. There are some who go so far as to re-enact slavery where they, white people, are the enslaved. I think you said some of these re-enact-ment retreats take place in some Caribbean countries…where white people can go and be put in chains, and black people play the role of the master. It was their way of trying to experience…

Sonia: Slavery.

April: Yeah. I remember it sparking a conversation amongst the three of us. That was an interesting dynamic, and it runs in contrast to some white people who believe that racism today is non-existent or that it has nothing to do with them or their status in society.

Sonia: Well, I think that enlightened and progressive whites understand that racism certainly did occur and is still occurring. The problem is do they want to help eradicate it?

April: What are some things white people can do to eradicate racism, things they can do specifically as a group?

Sonia: There are many things we all can do. I think that always the key is educating people. Teach black literature; teach women's literature; and teach black history. Go into the classroom and you look and you listen, and you learn and you understand some of the schisms that have developed between black women and white women, which came at the turn of the cen-tury when women's organizations were supposed to be organizing *but they really were not.* When some organizations tried to include black women, the southern white women said, "I'm not gonna be around those black women." They brought their racism up north to these organizations, and that's why black women, as an aside, organized their own women's organizations.

We've got to really look at each other and understand we are sisters and brothers. I always try to get my students to call each other sister and brother when they responded in class. I encourage them to be willing to really explore more about each other. You cannot talk about race and racism 'til we really look at what has happened in this country as it relates to us, including the rape of black women and black men by white men. It's part of the reason why we look the way we look in this country. We're saying that blacks and whites in America are bound by this twindom, what I call this secondary consciousness, this duality.

April: And we all have the "white is right" mentality right? Black people have it, white people have it.

Sonia: Well not everybody. The 60s caused something to happen. I'm on the circuit with university students all the time, and it pops up every now and then but, by the very fact that I'm onstage they know that white is not necessarily right, now. There's a different agenda with many of these young people, my dear sister.

April: So you see that there's a shift?

Sonia: I tell ya, life is funny. Ten years later students send you letters saying "Professor Sanchez, you were right." One of my students in the women's studies department I chaired at Temple says, "Professor Sanchez, you probably don't remember me. You came to speak at my college, and you told us 'You got to be truly satisfied with yourself. You have to really love yourself. You don't want to be somebody else. You want to be you.'" This is awareness; this is love of self. And when you love yourself you don't have to envy or kill someone, beat someone up, or want to enslave somebody, even.

Part of what has happened in America is Europeans that came here were not rich people. They came from countries that are what we would call bush countries. It's not like Europe now; these were whole other different countries. How do you then maintain your "civilized nature?" How do you not involve yourself with what they thought was non-civilized country? You had to have something to hold on to. And one of the things that they had to do—at some point—is that they had to hold on to whiteness, this European way. This whiteness was better than these Native Americans. They had to make themselves understand that they were better than these "savages." You had to, in a sense, raise your own light from Europe and darken the light of people who were already here. And most certainly when enslaved

Africans came, you really had to do that more because the point is you could become like them. There was always the danger of becoming like the people who were here. So how do you keep from doing that? You erect something that would make you certainly "not a native." Whiteness was the way in America.

April: And in the process degrading their own humanity…

Sonia: Of course. That goes with that, too. You had to be superior. Once you embarked on that train you had to keep to it. In this country there's been an interesting kind of progressive strand that runs through our history/herstory that we don't really talk about a great deal. Even Quakers, who were supposed to be coming here for freedom, owned slaves. I'm saying all this [because] I have been to many sites from New England to the South, and in the midst of reading a couple of poems I have been able to become attuned to something that has happened there, and I've literally cried as I read; literally sobbed because there are those areas where, from Native Americans to African-Americans, people have been slaughtered in this country. Witches, women have been burned because they tried to be much more human, different than people wanted them to be. I hope you can understand the connection. They were being burned because they also were probably women who saw something beyond what the majority of people were willing to see at that particular time as they just struggled to survive.

When you re-attune young people and identify these sites all over, then at some point we've got to understand we're opening up people's eyes to this history and herstory. Then they will begin to understand, indeed, why Blacks and Latinos and Asians and Native Americans and others have asked for Black Studies and Women Studies and Native American studies, and Asian studies, and Chicano studies, and Jewish studies, saying "we just want to learn something about ourselves at some point so that we can put it into perspective and truly understand, but at the same time we want *you* to learn."

April: And that brings us full circle. You have bought us back to what you have learned, what wisdom you have gleaned from relating to all kinds of people. Thank you, dear Sonia.

A Love Letter to White America...No, Seriously

Dear White America,

Forgive me for writing you one big letter, rather than taking the time to compose some 200 million separate ones, personalize 'em, and seal 'em with a great big kiss. But, I got some shit to do and not a lot of time in which to do it, so for now, just consider this a group hug.

Yeah, I know, a hug is not what you were expecting. Not from me anyway. I mean, I'm one of you—a member of the club, so to speak—but still, sometimes I get the impression that you think I don't much like you. In fact, just the other day, one of our number wrote me to ask why it was I hate white people so much.

Same stuff I hear on the regular: Tim Wise hates white people. Tim Wise hates himself. Crazy stuff. And I just wanted to make sure we were straight, you and me, 'cuz, ya' know, I don't want to be misunderstood. Besides, fact is, not only do I not hate you—I mean, us—I actually love you, blemishes and all; hell, oozing sores and all, I still love you. I don't always feel so hot about what you—I mean, we—have done. Nor am I real big on loving the unearned privileges and advantages we get just for lack of melanin. But hating that is not the same as hating white people. That stuff is about whiteness, which isn't the same as you, in case you didn't know that. Whiteness and white supremacy are systemic things, but you're just folks, caught up in the bullshit like everyone else. The only difference is, some of y'all don't know it yet.

Really it's sorta funny, ya know? To be accused of hating white people just because you speak out against white privilege and white racism. I mean, think it through with me: if being against white racism makes a person "anti-white," then doesn't that mean that racism is like the essence of being white? Doesn't it mean that being pro white racism is somehow the only way to show your love for white people? Doesn't it mean that white people and racism are pretty much synonymous? Or, at least like an old married couple? Messed up, dontcha' think? I mean, seriously, have you ever considered that? How ass-backwards it is to basically decide that we are collectively so evil, you and me, that we just can't help ourselves, and that trying to break free from the conditioning we've been exposed to is somehow to betray one another? It's sorta' like saying that for a man to critique rape is to be anti-male, which is to say that rape is the essence of masculinity. Now <u>that</u> is self-hating.

You see—and I may be wrong in this—I think you're better than that—that we are. I'm convinced we have choices. I know we do, because I've seen people exercise them and even made some myself. I know that for every Andrew Jackson—land stealing, Indian killing bastard that he was—there's a Jeremiah Evarts standing up against him and saying no. For every John Calhoun, defending the system of enslavement, there's a John Fee, challenging it, refusing to even provide communion to parishioners in his church so long as they owned other human beings and willing to be defrocked for his insolence. For every Bull Connor there's a Virginia Durr; for every George Wallace a Bob or Dottie Zellner. And yes, I know that for most of you, these names I mention in praise and in contrast to the others won't even be recognizable. And, I also know that there's a reason for that, and it's one you ought to ask yourself about from time to time.

Ask yourself why you know so well the names of those whose lives were defined by the cruelty they meted out to others, why you know the names and maybe even the biographies of the worst amongst us, but almost nothing about the best, almost nothing about those in our little tribe who placed their humanity—ours—above the conceit of skin alone. And trust me when I tell you, once you allow yourself to really think about why you know the one but not the other, the answers that will come to you won't be the comforting kind. They'll be answers you might wish you'd never known. The kind that make you realize that somewhere, along the way, whiteness tricked you, too. In this case, it made you identify with the perpetration of injustice and to jealously defend your own reputation from critique, even as you had these other role models all along, right there waiting for you to join them, to follow in their footsteps. And, had you joined them, your reputation wouldn't be half as sullied as it is now by virtue of your silence, your defensiveness, your denial.

So are you ready then? Are we? Ready to choose again and this time, perhaps, get it right? Ready to choose again and this time, to live in this skin differently? Ready to relinquish the bonds that we have placed around our own bodies and minds, thanks to white supremacy? Ready to join the circle of humanity but this time merely as equals, rather than as lords and masters?

I mean, it's your choice, and I'll keep loving you no matter what you decide. We're too tightly bound for me to do otherwise. But really now, the clock is ticking, time is tight, and all the world is dying, quite literally, for your answer. So think it over, but get back at me quickly. We have some shit to do. And not a lot of time in which to do it.

With Love,

Tim Wise

◈ ◈ ◈

"**I** imagine one of the reasons people cling to their hates so stubbornly is because they sense, once hate is gone, they will be forced to deal with pain."

--James Baldwin

Chapter 3

❧ *(Mis) Education & Socialization:*
You Are What You're Taught ❦

I have always agreed with a common sentiment that people are born whole, healthy, and full of love to give and receive; and slowly each person learns through social cues, through culture, through institutions, religion, and education, the "real deal." When facilitating workshops about white privilege I often ask adults when they first learned about racial differences and what they learned about them?

Many white adults share painful stories of the small but powerful moments when they were taught who they could play with and who they could not. Comments like "they are not the same as us" and "stick with your own" often come up during these discussions, and it's clear that, while the words themselves could pass as innocuous, the underlying message, repeated often enough, can create an ugly web of distrust, fear, and otherness that sets the foundation of insidious unconscious prejudice for whole generations. Combine the personal, family, and community socialization with the institutionalized educational socialization, and it is easy to see how individuals fell into (and continue to fall into) destructive belief systems.

So, how are we combatting the web of illusions that perpetuates racism and discrimination? Well, in the education field we have some very brave souls who have dedicated their lives to education for liberation and social justice. At San Diego State University, I was blessed to have mentors and teachers like the incredible Dr. Floyd Hayes III and Dr. Shirely Weber. Across the country there are educators of color and white educators who are taking a stand against institutionalized racism and white supremacy in the name of justice and equality. Two educators who you will hear from next, Héctor Calderón and Marcella Runell Hall, stand out as exceptional educators. Their work in this arena is widely respected, and I celebrate both of their commitments to *educate to liberate*.

❖ ❖ ❖

❧ The Schools We Need ❧

By *Héctor Calderón*

"Stakes is high," once proclaimed the celebrated Native Tongue crew De La Soul. And indeed, Stakes have never been higher for the educational future of our country. We live in a nation where every 26 seconds a student drops out of high school. That's 1.3 million students a year, according to the Alliance for Excellent Education. And, for those that graduate their diploma is not necessarily a validation of their preparation for college. This problem is particularly grave for young people of color who are victimized by an educational system that systematically deprives them of opportunities afforded to those in richer, whiter districts. This issue has been called the Achievement Gap. But the term "Achievement Gap" does not hold accountable the educational system that is complicit for the under achievement of young people of color. How does it feel to be a problem? The African-American intellectual W.E.B. Du Bois wondered in his 1903 classic *Souls of Black Folks*. He went on to say that race would be the defining issue of the 20th century, and some 109 years later it is still the defining issue today in terms of poverty, educational achievement, and the school-to-prison pipeline that particularly plagues Black and Latino men.

As a person of color, I am intimately aware of how schools can under serve young people of color. When my brother and I arrived from Dominican Republic in the late 70s, we landed in the heart of the South Bronx. From 555 Southern Boulevard, one of the few buildings where people resided on the block, you could see rows and rows of burnt-black brick buildings as far as the horizon. There were empty lots filled with all kinds of garbage and rubble. So much has been documented about the South Bronx in the 70s and 80s that I don't think it is worth going into a whole description of the conditions in which we lived. Watch *The Bronx is Burning, Wild Style, Fort Apache, The Bronx,* and many other documentaries and movies to get a glimpse of that period. Although a lot of the images and personages of these movies have been projections of stereotypes that confuse material poverty with poverty of spirit, there is truth to the physical conditions in which most people lived. The South Bronx was one of the poorest sectors in the country at that time. The choices of schools available to my parents and the choices they made for us really tell the story of the intersection of race, class, and education. Schools can be liberating spaces where intellectual curiosity and creativity is cultivated, or they can be oppressive spaces where you learn intimately to feel inferior and blindly obey authority.

I entered high school in the fall of 1979. The school was a large, comprehensive school that was housed in a beautifully designed Gothic building with a rich history. Established in 1897, it was the first public high school in the Bronx. But, by the time I got there, the school in no way matched the physical beauty of the building. It was considered one of the worst high schools in the nation. The first day of school there were hundreds of students milling about the front entrance long after the bell had rung for school to start. I remember large classrooms of 35 or more. For some reason, there were 21 year-olds in my classes. I never dared to go to the bathrooms because it was always filled with a cloud of smoke from students smoking all kinds of things. Teachers never dared walk through the front entrance. They preferred to walk in through the back entrance where there were guards and barbed-wire fences. The teachers were apathetic or at best overwhelmed by the immensity of their jobs. There was much blight in a place that was supposed to be a beacon of hope. Somehow, I began navigating through this large school to rescue what I could of my intellectual self. There were a handful of us who cared about how we did in school. However, the school had such low expectations for us. If you passed all your classes, you were put on the Honor Roll. If you came most days, you were given perfect attendance awards. Homework was a rare occurrence. At some level

Key Factors of Highly Successful Schools:

- Teaching focused on mastery
- Strong relationships between teachers and students
- Comprehensive social, emotional support services
- Effective school leadership
- Powerful school culture focused on an efficacy paradigm
- Aligned curriculum to high standards
- Data-driven instruction
- Effective observation and feedback for teachers and students
- Personalized professional development for staff
- Culturally relevant curriculum
- Strong parent and community involvement
- Provide opportunities for student leadership[1]

this made school easy for me, but I instinctively knew that I was not getting a good education. My parents knew it, too. One day my mother decided to take me to school, and what she saw petrified her. She saw all the gangs outside the school while police sat idly by. She saw firsthand how administrators didn't have control of the school. That same day, she heard about the school shooting in which three young people were killed. To be truthful, I was scared, too. Within a month, we left the South Bronx.

After we moved to Queens, I went to another large comprehensive high school, but the school was a lot more diverse and a lot less dysfunctional. I had never seen so many white students or, for that matter, students from any other ethnic/racial groups. I had only interacted with Blacks and Latinos. This was true of my neighborhood, too. We had a virtual UN. The diversity taught me to appreciate so many different cultural traditions and to value different perspectives. Interestingly, this also accelerated my learning of English. The school didn't have any English as a Second Language instruction. It was learn or fail, sink or swim. I learn to paddle my way through courses. Ultimately, I graduated from high school out of sheer resolve; I knew that there was no other option. My family needed me to graduate, and I needed it, too.

Learners should be the subject of education.

In 1993, I was part the founding team of community leaders who started the El Puente Academy for Peace and Justice. The mission of El Puente Academy for Peace and Justice is to inspire and nurture leadership for peace and justice. To this end, the Academy is guided by four core principles that serve as the foundation for all academic, programmatic, and institutional development. These are creating community, love and caring, mastery, and peace and justice. The Academy strives to achieve its vision in these three ways: by transforming its members into a comprehensive community learning institution; by integrating the resources of both the school and those of our community-based organization, El Puente; and by supporting the holistic development and the highest levels of achievement of Academy students, facilitators, and adult members.

By then, I understood that schools are a profoundly human institution. To paraphrase Wade Davis, schools are a flash of the human spirit. They are the vehicles through which the soul of every teacher and every student comes in to the material world. Schools are not just schools. Schools are sanctuaries of the mind. Schools are an ecosystem of academic, physical, and spiritual possibilities. Schools are community creations. The school is inextricably tied to issues of peace and justice within the community and in the larger community of the world. The purpose of education, especially within marginalized communities, is critically and explicitly attached to developing the self within the context of community and connecting learning to essential skills that students will need for their own intellectual development as well as the development of their community. The school is a fundamental institution in raising the village. I believe in a vision of school that does not separate the world from the world of school.

I'll never forget when I got to meet and learn from Paulo Freire, the renowned Brazilian educator. He became a pivotal figure in giving voice and vision to how I would approach curriculum design. I remember reading one verse in particular in his classic book, *Pedagogy of the Oppressed:* "Learners are the subject of the learning process and not the object, as they have to be the subject of their destiny." I had never thought about education in this way. I believed that an educated person was someone who was learned in all the things that schools deemed important. But, the idea that I was at the center of the learning process and that education should help me understand myself and my ontological stance in the context of the larger world, this was totally foreign to my understanding of what it meant to be educated. This became a critical realization as I began thinking about how I would address learning and eventually help create the El Puente Academy for Peace and Justice. In my learning process I sought to undo years of schooling that had been inculcated into my consciousness. I needed to let go of many notions and practices I associated with learning. I began developing curriculums, like Sankofa, which is a West African word that means "going back to the source to find out who you are" in collaboration with many other facilitators. The curriculum explored two existential questions that have captured the imagination of humanity since the very first pulsations of life were felt on Earth: Who am I? And Who are we? In short, the curriculum explored the questions of identity by using the lens of culture. These questions make up the first two years of the Academy's four-year vision.

So why a curriculum about identity? Identity gives meaning to one's existence. It is how we define ourselves politically, socially, and historically. Identity resonates with that primordial need for self-understanding. Young people, but in particular young people of color, have been systematically denied the quest for self-understanding, the quest for voice. Identity is self-definition. Self-definition is essential to self-determination. This is why I feel that schools should anchor themselves in the quest for self, in the quest for the soul, and in the understanding of community as an essential structure that supports this quest.

The responsibility of schools to their students is to enable students to see themselves as cultural, socio-historical beings. This process of self-understanding does not begin as an intellectual exercise, but it is the job of schools to structure activities that help students to navigate through this journey. In order to understand how schools can do this, it

> "Liberation as defined here, is the process of becoming fully human."

is important for me to explain three essential beliefs, which I hold as tenets in my work. The first tenet is the Freirean idea of education as the process of liberation. Liberation, as defined here, is the process of becoming fully human. All activities and work with young people and the community should be directed at helping them understand something essential about who they are in the larger context of the world. The second tenet is the idea that disciplines come out of the needs and experiences of people. Disciplines or ways of understanding are created to address the community's needs. Therefore, every culture and civilization has created its own disciplines to address its own concerns. If disciplines were meant to address the community's needs, we should not separate community organizing from schools. The third tenet is that knowledge is holistic. Knowledge in its natural state is not deconstructed into different branches of understanding. Instead, it is an integrated system of understanding. For example, a conch seashell can be studied from the perspective of a marine biologist or from the perspective of a cultural anthropologist when looking at how the Tainos, the indigenous people of the Caribbean, used it as way of signaling celebrations. At the same time its spiral design might be of interest to mathematicians who recognize in it the basic principles of acceleration and deceleration, also known as the Fibonacci sequence. There are many other contexts in which a seemingly simple seashell could be represented as knowledge, yet the seashell integrates all of it beautifully. When you use these tenets as a framework for designing schools, you begin to create learning communities in which the worlds of students are valuable funds of knowledge, in which parents, families, and community residents are a valuable resource. The school understands itself as a community creation, and therefore it's only natural that it celebrates the community's cultures and histories, as well as addressing its concerns and well-being.

Since its founding in 1993, El Puente Academy has created a legacy of academic achievement and community development. We generally have had a high graduation and college acceptance rate. Our graduates have attended a whole host of colleges, ranging from private universities to local SUNY and CUNY state colleges. Since 2007, we have earned four high A's in New York City's Progress Reports. For the past three years we have been in the top three percent of all NYC schools. I speak about this because it is important to declare success when warranted, but at the same time, I also want to acknowledge that this work is not easy. We have not always been able to work effectively with each class of students, and our data will show that also. Teaching is a sacred process. Every time we walk into a classroom with the intention to teach, we have entered into a sacred covenant with our students. It is our commitment that will declare to the world that we have a deep stake educating all children, regardless of race, color, or class. And, with our actions we can seal this commitment.

"Schools are an ecosystem of academic, physical, and spiritual possibilities. "

[1] Compiled by Héctor Calderón from the research of Paul Bambrick-Santoyo and Pedro Noguera.

❧ *Occupy the Spirit of Education* ❧

By *Marcella Runell Hall*

I am a mother, sister, friend, partner, scholar, supervisor, teacher, neighbor, author, lover, spiritual being, and more…and I occupy interracially intimate spaces in most areas of my life. I have a vested interest in interrogating my own "white" privilege and deconstructing racism in all facets of society, particularly education. I also identify as a social justice scholar and as a member of the Hip-Hop generation because of my long-standing relationship to the music and my passion for the culture. I cannot remember a time without Hip-Hop, but I do remember many times when it felt new, special, or under the radar. Hip-Hop has a major influence on how I see the world and how I experience my various social identities. And because it is a generation that I am a part of and something that I am continually thinking about in my professional experience as a social justice educator, I believe it is useful to explore as a strategy that can help us all to interrogate systems of oppression and can help us to "be the change we would like to see."

I remember first hearing the Boogie Down Productions (KRS-One) song, "*Love is Gonna Getcha*" in 1989, and it seemed to describe exactly what I was seeing in my life. I felt such a strong connection to that song because it was bearing witness to the counterintuitive things I was observing as the result of an unforgiving and ravishing drug culture. I had many friends who were in constant fear of getting caught up in the criminal justice system because they were hustling to make a few dollars selling illegal drugs. From that point, Hip-Hop always served as a counter-narrative and informer of current events in a way that no other medium could be for me.

As an educator, I began realizing that Hip-Hop might have the power and strength to create an identity and a political agenda, and that meant Hip-Hop might also work as critical pedagogy. That is, once I learned what critical pedagogy was and once I realized Hip-Hop had always been a public critical pedagogy for myself and many of my peers. Simply put, critical pedagogy is about naming societal conditions, reflecting on your part in the process, questioning the norms of the process, and finding or creating solutions to the problems. Although it would be sometime before I found other people who were working towards a similar goal, I felt that I was on the brink of witnessing a movement.

When I entered the Social Justice Education doctoral program, I came in ready to prove my theory that Hip-Hop as critical pedagogy was also social justice work. I was met with a lukewarm response at best. Most of the well-intentioned faculty and many of my fellow students asked, "Why Hip-Hop? Why would you study that?" How could I not? I thought, once I understood that people weren't making the connection between Hip-Hop and social justice. As I learned about Freire and the idea that "popular education" meant meeting students where they are in order to name, to reflect, and to act for/ create social change, I started to understand the power of using Hip-Hop to teach for social justice. The music and culture provided intrinsic value and seemed to be engaging and interesting for many students. Hip-Hop had provided me with my most powerful lessons in social justice throughout my childhood and continuing on into my adulthood through the work of artists, such as KRS-One, Sister Souljah, Public Enemy, and Queen Latifah.

> For all of the problems and passions it arouses, Hip-Hop connects with its youth constituency like nothing else can or will. When virtually nothing else could, Hip-Hop created a voice and vehicle for the young and dispossessed, giving them both hope and inspiration. (Watkins, 2004, p. 7)

However, I do not believe that Hip-Hop can provide answers for every educator or student searching for creative modalities to address issues of civic engagement or social injustice. And in fact, I spend a good deal of my academic writing cautioning against such quick-fixes or bandwagon approaches to teaching and learning. As two of my colleagues eloquently explain, the purpose of Hip-Hop pedagogy is to encourage critical thinking, not make Hip-Hop culture the next hegemonic approach to teaching.

> Our purpose as educators is not to simply replace one dominant ideology with another; the goal is not to make them slaves to a different (more politically correct) ideology. (Duncan-Andrade & Morrell, 2008, p.187)

Creating a model for utilizing Social Justice Hip-Hop Pedagogy is not about creating a new rigid set of requirements or a quick fix to major educational inequities. Wink (2005) defines critical pedagogy as being able to name, to reflect critically, and to act. But she stresses, "I doubt I can teach someone how to do critical pedagogy. We do not do critical pedagogy; we live it. Critical pedagogy is not a method; it is a way of life" (p. 120). I agree with this analysis and approach. Critical pedagogy, in its essence, is where civic engagement and interdisciplinary thought merge and the ability to create new knowledge is born.

I believe that there are many aspects of teaching and learning that speak to my personal teaching philosophy. In the spirit of intersectional pioneers, such as Audre Lorde, I am informed by my own interdisciplinary background, and I excel in creative approaches that honor multiple learning styles. I enjoy diverging opinions and lively dialogue in spaces that are constructed to encourage such exchange. I appreciate multiple learning styles, and strongly believe that experiential learning can be a rich and profound opportunity for learning. However, I do believe that in all facets of educational experiences, excellence and rigor should not be sacrificed under the guise of creativity. Theory, research, and the acceptance of intellectualism as being an important facet of democracy must always be protected. For this reason, I believe in organization, equity, and consistency as a teacher and believe we can be pragmatic, socially active, and intellectually curious all at the same time. As bell hooks describes the intersection of emotion and intellectualism and the power of theory in questions of social justice and civic engagement,

> I came to theory because I was hurting—the pain within me was so intense that I could not go on living. I came to theory desperate, wanting to comprehend, to grasp what was happening around and within me. Most importantly, I wanted to make the hurt go away. I saw in theory then a location for healing. (hooks, 1994, p.59)

hooks's description of the significance of theory and its usefulness in her journey is a poignant commentary on the quest to theorize Hip-Hop as pedagogy. The practical applications of Hip-Hop as pedagogy are being demonstrated daily in classrooms across the U.S. Yet, the justification for this pedagogical application of Hip-Hop remains under-theorized. It is my hope that as an academic I will continue to contribute to this conversation, as a point of healing and to engage future scholars.

It is fairly common knowledge that the overall cultural disconnect between teachers and students inherent in most U.S. classrooms (Ladson-Billings, 2001) has seemingly grown since Brown v. Board of Education (Love, 2004). At present in the United States, approximately 41% of school-age children in grades K-12 identify as Black or Latino (National Center for

Educational Statistics, 2005). In contrast, 80% of the teachers in U.S. schools are white women (National Collaborative on Diversity of the Teaching Force, 2004). In fact, almost half of U.S. schools do not have a single teacher of color on staff (Jordon-Irvine, 2003). This means that most students of all backgrounds will graduate from high school having been taught primarily by white women. While it is understood that race and gender are only two salient social identities in educational settings, they are important in how students navigate "success" in educational spaces and often serve as indicators of who will be successful in formal school settings (Ladson- Billings, 2001). Despite the positive results reported by many educators (Hill, 2009; Runell & Diaz, 2007, Parmar, 2005), it has been an uphill battle to prove the merits of formally infusing Hip-Hop into education. Blackman (Runell, 2006) recalls, "It's only recently that Hip-Hop in education has been embraced. I remember getting cancelled by the principal the day of an event, they didn't care that I had a Masters degree, they didn't give a damn that I traveled the world, all they knew is that this girl is… a rapper" (p.3).

It has also become exceedingly obvious that there is a hidden curriculum and a ceiling that is imposed by the opportunity gap for students of color (Baszile, 2009; Love, 2004; Apple & King, 1983). The opportunity gap for students of color in the United States is often mistakenly referred to as an achievement gap, which measures Black and Latino students' standardized test scores in comparison to white students. This is a mistake because over the course of U.S. history, public schools have repeatedly failed to create equitable educational opportunities for students of color (Love, 2004) as evidenced in monumental court decisions, such as Plessy v. Ferguson 1896, which required separate and equal schools.

And then, Brown v. Board of Education 1954 was meant to be an "equalizer" for students of color by creating access to well-funded predominantly white schools. Unfortunately, rather than measure the "achievement" of such legal decisions, school policies, school administrators, curriculum developers, or teachers, it has been erroneously framed as a student achievement gap. Solely measuring the achievement of the students is a byproduct of misguided policies and decision-making. The achievement problem is more of an opportunity gap (Noguera, 2008). The use of Hip-Hop as pedagogy will not be able to change the history or the obvious policy-maker "achievement" gap that is present in schools; however, it does offer a new way for teachers to think about student culture and an opportunity to create more culturally relevant teaching methods (Ladson-Billings, 2001), which are reflective not only of the often hegemonic, white, male version of American culture (i.e. hidden curriculum) but in fact are reflective of all students; which has proven to create more opportunity for student success for all students (hooks, 1995). As I began this essay, I, like most people, am a fairly complex person full of contradictions with my own multiple identities and a salient passion for healing oppression. I believe the solutions are right at our fingertips, but the time is now. We are required to occupy the spirit of education by demanding more from ourselves, our teachers, schools, curriculum developers, leaders…and each other. The world needs us to activate our collective conscience.

Apple, M. W., & King, N. R. (1978). What do schools teach? In G. Willis (Ed.). Concepts and cases in curriculum criticism (pp. 446-465). Berkeley, CA: McCutchan.

Baszile, D. T. (2009). Deal with it we must: Education, social justice, and the curriculum of hip hop culture. Equity and Excellence in Education, 42(1), 6-19.

Duncan-Andrade, J.M.R., & Morrell, E. (2002). Promoting academic literacy with urban youth through engaging hip hop culture. English Journal, 91(6), 88-92.

Duncan-Andrade, J. M. & Morrell, E. (2008). Art of critical pedagogy possibilities for moving from theory to practice in urban schools. New York: Peter Lang.

Jordan-Irvine, J. J. (2003). Educating teachers for diversity: Seeing with a cultural eye. New York: Teachers College Press.

Ladson-Billings, G., & Tate, W. F., IV. (1995). Toward a critical race theory of education. Teachers College Record, 97(1), 47-68.

Hill, M. L. (2009). Beats, Rhymes, and Classroom Life: Hip-Hop Pedagogy and the Politics of Identity. New York: Teachers College Press.

hooks, b. (1994). Teaching to Transgress. New York: New Press.

Love, B. J. (2004). Brown plus 50 counter-storytelling: A critical race theory analysis of the "majoritarian achievement gap" story. Equity and Excellence in Education, 37, 227-246.

National Center for Educational Statistics (2005) Estimates of resident population, by race/ethnicity and age group: Selected years, 1980 through 2004 [Data file]. Available from the Digest of Education Web site: http://nces.ed.gov/programs/digest/index.asp

National Collaborative on Diversity in the Teaching Force. (2004). Assessment of diversity in America's teaching force: A call to action. Washington, DC: National Education Association.

Noguera, P.A. (2008). The Trouble With Black Boys: And Other Reflections On Race, Equity, And The Future Of Public Education. San Francisco: Jossey-Bass.

Parmar, P. (2005). Cultural studies and rap: The poetry of an urban lyricist. Taboo: The Journal of Culture and Education, 9(1), 5-15.

Runell Hall, M. (2006, September). Hip-hop education 101. Vibe Online Exclusive (www.vibe.com/news/online_exclusives/2006/09/hip_hop_education_101/ Retrieved July 1, 2008).

Runell Hall, M., & Diaz, M. (2007). The Hip-Hop Education Guidebook: Volume 1. New York City: Hip-Hop Association

Watkins, C. S. (2005). Hip Hop Matters Politics, Popular Culture, and the Struggle for the Soul of a Movement. New York: Beacon Press.

Wink, J. (2004) Critical Pedagogy: Notes from the Real World. New York City: Allyn & Bacon

❖ ❖ ❖

My good friend, the brilliant activist-scholar Rosa Clemente, introduced me to Dr. Jared Ball at a Hip-Hop conference. The word "lecture" doesn't even begin to capture the experience we had watching the "Dr. Jared Ball Experience": DJ, multi-media images on a big screen, lecture/emceeing, spoken word throughout. Droppin' knowledge so hard it made my head spin.

Jared and I got to talking, and when he told me his story I was caught up in the intrigue of it all. It got to the heart of how education, socialization, and upbringing contribute to our worldview and gave insight into what is possible, given the right nurturing from family to institutions and community.

Jared's life story is an example of going against societal norms and creating justice in your own sphere of influence. His mother Arnette did what she thought was right in raising her son, which was her sphere of influence. Her son now reaches a huge number of students through his teachings and his books, giving rise to ever-greater spheres. His story shows us how, brick by brick, we can take control in our world and dismantle racism.

❧ *A Black Nationalist Raised by a White Jew?* ❧

An Interview with *Dr. Jared Ball and his mother, Arnette Ball conducted by JLove Calderón*

JLove: How did a white Jewish woman raise a Black nationalist?

Arnette: I have no idea! My family were Jewish leftists, so there already existed that radical environment. Jared's father was an activist and very committed to the struggle for civil rights, but our marriage didn't last long, and I became the single parent of a Black child. It just sort of came natural to me that he could see that he was the product of two great traditions: the Jews and the Africans. But I don't remember forcefully teaching him to be an activist. He came to that at an early age. He was maybe fourteen or fifteen, and we were talking about racism and some of the experiences he had as a bi-racial child at school, and he asked me where racism came from. And, why it existed. And, I caught a glimmer in his eye. He really came to it on his own.

Jared: One of the things that happened fundamentally is that my mother taught that all humanity deserved to be treated equally. She has this deep concern for progressivism and change and equality. What she did for me was teach me that Blackness was equal to all, and that Black men in particular were equal and powerful. I had the reverse mythology. All people need and have myths used to manufacture cohesion (or "consent" as has been famously said). This is the purpose of national anthems and pledges of allegiance, for instance, to create even the illusion of unity. The mythology in my house included the fundamental equality of humanity, and specifically, that Black people are as much a part of humanity as anyone else. So I never had feelings of inferiority related to Blackness. I also took it all to mean that I deserved to be treated as well as anyone else, what some call being spoiled, but what I prefer to see as John Henrik Clarke's "essential selfishness of survival." I was selfish enough to think I deserved all the good that anyone else got. I hope I've matured to extend that to "we" deserve all the good that there is to have.

JLove: How do you feel you learned how to be a strong Black man being raised by a white woman?

Jared: Much like everyone else, I had no choice but to be. In this regard I am no different from any other Black man. This racist society identified me, for the most part, in relationship to its own anti-Black definition of Black. It was either toughen up or be crushed. My mother did not have the readily available tools that, perhaps, a Black woman would have, so she did the best she could to manufacture them. Again, one of her tools was myth. It helped that she first developed a positive mythology about my father. This was essential. The myth of him and of even why he wasn't around was powerful even if obviously incomplete. So for me the myth of Blackness (one to which I still adhere, by the way) was one of beauty, intellectualism, art, and, most importantly, one that equated Blackness with a deep commitment to radical politics. And as an intellectual my mother always had all kinds of books in the house that even if I didn't initially read, I always took as just being normal. It took me a long time to even realize that these cats were considered "radical" or anything abnormal: works by and about Malcolm X, Kwame Ture (Stokey Carmichael), and definitely Paul Robeson; he, I think, is still my mother's favorite artist/intellectual/activist. And even James Baldwin, whose sexual orientation may not have been mine but whose own particular brand of Black masculinity ultimately remains as impressive a standard as any. As I got older and started to actually read the books I had seen around all those years, it just became clear that, really, what my mother did was instill the fundamentals. Be a good human being, which meant simply seeing the equal humanity in everyone and applying all attendant principles. If humanity meant belonging to and benefitting from society, then everyone must belong, too, and benefit. And if I am being denied based on my Blackness, then that which denies me must be dealt with directly, proudly, immediately. So that's why I say that in a Black nationalist being born to and raised by a Jew I see no contradiction. If the principles of humanity as they currently exist are extended to my mother's people, then the same must be applied to my father's. Same rules, same freedoms, same sovereignty. Now, I am not naïve. I know that these rules currently do not include my father's people as part of the human family, and herein lies the tension that is often deridingly dismissed as the tragedy of the mulatto. But, I am not confused and lost "between" two worlds. I am the conscious product of two unequal and hostile worlds whose hostility intends to create a myth of liminality.

One way I reject any attempt to place me in some mythological 'nowhere' is by aggressively demanding, claiming and acting upon the equal humanity of my father's people – of Black people. And of course I should.

This is not a denial of my mother but the logical and loving conclusion she taught me to reach. It is something like what dream hampton said to me once, that her political and cultural identity as Black is no more a denial of her white mother than her self-concept as woman is a denial of her father. And to me Black Nationalism is the necessary and logical initial step (a kind of micro version of Kwame Nkrumah's process of nationalism to pan-Africanism to socialism) to addressing these issues of race or "multiraciality" and toward bringing about real change assuring that currently hostile races or nations meet again one day on new, improved terms.

JLove: Can you breakdown just what a Black Nationalist is, because different people look at it in different ways. Some people think that Black nationalists hate all white people.

Jared: Well, there are various nationalisms and some nationalists do hate all white people. And while I have to love at least one [smile], I don't begrudge anyone for hating white people. The real question should always be, given the principle of equal humanity, what has been the result or impact on the world of a collective whiteness? What are those self-defining as "white" doing that causes some to react with hatred or what is deemed as hatred but is really self-defense? For me, again similar to Nkrumah or as made more plain by Malcolm X, if we are already to be an isolated and colonized community—as it is in this country with a de facto segregation that rivals any period in this country's past, the nation within a nation, or as Charise Cheney put it, a "nation without a nation"—then there must first be a struggle for a kind of national liberation. So nationalism is controlling the economics, the politics, and social lives (culture) of that community and, especially given a worsening crisis of mass incarceration and police brutality, you have to have control over the policing of that community as well. I look at Black America as an internal colony and to that extent theoretically, at least, try to approach the problems and the conditions of Black people as you would any people in need of decolonization. And, again, I think nationalism is the first essential part of that revolutionary decolonizing process.

JLove: So, Arnette, how do you feel hearing your son talking about this? And how does it impact your relationship with each other?

Arnette: He's far more knowledgeable than I am, and he's made it a life study. With me, it's been more of just the way that I am and need to be.

JLove: I wanted to explore the impact of your social beliefs on your relationship.

Arnette: I think the impact is positive. For one thing, I learn a lot more about what's really going on. I think that I am more integrationist than he is so that I would like to see all of the oppressed people or the people without the power have the power and work with each other to make things better. At the same time, the older I get the more cynical and less hopeful I get.

JLove: Where do white people fit into that equation—or do they?

Arnette: I think we do. I think the other part is that I don't really whole-heartedly consider myself white.

Jared: That's the whole other part of the origins of me that has to be under-stood. My own politics have always been impacted by my mother's definitions of "Jew" and "whiteness." Her own class position and non-white self-concept all play big here.

Arnette: When I was growing up, because I am a Jew—not that we were religious by any means—I already knew I wasn't part of the world of power. The older I got, the more I think I never wanted to be a part of that world. Again, I am not religious; in fact, I am an atheist. But, I became more and more distressed by the feeling that I was being forced to be something I was not. I remember feeling that distress strongly when we were forced to insert "under God" into the pledge of allegiance. It was one more proof that I, as a Jew, as a child from a Leftist family, and as a poor person, was not white because white meant the power structure, the people who got everything and did everything. I was a Jew. We were poor and lived in a housing project, not a Jewish neighborhood, and the overwhelming cultural understanding was that white and Christian meant acceptance and success. I knew I wasn't part of that world.

JLove: How did you interact, though, with people of color? Because even though Jewish, you had the white skin and privileged rights that go with it?

Arnette: The funny thing is that I grew up in the Fort Green Housing Project in Brooklyn. I moved there when I was nine. There was every kind of person there: Latino, Irish, Italian, Catholic, Jewish, Black, and so when I was older I was comfortable in any environment, save for that of the white upper-class. We lived in the projects until I was in my early twenties. So I never felt that I was going into another world when I was with Black people or Latino people. I never felt apart from them as I did from the world of power.

JLove: So you felt more comfortable with people of color than with white people?

Arnette: Well, it depends on who the white people were. I socialized with leftists, with the folk singers, and Bohemians. So the white people that I met were more like I was. I identified white with power and was aware that I had little to do with that.

JLove: What was your idea of racism growing up like that?

Arnette: I knew what racism was. I knew that it mostly happened down South. I knew that there were horrific things happening to Black people in certain areas but they didn't happen where I grew up that I was aware of or that I could see. I just knew that such things were wrong.

JLove: How did you know they were wrong?

Arnette: I suppose because of my parents, what my parents would talk about or what I would read in the newspapers. Politically, I was involved with leftist youth groups and there such things were talked about. As I got older, I became more aware and understood the bigger picture and I chose to do whatever I could.

JLove: What's your definition of white?

Arnette: To me, it means Christian, wealthy, and, therefore, powerful. When I fill out forms I do not check white. I am uncomfortable checking white. So I write Jew, or I'll put Other. I am very aware of and concerned about this white privilege business.

Jared: Whiteness. This is what it has become: a political-cultural construction that protects the only true minority in the world worthy of the label—elite white men. It is they who set up the construction, defined and set its parameters, and who did so to protect their own interests. And to this day, quite predictably, they are the only ones who truly benefit from their construct.

JLove: How does white privilege and white supremacy fit into that?

Jared: There is no need for a "fit." It simply is. The privilege extends from the supremacy and the supremacy extends from, as Fanon said, first, the physical violence of imperial conquest and then the polydimensional method of psychological violence waged to maintain order. The supremacy is required to protect and justify the treatment of the world's majority and out of necessity defines and oppresses its opposite. So a myth of white supremacy requires a myth of Black inferiority. Again, these myths are essential.

JLove: What is the most pressing issue facing us today in your opinion?

Arnette: I think it is economics, which has all of the racial under- and overtones. From economics flow the racism and the destruction of the planet. Somehow we have to find a way to live in this world so that everyone has a decent life.

Jared: You can't divorce white supremacy from capitalism; neither could exist without the other. The attempt to separate them makes the point harder to see. They are so intertwined. But I would also just say that imperialism, colonialism, and capitalism are the most pressing issues. They create all the other problems we continue to struggle with.

JLove: What are some insights about racism in America based on your relationship?

Arnette: Respect. When you are walking down the street and there is another human being, just respect. I breathe, you breathe. We cry, we fight, we laugh. What's the difference? I could never understand that. The difference is imposed, and it's imposed because of economics.

Jared: I would say that our relationship teaches that in-home concepts are ultimately subservient to those held by the larger society. The loving relationship my mother and I share says absolutely nothing about my relationship to white people or society and says nothing about macrorelationships between Black people and whites or Black people and Jews. It is not enough to stop at personal or individual self-concepts or intra-family bonds.

I love Lorraine Hansberry's response to a question about the tense nature of being a Black artist and dealing with all the real or perceived differences between herself and her community. She said that "to destroy the abstraction for the sake of the specific is, in this case, in error." I think her point there is mine here. To apply her particular experience as a successful artist to the conditions of her community was to her as much a foolish mistake as I feel it would be to assume an extension of the love my mother and I have for each other or that which my mother and father had briefly to the larger communities involved. Society must ultimately be changed, and the contradictions exemplified in the differences between my life with my mother and my life with the broader world must be confronted on the most radical terms possible.

JLove: What will it take to eradicate racism?

Arnette: A new world order (laughs). I don't know— if people would just be honest. We always hear "American values." If they would just be friggin' honest and really behave as if they really believed in those values we'd be on the right road, at least.

Jared: White people as we currently know them must cease to exist. We could begin by fighting for a greater distribution of wealth, goods, and services and leveling some playing fields. But really, I think it will take a movement led by the world's majority that forces those now defined as white to make the necessary psychological breaks with their own self-concept. How this break comes or by whose hand I cannot say. I really don't care, as long as it happens. But it is hard to envision, so I tend to agree with those like Fanon, Cesaire, or Frank Wilderson that we just need to strive for an end to the world as we know it. Scratch this joint, and start over.

JLove: How do you feel about the rise of a white antiracist movement?

Arnette: I didn't know there was such a movement.

Jared: Let's hope we see one come out of this Occupy campaign. But, we see so much of the historical trend of white inability to deal with Black and Brown people and their histories, experiences, or analyses. So much of what has been reported about the experiences of Black and Brown people within the Occupy effort has reflected this. And, one sign of this is the persistent inability of the white left to recognize or incorporate the experiences or thoughts of political prisoners, even their white ones. So we see the Occupy folks routinely point to the regulars for analysis—Chris Hedges, Michael Moore, Amy Goodman, and so on. Why not invite the ideas of David Gilbert or Claude Marks? How about Laura Whitehorn? Shoot, with all the talk of the political imprisonment of Bradley Manning one might think this trend could be bucked, but they didn't talk to Marilyn Buck—pun intended!—either. Bradley isn't even the only White political prisoner and not nearly the longest-running one either. What might Tom Manning say to this generation of white potential radicals? What might any of these folks have to say to whites about white involvement in radical politics? I am now convinced, and I am late to this, that this community of young white radicals must be consulted and raised to the level of importance currently held by the Chomskys and Tim Wises. Political prisoners, white and Black, should have their histories play a larger role in today's activist efforts. They have so much to offer regarding interracial coalition-building and antiracist work. They would be a great resource and their involvement with today's white-led Occupation campaign—one that could still yet prove to be radical and genuinely antiracist—would be a huge sign of genuine change in the right direction.

A Love Letter to My European American Brothers and Sisters

Race is a loaded issue in our society, and people have many feelings about it. It's personal and impersonal, complex and simple. Race in our society denies us things we need in our lives, while at the same time cultural difference often affirms our experience. So what happens when white people and people of color come together "at the table" over matters of race?

Many white people feel a strong need for relationships with people of color. In broad strokes, we are looking for love and affirmation of our shared humanity. This is the very thing race denies us. White identity, historically and presently, depends on separation and contrast from people of color. Many white people feel this separation and want to heal that wound within ourselves.

Countless writings and spoken testimonies by people of color tell us that relationship with white people is not the most compelling reason bringing people of color to the table. Surely, people of color often want to share relationships across racial lines, but they receive affirmation of their humanity from the rich cultural experiences in which they already partake. People of color want justice. This may be equality; it may be a level playing field; it may be recognition and action on issues, such as police brutality and economic discrimination. White people can be significant allies in the struggle to achieve racial justice. So what happens when we come to the table? White people find ourselves in relationship with people of color. We receive the acceptance and love that so deeply motivate us. We are affirmed. But, coming to the table does not in itself bring justice to people of color. At best it is a promise of future action—a promise that often is not kept.

Over the years I have seen white people often confused on this matter. Relating to people of color becomes an end in itself, almost like a drug. We can't envision any other goal or any other method. Sometimes white people will shape their lives around relating to people of color, but if you ask them to work with other white people (as people of color often do ask them) they reject that work. Those of us who honor that request to work with our fellow white people—and this request goes back at least to Malcolm X, Stokley Carmichael, and Bayard Rustin—often find some of our white brothers and sisters cannot remove themselves from the immediacy of interracial relationship to help us work for racial justice where it counts most, in our own white community.

No community can stand for long without both love and justice. Each must be present. Love without justice is superficial at best. People of color working for justice are often accused of being "divisive," but a community bound by love that allows systemic injustice to go unchallenged is a community that will permit anything, including slavery and economic exploitation. In effect, it is not a true community at all.

With Love,

Jeff Hitchcock
January 30, 2012

❖❖❖

8 Strategies for Speaking Up About Race

From the book *Witnessing Whiteness; The Need to Talk About Race and How To Do It* by Shelly Tochluk. Excerpted with permission.

- ❖ Begin slowly. No need to speak out on every new piece of knowledge all at one time if our friends or family are not asking for more. These are our closest relationships. We have plenty of time to initiate people into this way of seeing the world. Besides, jumping in too quickly might very likely only push them away.

- ❖ Speak from the heart. Refer to recently-acquired information and how it has been personally affecting. Ask only for them to listen and try and understand why you feel as you do.

- ❖ Demonstrate excitement. If we offer some of our realizations with excitement and interest, we stand a better chance of getting people on board. A sudden shift into anger alienates and makes our journey less appealing.

- ❖ Challenge sensitively. Using the previously-described strategy of expressing personal emotional reaction to statements can be extremely helpful when we need to challenge something said within a dialogue.

- ❖ Be humble. Becoming angry with our families, friends, and colleagues for not seeing issues of race as we do is sure a way to get shut down and to turn them off.

- Pick battles carefully. Some people just are not ready to hear what we have to say. Reserve energy for moments when our effort can make a difference. Retreat and come back a different day or a different year, depending on the individual.

- Plant seeds. Know that we plant seeds every time we witness actively. We might not see immediate results, but some new epiphany might be growing in someone that will someday emerge, even if we never see the tangible results.

- Extend the invitation. Invite family, friends, and colleagues to join this journey with you. Give this book as a present to someone. Ask someone to watch a movie that features a racially provocative theme with you. Invite someone to attend a culturally or racially diverse art show, musical performance, or other event with you. Ask questions and prompt conversation to see what people are thinking.

For more information and tons of free resources go to:
www.witnessingwhiteness.com

❖ ❖ ❖

"Love is what we are born with. Fear is what we learn. The spiritual journey is the unlearning of fear and prejudices and the acceptance of love back in our hearts. Love is the essential reality and our purpose on earth. To be consciously aware of it, to experience love in ourselves and others, is the meaning of life. Meaning does not lie in things. Meaning lies in us."

--Marianne Williamson

Chapter 4

❧ *Appropriation or Appreciation* ❧

"I wish White people would find their own damn culture and leave ours alone!"

The anger radiating off my fellow panelist was unmistakable. As the only white person on the Hip-Hop and Activism panel at the conference in Denver, I had the urge to get up and run out of the crowded auditorium. I hate conflict, which is odd given that I'm an activist and that engaging in conflict is pretty much a daily occurrence. Alas, sprinting for the door wouldn't help my cause any, so I had to stand my ground. But what ground was I standing on?

Although the guy didn't say it outright, I was being accused of being a culture vulture. It wasn't the first time. I knew the audience was waiting for a response; he dissed me in front of all them. So I said what was in my heart. "Maybe you are right." I turned and saw a look of surprise come over his face. "Maybe because I love this culture so much, I need to leave it."

Many late night conversations with Hip-Hop activists end up with the discussion of white people's role in the culture, so my involvement in it had been on my mind for a while. There's always much groaning over the latest corporate take-over of Hip-Hop with the white execs strangling every drop of money they possibly can through the fashion, cell phones, even children's cartoons, to name just a few "revenue streams." During these spirited discussions, our overall concerns boiled down to this: Will Hip-Hop end up like jazz and rock-n-roll? Many Americans have no idea that rock-n-roll was started by Black people. My friend Baba Israel always talks about Eminem being the new Elvis. Is history bound to repeat itself?

As a young white girl enchanted by rap music and graffiti in my early teens (and later enchanted by everything Hip-Hop), there came a low point where I attempted to be "Blacker" than any Black person around. I really hated being white, so I compensated. I over-compensated. What started as mild appreciation became an obsession. My love for the music and culture was genuine, but how I used it was not. I was so absorbed in Hip-Hop culture and Black culture that I lost myself, and that's what I wanted—to lose myself. What is white culture, anyway? What are white values? What are white dance styles and food? I was oversimplifying. But that's how I saw things. I didn't value what I had.

Part of what happened to me was that I wasn't taught much of anything about my own cultural heritage. I never said I was Irish or Irish-American when asked what I was. Just white. The same was true for lots of my friends. They weren't Italian or Italian-American or Greek or Greek-American; they were just white.

I don't blame my parents. They took me to the St. Patrick's Day parade every year, where I wore a huge button that said "Kiss me, I'm Irish!" But, beyond that and my very Irish given surname, I knew little else of my heritage. I'm not sure how much my parents knew, either. This was, in fact, part of the cultural assimilation white America demanded of new citizens: give up your culture and history and become part of the great Melting Pot. I don't think my great great-grandparents were aware of how devastating their decision to go along with that demand would be.

CULTURE:
The beliefs, customs, practices, and social behaviors of a particular nation or people.

The more I learned about racism in middle school and high school, the more I saw with new eyes what was going on in my community and school. AP classes were filled with white kids in my predominantly black school; teachers and police had distinctly different expectations of black and brown kids versus white ones, and the contrasts between the Black and Mexican neighborhoods and the white ones were stark and undeniable. Ferocious shame and guilt took hold. I wanted nothing to do with being white. To me, it equaled being boring, corny, rich, ignorant, egotistical, racist, punctual, stingy, prudish, having no rhythm… the list goes on. So I asked the quintessential question of the 90s that still plays out today: How can I be down?

Being down meant proving oneself. In my case, this meant proving myself to the Hip-Hop community. Mentors taught me that being down was about respect. Respect the culture's originators. Learn its history. Understand its context and importance: Hip-Hop's beginnings were partly about unity and having fun, but it was also created in reaction to the dismal poverty in urban communities. Many Hip-Hop historians consider it a rebellion against racism and inequality.

This knowledge, coupled with a lack of cultural identity to keep me grounded, made me love Hip-Hop. And I found out Hip-Hop, for the most part, loved me back. I co-opted, happily twisting and squeezing my way in. I decided that refusing to participate in racism meant rejecting my whiteness and abandoning my white family, church, and community. I didn't see another way out.

I was more a party girl than a politically conscious activist. And, I was never self-critical. I never really reflected much on what I was doing, beyond thinking about ways to ensure that I was still down. I didn't get that what I was doing was wrong; it felt like a personal choice. I never saw it in a larger context of claiming to be part of something without fully knowing the social and political implications.

More Than Just Music

Fast forward. I was a pretty well-established Hip-Hop journalist and activist. I lived, worked, and played exclusively in communities of color. I believed I was being true to myself, but in fact I was cutting out a substantial piece of who I was, using Hip-Hop to deny my whiteness in any way I could. It was my shield, a way of saying to the world, "I'm not, like, a *regular* white person."

Over time and with the help of mentors, wisdom from lyrics, books (*A Promise and A Way of Life* by Becky Thompson and *Uprooting Racism* by Paul Kivel were two of the most important), and friends, I gently filled into a new shape. Or maybe it was my old shape with new dimensions. Whatever it was, it meant embracing my full identity, which includes both white skin and a soul desire for justice and equality. Some call this identity "antiracism," but my favorite term is from an organization called AWARE- LA (Alliance of White Antiracists Everywhere-Los Angeles). The term is *Radical White Identity*. Radical White Identity allows me to love being white and love fighting racism. You will hear from the creators of the Radical White Identity Model later in the book.

I love Hip-Hop. I'm choosing to stay in this cipher for the rest of my life. It's been family for so long now that it's truly part of me. I don't think I could leave it behind if I tried. I celebrate it for all it has done to bring diverse people together around the world.

I will always strive to do my part to learn, reflect, and act. Being antiracist, or embracing a radical white identity, is a life-long process and a commitment I am proud to make.

❖ ❖ ❖

Part of evolving into the people we want to become is searching for the knowledge-makers and the cultural creatives who can stir up our thinking, open our eyes, and spark our imagination. Jeff Chang does all three of these things at once. A warrior for Hip-Hop culture for decades, he has written seminal volumes on it so that Hip-Hop history is accurately portrayed by people from within as opposed to how it usually happens: outsiders depicting something they do not know or understand.

❧ *Hip-Hop's Stepchild* ❧

By *Jeff Chang*

In 2005, my first book, *Can't Stop Won't Stop: A History of the Hip-Hop Generation*, hit the stores. After working on it for so many years, I was excited to get out and talk about it. But almost everywhere I went I was greeted as something of a curiosity. How is it, I was constantly asked, that an Asian Pacific Islander who grew up in the suburbs and country-side of Hawai'i could come to write a 500+ book on Hip-Hop?

Most who asked—whether journalists, radio hosts, friends, or simply folks who had come to check out a reading—had no idea how much the question irked me. To be fair, it was almost never asked in an accusatory scandal-scrum kind of way. This was soft-toss, warm-up stuff. Clearly I had to understand why the red light was screaming in my head.

The theorist in me usually responded first. The question only made sense if one assumed Hip-Hop was a Black thing, and Asians—not being Black, because that was why Sonny in the "Do The Right Thing" was so funny, right?—could be questioned as if they were whites. Latinos were just too confusing to figure into this conversation. The question already came stereotype-loaded-for-bear.

Look, I would say, Hip-Hop began from an Afrodiasporic foundation. (Your Latino question, answered.) This was undeniable—and anyone who had actually read the book should have come away clear on this. But it had transformed a million times since, in the looping circuits of culture and people and ideas and sounds and images and motion. So here I turned the question on the questioner: Is every instance now of an Asian or Pacific Islander picking up a mic or scratching a record or executing a handspin just an opportunity for you to trot out that tired old 80s word: "appropriation"? If a Black producer samples a koto, ukulele, or a dhol, do you really believe it's an inauthentic act? None of this stuff is transgressive anymore, right? It is just the way things are. So, I mean, how dumb is your question really?

But that was not the whole answer, not even part of the answer, and it presumed the questioner was not only proceeding on bad faith but had just awoken from a two-three decade slumber and missed the point when the young world—aided in no small part by Black genius in the gift of Hip-Hop—had gone beyond multicultural to global. It was wrong for me to assume they were trying to be assholes for asking because, obviously, most of them weren't.

The question was really a two-parter. The first was a challenge: What qualifies you to write this history? The second was infinitely more difficult: Are you displacing other voices by raising your own?

I had no problem answering the first part, although it meant having to tediously recite my bio. I decided that if people couldn't get with the fact that I, like millions of other kids around the world, had been thoroughly moved and inspired by the creativity of Black and Latino kids from New York City's abandoned neighborhoods in the late 70s and early 80s, that it had set off all kinds of creative impulses in me, and that what those kids did back then continues to shape my worldview and my life work, well, there was not much more I could explain.

But invariably I added a philosophical point about Hip-Hop. It is a movement, I would say, that is centered on the cypher. You either step in and show-and-prove, or you get laughed out of the cypher until you can come up with something that demands respect. In my time, I said, I was a wack popper, better at graf but far from famous, and a decent DJ. But once I got with writing, I was slowly and surely able to earn my props in the journalistic/scholarly cypher. Hip-Hop relies on call and response. I was called. I responded. I called, you responded. Your turn.

This answer felt right. I could defend it. It felt true too. It was the rhetorical equivalent of a b-boy routine, finished off with a hardcore stare-down freeze that dared the interrogator to come with a tougher follow-up question. And, it worked. Few did.

But sometimes the conversation moved to the second question. One day, while I was doing an interview on a radio show in San Francisco, my own turf, a caller—an African-American elder, a well-known author from the Black Arts era—phoned in to challenge me. "We don't need a Chang to tell these stories," he said, dipping my surname into more than a little bile. "We need the pioneers to tell their stories."

The white host turned to me. "So what do you think? Why can't an Asian American write about Hip-Hop?" he asked, probably hoping to turn the discussion into one about the permeability of pop, the ability of commodity culture to eventually redeem even the white bluesman, the Asian American Hip-Hop head.

I replied that I thought the elder was right on the mark. The real question, I said, was why more people of color—especially first voices—could not tell their stories in a white-dominated publishing industry. The host quickly changed the topic.

Later, crew, friends, and colleagues reassured me that they thought the elder was wrong to put me on blast, that he had no idea who I was, what I had done, or what I was doing in the community. Did he even read the intro by DJ Kool Herc? Had he ever reflected on whether he had given adequate voice to blues and jazz pioneers in his work? But, I was haunted by the question.

I remain aware of how it feels to have someone else tell you and others the what, how, and why of who you are. It's why I got into writing. I have also seen far too many of my fellow A/PIs use their minority status to aggrandize themselves and to push down other communities of color. In a time when the color lines are becoming more complicated, there is a fine line between solidarity and erasure.

I was pretty sure I knew where I stood. But, the questions lingered. Was I writing to express empathy or to aggrandize myself? How damaging could good intentions be? In the process of raising my voice was I silencing others?

Any intellectually honest student is always keenly aware how much he or she owes to the knowledge and wisdom of elders and peers. In Hip-Hop, as in a lot of cultures and movements, people do not take you under their wing lightly. You hold the stories you tell, just as you do the storytellers, with the highest regard and care. Your responsibility includes the imperative never to silence those first voices but to amplify them. Yet even if you have chosen to be the documentarian, you're still not the griot. One day if you've done your job well enough, you will know. But, it is never your choice. It is, as DJ Kool Herc says, "the people's choice."

I had written that *Can't Stop Won't Stop* was "but one version, this dub history—a gift from those who have illuminated and inspired, all defects of which are my own. There are many more versions to be heard. May they all be."

I believe in my words. I stand by them, and I take them as my personal law. But, words never inoculate. In the end, the second question is not for me to answer. It needs to be decided in the cypher with the community as the final arbiter. So these days, if the conversation comes this far, I give the most honest answer I can: "Judge me by what I do, not what I say."

It feels true. And, it's as Hip-Hop as I can be.

❧ *America's Original Sin: Race, Respect, and Keeping the Dialogue Alive* ❧

An Interview with
Hip-Hop Artist *Talib Kweli & his father, Dr. Perry Greene*
conducted by JLove Calderón

I asked Talib Kweli and his father, Dr. Perry Greene, to expand on the concept of cultural appropriation, race, and privilege. I wanted to hear an intergenerational father-son dialogue to get the richness of a historical perspective.

Talib Kweli rocks superstar sunglasses while slinging urban Afrocentric knowledge on a beautiful day in Brooklyn. His father, Dr. Perry Greene, the Provost and Dean at Adelphi University in Long Island, is poised and present, complimenting Talib's flow with deep wisdom emanating not just from his intellect but from his soul. We dip in and out of history, family, legacy, and life.

JLove: I would love for you guys to talk about the history of Hip-Hop and where is it now in terms of race?

Perry: I think that Hip-Hop has two faces, and I'm talking as a person who is a relative outsider. I'm reminded of the birth of minstrel in the 1830s. Black performers weren't allowed on the stage. So white performers who wanted to pretend to be black would put on blackface. What's interesting in that historical context is that the minstrel shows were developed as a parody of slaves on the auction block. Fast forward to today, and for some—if they're attending to one face of Hip-Hop—it's not that different than the minstrel show in some ways. There is the face that is born of materialism, of money, and of violence. And then there is the face of anti-violence, grassroots activism, and positive energy. Which face is the true face of Hip-Hop? The true face of Hip-Hop is the second one because it started out as an anti-gang, anti-violence, anti-drug movement in the South Bronx—a South Bronx that had been left to die. And so those people who choose to pay attention to that first face only and then pick up and put on the metaphorical blackface, are doing harm to the culture. Those who honor it—white or black—are of a positive influence.

Talib: To add to your point about the minstrel show, I think now people embrace what they think is blackness. So people are proud to be black, but it seems like they are proud for the wrong reasons. The historical context isn't there; the knowledge isn't there. Being black means being hip or embracing a stereotype. I think that's where you get the minstrel-show thing; we don't need white people to show us how to embrace a limiting stereotype. We do it ourselves.

JLove: How do you feel about white people in Hip-Hop?

Talib: Well, I would say that I grew up inherently nationalistic. I truly believe that any group of people—black, Irish, Russian—has to work out the problems in their own family. And you can't appreciate somebody else's culture unless you have a full appreciation of your own culture. Hip-Hop is the first thing I've seen in my lifetime that is truly multi-cultural. So I come from a nationalist ideology, but I participate in this multi-cultural thing. It conflicts sometimes. There are white people that have been down with Hip-Hop from the beginning; white people now who are artists, producers, and business people in Hip-Hop who truly have the love for the culture and for the music. I would never say that because Hip-Hop was started by Blacks and Latinos in the Bronx, it's just for us. But at the same time when you're dealing with the real issue of racism, that same white kid that grew up in Massachusetts and who took the Metro North down to go to clubs…he's probably, you know, president of some label or some big A&R making hundreds of thousands of dollars. Whereas, his good friend is trying to make a demo tape or something. So the racism is real, whether someone has a love for the culture or not. That's just the reality of racism in this country. I know people who were doing the same thing as me back in the day and they are making way more money than I am now.

JLove: Because they're white?

Talib: Because they're white. And because there's more opportunities for them just in general. This is an issue people don't really, truly understand. I don't hear people talking about white power. I don't hear black people talking about white privilege.

Perry: If all things were equal? I'd have absolutely no problem with anybody doing anybody else's music. It's a beautiful thing.

JLove: But the problem is it's not all equal, right?

Perry: Well, you can't help but be a little burned by history. When you think about Elvis Presley, you don't think about Big Mama Thornton. There's nothing wrong with Elvis Presley, but I want people to know that his mama—musically speaking—was a black woman named Big Mama Thornton, and he got many of his lyrics, many of his songs from her. You go to some places and you start talking about rock and roll and some people go, "Oh, that's white folks' music." Before Elvis, it was race music. And in less polite circles it was nigger music. When you think about jazz—something I'm very fond of—and, frankly, it is sad that you go where jazz artists are singing and performing and playing, and it's getting harder and harder to find black musicians.

I was at the Blue Note a couple of weeks ago, and I noted there was one black performer, and no one working in the Blue Note was Black. And, I can't help thinking, looking at the walls, seeing all of the jazz artists of the past, this place was built on the artistry of these men and women. Where are they now? What's wrong with this picture? There need to be black artists and white artists. But, we're coming to a point where the black jazz artists are far and few between because some of that unconscious racism that we talked about earlier, that racism says it's either all mine or it's nobody's. And in that, I have a problem.

> **APPROPRIATE:** To take or use something forcefully or without permission.

JLove: So what's important for white people to know when engaging in cultures and music and art that are from indigenous folks or people of color?

Talib: I think Eminem has written the best song about this particular issue that I've ever heard. That song, "White America," is a song about the idea that he's accepted and he has success because he does black music and brings it to white kids. And how white kids relate to him because his hair is blonde. This song is the most honest piece of work that I've heard about this issue. And, I think it had to come from a white person to really address that issue. I love that record. But I think he's in a position where he, as an artist, can be completely honest where most people can't be completely honest.

The first thing we learn in elementary school—the idea of the melting pot—is the biggest obstacle because that's the get out of jail free pass: "Hey, this is America. This is a melting pot." You're supposed to come to Ellis Island, forget whatever it is you were dealing with before you got there—brand new identity. Well, that works if you're there on your own free will. Or even if your country was so messed up that you made a choice to leave the country and seek opportunity here. That doesn't happen for Africans. And so there's a privilege that other people in this country have that we just don't have.

JLove: I would push back on that a little bit in terms of the Ellis Island conversation, though. I don't know if you guys have heard of Tim Wise. He talks about how his family are immigrants that came over through Ellis Island and were forced to give up their culture in order to succeed. Many white people seem to feel an emptiness, a cultural void. So how do we look at white people and our constant need to take other people's stuff because we have nothing of our own?

Perry: What's interesting is that a critical look at histories will see that there are a lot of similarities. In America there is a big backlash against Hispanic folk; whether we're talking about language acquisition, bilingualism, socio-economic status, you can look particularly at the Italians, the Irish, at Jews and see that they were treated very similarly to the way that we are treating the Hispanics today. When you look at it that way, American culture is, in fact, that treatment. The interesting thing about African-Americans and our involuntary status is we really haven't been part of that ebb and flow. We have been fairly static. We have been a permanent underclass. And the reason for that is we started out as a product of guilt. I don't mean as a people but our role in America, because America couldn't deal with the notion that they were enslaving people for the rest of their lives. So they had to define those people as not human. I want to argue that that original sin is with us today. That definition of who Black people are, that's still with us today, woven right into American culture. Not a very pretty thought, but our historical roots are part of our culture. What we did as a country frames who we are.

JLove: A friend of mine named Asia-One is a B-Girl and graffiti artist. She wanted me to ask you why it is that in Hip-Hop if you have skills it doesn't matter what race you are, but in regular society race is such a big thing. Any thoughts about that?

Talib: In society if you're not white, in order to make it you have to be more skilled. I would venture to say that for Hip-Hop it's the reverse. I would say that Eminem, for example, is successful because at the time he came out he was better than almost anybody. And that was the only way that we could accept a white rapper. You gotta be better than everybody. That's the only way.

Perry: I think Talib is absolutely right. I don't know if Hip-Hop has rid itself of the divisions and divisiveness that affect the larger society. But I do think it has a better chance than the Republican party.

JLove: Final Comments?

Perry: What's worrisome is that as long as in places like New York City where there's 50% unemployment among Black men, where Black children still die at twice the rate at birth as white children; as long as in some parts of the country where there are Black and Latino children who remain two or three years behind their white counterparts…as long as there are people directed into what communities they can and cannot live in and what loans they can get and what small business protection they get; as long as there are Katrinas, as long as we are willing to suspend the rights of young Black men in the streets all across America just because they're young Black men; as long as the Rockefeller laws still imprison Black youth at higher rates than their white counterparts…We should be paying attention. Serious attention. So what I ask of people is: don't let the conversation die. Because if you let it die, then being arrested for a little bit of crack can get you 20 years if you're black; being arrested with a bundle of cocaine can get you a slap on the hand if your white. As long as those kinds of things are still going on, as long as the Sean Bells of the world still have fifty bullets shot at them, as long as there's still racial profiling, if we stop the conversation then we get frozen in time. And Sean Bell becomes okay. And Trayvon Martin becomes okay. It's not okay.

So if I had to say something to somebody, it would be: don't stop. We have to have the conversation until the game is over. And the game's not over until America comes to terms with its past. And it hasn't.

❖ ❖ ❖

Artist/Activist Baba Israel was the first white boy I met who was down, had incredible skills on the mic, was respected by black and brown communities, and spoke honestly about being white in the game. Very few white rappers back in the late 90s were 'bout 'bout it.

What was also dope was his disinterest in the "white on white" competition to be most down, so when we first met at a conference on the prison in-dustrial complex he was warm and friendly. I learned what it meant to have an ally who understands me inside out because we shared similar struggles. Our generation was very different because in our youth Hip-Hop culture was for black and brown people. It was rare to find white people at the Hip-Hop clubs. In fact, in many places clubs were defined on the street as "black" or "white." A homey might call and say, "You wanna roll to a black club tonight?"

Through Hip-Hop, I learned a bit of what it feels like to be in the minor-ity. During its Afrocentric phase, I was unpopular. I sure dressed the part, rocking baggy pants, the right sneakers, and medallions. But I had experi-ences where my skin color was not the right color, my body was not consid-ered beautiful, my hair wasn't good with the "in" hairstyles. I had physical attributes you cannot hide, and I felt ugly and unworthy because I didn't fit in.

I reflect on that time in my life, and for all the pain I felt over being judged based on physical traits I couldn't change—skin, hair, eyes—I know I will not ever be able to understand what it must be like for people of color enduring this every day of their lives. White people, you may have had some similar experiences, but it doesn't mean that you can relate to what it means to live with racism as a person of color in the United States.

Things are very different now when it comes to Hip-Hop. The posi-tives are its power to unite people from all over the world, the inspiration it provides to help build movements for change, and the way it fosters the continuation of the creative expression of people.

The negatives are the rap industry, which has taken over the airwaves, and the corporate commercializing of Hip-Hop culture, always figuring a way to earn another nickel, dime, and dollar. We see more and more the craft of the emcee, or rapper, co-opted into its own bastard child. The wack-est get the most play. The intelligent is underground. Corporations decide who makes it big.

Another negative—a consequence of the rap industry—is that rap mu-sic, Hip-Hop music, is enjoyed by millions of white people. I am talking about white people who are The Majority, who don't know the culture's history. They think they are down because they listen to some songs yet do not know one damn thing about the group of people from which it came. What they do know comes from watching videos and listening to the lyrics. They are fully educated on Lil Wayne's version of Black America, Young Jeezy's lifestyle, and Rick Ross, using those archetypes to access an entire culture.

We need white people like Baba Israel who respect and understand white privilege, cultural appropriation, and the history of Hip-Hop culture. We need songs like his "Black Music" on the airwaves to teach, to role model, to bring forth new ways of interacting respectfully with cultures that are not our own.

❧ *I Ain't White, Not in My Mind's Eye* ❧

By *Baba Israel*

It was a Saturday night, 1985, and I remember listening to the radio, huddled close to its sound. It was silver and blue, a Panasonic adorned with graffiti scrawling. I loved the LED lights that would flicker to the beat. The music was Hip-Hop, and it filled my ears late at night. It was a moment of discovery that took me from one world into another. It took me from the world of sixties counterculture, Jazz, and utopian dreams to the intensity of New York City life with the radio waves translating emotions into tangible audio bytes.

The radio program was the Mr. Magic show, and I waited eagerly as each new song would enter the mix. Beats pulsed, and my imagination ran to the futuristic sounds of "Planet Rock" and "Jam on It." These were songs produced by Afrika Bambaataa and the Soulsonic Force and Nucleus. They were part funk, part electronic, and out of this world—Hip-Hop, the perfect soundtrack for a kid into science fiction and political awareness. I was born in 1974, and my parents raised me with a sixties ethic, a diet of non-violent anarchist revolution in the wrappings of poetry, story, and imagery. Hip-Hop music fused the world of thought and tone. It was the future, and my ears had found it.

The movements and fashion of Hip-Hop were from the future, too, blending graffiti and the space age aesthetic of performers Sun Ra and Parliament combined with the traditional imagery of Egypt, Zulu, Native American, and eastern martial arts. The human instinct for mythology was satisfied for the youth of my generation via heroic and villainous characters found in the pages of Marvel comics and in the Saturday morning cartoons. The Robotic movements and dance styles of popping and electric-boogalo brought these animated images to life.

How did a white kid in Soho connect to this rich culture from the Bronx? The graffiti on the trains was a smoke signal, sending a beacon of artistic reverie in the form of gigantic murals or burners that brought color and breath to lifeless metal. Every morning my eyes gazed in wonder as the trains pulled into the station, bringing with them tales of adventure, whispered and proclaimed in bold characters and images found on the subway's skin. The New York of the mid eighties was Hip-Hop. It began in the Bronx but made its way to me through a very connected New York. No matter what neighborhood you came from, you could get on a train and make money or get fame in any borough of the city. A lot of dancers and artists came to Soho to street perform and hang in the downtown art scene. That was my first exposure to Hip-Hop culture—live and direct.

At the age of eleven I didn't really question the fact that I was white and into Hip-Hop, but I did begin to distance myself from white culture. I would fight with my mother and get angry when she brought up our English heritage. Cursing England's imperial history of colonization and exploitation, I slowly built a wall.

Hip-Hop lived for me in my Walkman; I would make mix tapes that became the soundtrack of my life. Songs blended and shifted, telling stories that grounded me, energized me, angered me, and motivated me. With the arrival of Third Bass, I saw on TV a white rapper, Serch, who moved, danced, rapped, and even wore his hair in a Black Style, the "flat top." This gave me and my other white friends in to Hip-Hop a private affirmation that there was indeed a place for us within this culture. The fact that Serch was Jewish and used his lyrics to address racism made us feel good about him being a white emcee.

I felt that I was Hip-Hop, and my whiteness faded into a distant memory. It was like my skin no longer existed; I was a psyche carried in a cultural form. Adorned in the proper clothes, moving with the proper sway, my voice and accent shifted. My whole being had transformed. I felt at home, and I felt connected. These were two feelings that I had sought with a quiet desperation. I had longed for a feeling of connection because my parents had made the choice to live as radical artists that isolated us from any larger family of cousins, brothers, nieces, aunts, and uncles who were majority conservative and looked down on our family. There had been connection with my parents' artistic community, but the contact was infrequent, and there was a generation gap. I began to find a home and community of my own—though at this time my community members existed more as voices on CD only later to be replaced by real people, who were fellow artists of my generation.

At the poetry readings I attended, the white devil lyrics that I had heard from the safety of my room now filled the space and caught around my neck, closing in on my force field. They burned a fire in my stomach, and at some point I asked "Is that about me?" "Can I still be down?" I sat through those lyrics, and I stepped up and did my thing. I felt a responsibility to the white people I knew who sat in the skin of a whole and vibrant humanity, a responsibility to show there was another side to the white experience.

I am at the Nuyorican Poets Café in the Lower east side of Manhattan in the early nineties, and the poetry is filled with anti-white and "white devil" content. The heat is rising, and, of course, the white folks are heading for the door. Something in my spirit told me to stay. The choice to run away is a product of white privilege. To be able to choose when or when not to deal with race is at the heart of white privilege. To sit and listen and burn that wood is the beginning of something else. It is the beginning of genuine empathy, not pity, and genuine understanding, not condescending posturing. It is the beginning of an attempt to carve away the space to really feel someone else's experience.

As a performer, I was received with a consistent appreciation and respect from black audiences. This reception was encouraging and gave me hope for a new way of relating to the world. As a young adult this was an important affirmation. I eventually developed an intention that had less to do with feeling good and more to do with a big picture view of my place in the world as a white man, struggling with privilege and antiracism intention.

At this time, I found it a mission to consistently represent an "alternative" white expression in black and multi-racial environments. This departure from white culture and entrance into a majority community of color was in fact another serious example of white privilege. The ability to move somewhat fluidly between worlds is not often an option for people of color.

I have often struggled with the frequent white response to accusations of racism: "I have a black friend," or "some of my best friends are black." This answer has always felt defensive and somewhat superficial, and yet it was the fact that I had black friends in high school and college that did help to shape my antiracist views. Joe Feagin and Hernan Vera offer in their essay *Confronting Ones Own Racism* "... Real friendships across the racial barrier have enabled her to withstand the daily drum beat of racism all around her." There is some comfort that comes from this line of thought, that through real and tangible friendships with people of color I am able to transcend and move beyond racism. I would later learn that that comfort could be easily tested with even deeper and more radical notions. As Wildman and Davis write in their essay "Making systems of white privilege visible" from *White Privilege: Essential Readings on the Other Side of Racism* "...The perpetuation of white supremacy is racist. All whites are racist in the use of this term, because we benefit from systemic white privilege. A big step would be for whites to admit that we are racist and then to consider what to do about it." This viewpoint that sets all white people as default racist is both terrifying to accept, as it connects all white people to the heinous history of racism, and also sobering, as it gives us a solid and non-defensive place to work from.

Facing my whiteness

White privilege creates a sense of entitlement that hardens our ability to live as full and whole human beings. Though white people can be challenged through gender, sexual orientation, and class, there is still a fundamental and longstanding history of white supremacy that inhabits our behavior. This presence, this psychic infection, this perversion of humanity creeps into our beings and if not challenged cuts us off from an awareness of other people's experience in this country and in the world. This detachment makes it difficult to be aware in our bodies, if not our minds, of the struggle that people of color face. As I grasp to communicate this I only touch the surface. This lack of awareness can result in a condescending response or, worse, white guilt. So, whether as white people we negotiate the pitfalls of racism, condescending compassion, or white guilt, we rarely reach a place of true openness to people of color.

What does it mean to be a white emcee?

In my own practice as an emcee I look to make a conscious effort to think about my place in the culture. Do I make the "I am a white emcee song"? When I was younger it had more to do with having something to prove, like "Yeah I am white but I am nice on the mic, not the great white hype but tight with the lyrics I recite." I have taken a subtler route, and there is still a lot about me that I feel has not made it into the platform of my rhyming. Now, it has more to do with trying to bring my own story into my lyrics and also to write from a greater understanding of privilege and racial dynamic.

Black Music

this is the music that originates
in African landscapes
now broadcast on mix tapes
I got the privilege to be a part of this culture

respect this
This is Black music

I am a guest at best blessed to express stress over beats with finesse
Elvis was a tragic star that fell so far from what music meant
pimped by his management
the cross over sex appeal
let's get real

                rock and roll

was a code for soul
to get RnB played on White radio
it's not long hair and guitars
that came later

The British invader

singing the Blues without paying dues
this country is infused with African philosophy
this music is African property and should be respected properly

the transcendental state of Blackness

I want to have this
but to think it's mine is madness
to bear the bounce but not the burden
all I can possess is the presence of mind
not to be blind
and look beyond the curtain
what's on the stage?
unfair wage and prison cage?
racist policy human mockery
a militant monopoly that absorbs culture into a commodity

so White kids let's not make the same mistake, musical rape
respect build trust in order to integrate
know our privilege is power unchecked at the gate

I have felt alone in a world that is cold
found peace and strength in stories told
Hip-Hop molds my flow language and soul
so to this I owe humility
yeah I'm nice on the mic
my spirit would recite poetic transmissions whether Black or White
these words were given form and function
through African diction and tradition
as I find my way is this contradiction?
should I hang up the mic and seek somewhere else

I know Hip-Hop   like I know myself

I remember coming up
pumping X-Clan
like I can't be a White man
used to get love from my Black fam
it was like I wanted to change who I was
measure myself by the thickness of my blood
and the depth of my love

always stepped with sincerity
got love from the crowd staring at me
it was a spiritual calling
that I could not refuse
this path I had to choose it
but let's not forget this is   Black music

Cultural appropriation is the adoption of some specific elements of one culture by a different cultural group. It denotes acculturation or assimilation, but often connotes a negative view towards acculturation from a minority culture by a dominant culture. It can include the introduction of forms of dress or personal adornment, music and art, religion, language, or social behavior. These elements, once removed from their indigenous cultural contexts, may take on meanings that are significantly divergent from, or merely less nuanced than, those they originally held. Or, they may be stripped of meaning altogether. (source, Wikipedia)

A Love Letter to White Allies in the Struggle for Racial Justice

I can only imagine what you were expecting, but I'm pretty sure it wasn't this. You've shown up to every meeting. You're mindful of how much space you take (except that you're the first to call out anything that carries the remotest odor of racism). You laugh at the "white people" comments, your own barbs at the most egregious and deserving targets ranking among the funniest.

And then it happened.

You said one thing or did another, and now everyone looks at you differently. You didn't mean anything by it. You're so ready to make things right, but it seems the harder you try, the worst it gets. That's not you, you insist. Still with one small act, the trust seems to have been irrevocably broken. In fact, the good will was so easily shattered, you start to question if it were ever there.

You go from embarrassed to hurt to angry (although that you keep to yourself). You feel set up. You want to yell, "I've been bamboozled!," but you know that'll just get you into more trouble, and so you don't. You don't think you'll ever speak freely in mixed company again. You wonder if you should just walk away and take on another cause.

This is what racism has wrought.

You may not believe this, but some of us do stand up for you. We knew this day would come—it always does—and we have learned that this is par for the course in the quest for racial justice. It's not that we aren't hurt or angry by what you said or did. We just get that this is what it means to have multiracial alliances.

If we have our way, we will mine the conflict for opportunities to deepen the connection we have with you.

But as you can see, it's extremely difficult to convince the others that sometimes a White person has earned the right to be struggled with, and that struggle is part of building movement and creating change.

I write this love letter to see if I can make you understand why it is so difficult. Have you ever seen the film The Mirror of Privilege: Making Whiteness Visible? In that documentary, a White woman says that she "got" it when an African-American woman explained the difference between the way White Folks and People of Color approach the possibility of interracial friendship. She said that when a White person wants to be friends with a Black person, all she has to do is walk across the room, extend her hand, and introduce herself. When a Black person makes that decision—and I'm paraphrasing here—she is crawling across the room across the shards of broken relationships with White people in the past. Ain't no way to start a friendship, is it?

But this is what racism has wrought.

You cannot imagine how many times, for example, women of color have had White women shut down a conversation about race under the guise of focusing on "all women?" How often have White people in the media advanced their careers telling stories about People of Color, making it almost impossible for us to produce our own narratives? Do you know how many times organizing groups headed by well-meaning White leaders have parachuted into our communities and then almost instantaneously commanded all the funding as if organizations with indigenous leadership and in need of resources did not already exist in those neighborhoods? If you were to pick up any of the shards of which that African-American woman spoke, these are just three of the million reflections you would see.

I know. You have seen some of these things. You might have even spoken out against them. And, no, it is not your responsibility alone to address them. You are only one person, and we are supposed to do it together. That is precisely why you showed up in the first place.

But you must grasp just how outnumbered you are. We have come to value you so much that we venture out in search of more of your kind only to have our hearts broken. What you are going through right now happens to us all the time. Do you know how many times we were made to feel safe in a predominantly White space only to be alienated once we brought up anything about race? Do you know how pervasive "color-blind racism" has become? (Once you've watched Mirrors of Privilege, cop Eduardo Bonilla-Silva's Racism Without Racists.) Do you know what the average White person does when the dialogue ceases to be about other faceless White people of the past and focuses on the present—specifically on how, to this very day, she or he benefits from what those long-dead white people did?

She packs up her privilege and leaves. The ability to trump one's Whiteness with some other identity—"I'm a woman, I'm working-class, I'm a good person, etc."—all without giving up the spoils of supremacy, is perhaps the biggest privilege of Whiteness of all. Ironic, isn't it?

And this is why we seek to separate, whether by creating our own organization or claiming our own table. We need to separate sometimes for our own welfare. And so when we meet folks like you and take the risk to integrate our spaces, even the most honest of mistakes can feel like hammering open a cast before the bone has fully healed. And if the mistake seems less than honest ....

I know. No one wants to have his goodness called into question. Least of all when all he did was be imperfect. Especially when, unlike others of the same privilege, he has chosen to step up for change. Trust me, I get it. As a heterosexual ally for queer liberation, I've been there. I know some men involved in the feminist movement who have been there, too. We can go down the identity checklist and draw parallels all day long, but I hope you understand that herein lies the rub.

Because of what racism has wrought, this is what it means to be an ally.

I cannot tell you whether you should stay or go. You may not even have a choice in the matter. But if you do go, I encourage you to ask yourself, "Am I just picking up my privilege and walking away?" At the heart of that question is what it means to be an ally. An ally sits in the fire that we cannot easily flee. And you know what? That includes those occasional fires that—for whatever reasons—we may have set ourselves.

How about if I make a deal with you? You have my word that some of us will continue to advocate for your essential goodness. We will take on the discomfort that ensues when we point out the dissonance between demanding that White people be allies only to show them the door the second they reveal themselves to be human. We will remind our kin that you are not there to save us but to liberate yourself, and that it is not acceptable for us to take out on you our rage at other White people. We will raise the painful question of just how effective we are being in empowering ourselves if we remain so easily threatened by the few White bodies in the room.

In return, I ask you to separate your intentions from your impact and to be willing to be accountable for what you say and do. I request you expand your contribution to racial justice to include your building with other like-minded White folks and finding the courage to discuss White privilege with those who deny that it exists. I caution you to attend to your guilt because it has a counterproductive tendency to hear things that were never said, serving no one, least of all you.

Most of all, if we are truly in this together, and you want me to go to bat for you when your fallibility makes you seem too much like the racists they have encountered before, the last thing you should do is pack up your privilege and leave.

Sofia Quintero

> "In every age, no matter how cruel the oppression carried on by those in power, there have been those who struggled for a different world. I believe this is the genius of humankind, the thing that makes us half divine: the fact that some human beings can envision a world that has never existed."
>
> --Anne Braden

Chapter 5

❧ *Media Power:*
Exporting Racism By Remote Control ❦

I have a love/hate relationship with the media because I have been a huge critic of it, yet here I am creating and producing TV and film. My desire sparked when my first book, *That White Girl*, got optioned for film. I wanted to stay a part of the process because the book is inspired by my life story. I was brought on as a producer, and I fell in love with the possibility that film offers.

As I continued down the production path, though, I developed a sheer disgust with the reality of reality TV. From my perspective, the shows millions of people are watching do very real damage around race and gender. From *Jersey Shore* to *Bad Girls Club*, to *Real Housewives* to *Basketball Wives*, the totality of what a woman is, I learned, amounted to being gold digging, alcoholic, weak-minded, dumb, boy-crazy, low-self-esteem having hoes. Women of color get a bonus: an extra layer of racism (skin lightening, anyone?) heaped on, serving up a little more dysfunction to really make sure the message gets across.

What to do?

Three routes, all important and valid.

One possibility is to wage a campaign against the racist, misogynistic machine messing up our kids and our society. Online petition (change.org anyone?), write an article, march in front of some offices, and show them what's up.

A second route: Create our own media. Go outside the system and create *our* version of reality, one that speaks to our values, vision, and highest purpose. Entertain, educate, and inspire. Use the collective brilliance to outdo and undo what mainstream media has had a lockdown on for so long.

Three, work within the system. Take out old Hollywood, and create New Hollywood. Make smart the new sexy. Shine a light on the dumbing down of the U.S. Raise some standards. Thought-provoking, politically edgy TV and film is attractive—we can win audiences back when we do it right.

Studies show that children are watching between five to seven hours of

TV a day. So not only does the media control our lives, but it's been raising our kids. No longer are parents or teachers the most influential adults in a child's life, producers are. Scary thought, seeing that their goal is to make money, not raise emotionally healthy humans.

There are some fundamental questions we need to engage in as a community: How do the media continue to maintain and control the racist status quo? Who owns the media, and what are the owners' agendas and political views? And who controls the controller? Let's get active, using media's power to create social justice, not perpetuate a racist, sexist, and downright stupid country.

❧ *My Media Roots* ❧

By *April R. Silver*
January 2012

January 1977. I was nine years old when the television mini-series, *Roots*, aired on ABC. A groundbreaking event of its day, the series was based on Alex Haley's novel of the same name. My family and I watched *Roots* every evening during the week that it aired. This, my first "up close and personal" depiction of what racism looked like, would change my life forever.

At nine, in an all Black part of Queens, New York, I had not yet been introduced to the ugliness of some White people. I had no concept that human beings had ever treated other human beings so inhumanely until I saw *Roots*—until I saw a machete sever Kunte Kinte's toes. It was a traumatizing scene, one that helped shape me into the activist that I am today. And when Fiddler (Louis Gossett, Jr.) tells Kunte Kinte (who always tried to escape from slavery, which bothered the hell out of Fiddler): "I don't know how to be free…" well, I was shook by that, too. "What does he mean he don't know how to be free?" my simple mind wondered. His question haunts me to this day. The thought that there are people in the world scared of freedom is something that didn't and does not bode well for me. I didn't know it at the time, but I'd spend my days trying to escape any semblance of slavery.

Two years later: October 1979. I was eleven years old when the feature film, *10*, was released. The romantic comedy was popular (it was nominated for two Oscars) and profitable (it pulled in over $74 million at the box office). *10* centered on a voluptuous blonde woman named Jenny Hanly (Bo Derek), who is the object of George Webber's (Dudley Moore's) obsession. Commercials for the movie featured Jenny and her jiggling breasts bouncing—in slow motion, of course—along a serene beach. A sheer beige bathing suit seems painted on her glistening beige body. She was the American/European picture of perfect beauty. On a scale of 1 to 10, she was a "10."

But here's the rub: Jenny was sultry and highly desirous...*and she was sporting cornrows*, an exotic "new" hairstyle rarely, if ever, seen by White people. The word on the street (Hollywood's streets) was that Bo Derek had created a "new" hairstyle for her character and that hairstyle was mysteriously known as *cornrows*.

With *Roots*, I was traumatized. With *10*, my feelings were deeply hurt. The lie about Bo Derek creating cornrows was a profound betrayal. I couldn't express my outrage fast enough; I couldn't yell at the idiot box loud enough. "HOW DARE THEY? BO DEREK CREATED CORNROWS?!?! OH MY GOD! My mother has been braiding my hair in cornrows since I was a lil' girl. All my cousins and friends wear cornrows, too...since forever!! How they gon' give credit for our stuff to Bo Derek?? *That's not fair!* How can they get away with that lie??"

I wanted to cry, kick, and scream. I wanted to tell "them" to stop lying on us: me, my girlfriends, my mother, my aunts, my grandmothers, and my family. I was convinced, at that point, that the world was not safe and that White people use television and film to tell the biggest lies to the most people, all at one time. I hurled imaginary rocks at an abstract "they" in the middle of a war that I didn't know existed until then. This battle felt like a relentless, sensational assault at the bottom of a very dark valley: deafening sirens, urgent flashing strobe lights, thunderous helicopters hovering inches above my head. Riot police, with full body shields and Darth Vader-esque masks, surrounded me from every angle. But, my make-believe rocks—more like pebbles—weren't big enough to combat the make-believe boulders being pushed down the make-believe hill. I could scream and cry about the unfairness of it all...but I would not be heard.

And that is how I was introduced to "the media" from an early age. I discovered that this thing was awesome and omnipresent, yet abstract. It was as inescapable as the air we breathe, and it was very powerful. "It,"

"They"—the media—had the ability to re-tell history to millions of people worldwide and "it," they"—the media—also had the ability to "make believe." The media's "make believe," though, was a world run by evil White people who enslaved and tortured Black people and who lied about our hair. I be damned if "the media" was going to make me believe anything they said. Liars. Somehow I knew my life was going to be a series of constant righteous reactions to and deconstructions of horrible lies.

And we can start with this notion of "White supremacy." The thing that people need to get most about "white supremacy" is that it doesn't exist. Racism exists, yes, but White people and "whiteness" are not supreme. The very creation and use of the phrase reveals how oppressive language and media are, even in the social justice communities. By extension, the thing that people need to get most about media, I've come to learn, is that when it is stripped down to its barest form, it doesn't exist to dominate, propagandize, or generate profit. It is neutral. Institutional, corporate media, however, has a more precise function. Specifically, the individuals or legal entities who own giant media companies are singularly focused on making big profits. There is no other reason for them to be in business. And, with reference to the standard American approach for successful business ownership, one must stay relevant and agile, and one must be fiercely competitive. Nappy-headed Black girls yelling at the White people on their TV screen have no standing in Hollywood's media and marketing offices.

Media, born neutral, is what we make of it. While it is true that media plays a well-documented role in negatively impacting the self-esteem of Black and Brown communities, it is simultaneously true that media has been a liberating force for those very same communities around the globe. Citing just three examples of recent memory, one can reference how the national Black community used Black radio and social media for the *Free the Jena 6* campaign; how the media was used during the so-called Arab spring of 2010; and, more locally, in New York City how WBAI Radio's popular weekly segment "The Spin,"—a media roundtable featuring only women of color—enlightens 19 million listeners every week.

At Sundance Film Fest 2012, Ava DuVernay became the first Black woman to receive the Best Director award for her film, *Middle of Nowhere*. As a guest on The Spin, actress Karen Chilton reminded the audience about the profound significance of that accomplishment. As an insider, Chilton attests to how Sundance represents a film world that is "so White and so male;" so competitive and so very exclusionary. By extension, the award for DuVernay is earth-shattering. But to hear a grateful DuVernay speak about being accepted into Sundance, it's easy to surmise that she would have likely been fine without the award. The Compton native, a former film publicist by trade, is an activist at heart. In addition to making films, DuVernay founded AFFRM (African-American Film Festival Releasing Movement), a "theatrical distribution entity powered by the nation's finest black film festival organizations." Like so many other progressive media makers and social entrepreneurs before her, DuVernay recognizes that Black people have no voice that Hollywood is bound to amplify; we have no story to tell that media giants are bound to respect. And so she took matters into her own hands. In DuVernay and others, we have a few truths affirmed: That media is what you make of it, that White supremacy is not, and that we have choices.

"The thing that people need to get most about 'white supremacy' is that it doesn't exist. Racism exists, yes, but White people and "whiteness" are not supreme."

❖ ❖ ❖

❧ *Media, White Privilege, and Racism* ❧

An Interview with *Danny Hoch conducted by JLove Calderón*

JLove: I would love to hear your thoughts about *Curb Your Enthusiasm*, and shows like it.

Danny: (Laughs) Well, *Curb Your Enthusiasm* is a really good fodder to dissect, because I think the show is really funny. It's funny because Larry David as a main character is someone who, no matter what your background is, you love to see him go down. And you love to see him sort of fail in his good intentions because I think a lot of people can identify with having good intentions and failing. Right? Particularly liberal white folks. Or having good intentions and not being accepted. Right? So I think that the way that the show deals with issues of race is probably unprecedented—except maybe All In The Family. But for me, there's a problem at the same time. And the problem is that even though we're dealing with issues of white people's fear and unspoken, day-to-day in your face racism, the bigger racism is that we're watching a show about a rich, white, Jewish Hollywood media broker who, in every show, is a victim. And that is not ever dealt with in the show. So at the same time that it may be addressing these day-to-day issues, it's completely ignoring and not acknowledging at all the *Seinfeld* factor. And it's not ironic that Larry David was the creator and producer of *Seinfeld* and that Seinfeld's character was based on him, because what S*einfeld* did, as *Curb Your Enthusiasm* does is enforce this idea that there is no white privilege. It reinforces and bolsters the idea that, "Hey! I'm just trying to live!" You know? Like, "Why is this stuff happening to me when I'm a good guy?" And you kinda laugh at him because he's a schlep. But yet, at the end of each show, it's like he's done nothing wrong and he's a victim of just being. He's not really responsible for institutional racism. He's not really responsible for any of his actions, except for the ones that piss people off in a funny scene.

JLove: What are the implications of that for white people especially?

Danny: The implications of that are we're reinforced into thinking that white privilege doesn't exist. And, by embracing this kind of show, we are trained to be more comfortable in our white privilege.

JLove: Is this a conspiracy thing? Is it something premeditated, something that they think about?

Danny: They didn't sit down to make the show to say, "We want to reinforce white privilege." However, it is clearly symptomatic of something that white people feel. Which is that no matter how much privilege we have, we still feel like we're the ones who are mostly struggling. We feel like: Why are these things happening to us? Why are we the victim if we're just good people? The fact that *Seinfeld* is the largest grossing show in television history pretty much confirms the fact white privilege exists because if there was a black person or a Latino person or, better yet, if there was a Native American who had a television show about, 'Why is all this stuff happening to me?,' not only would it not be the highest grossing television show history, but it would not even get on the air. So, that's the implication of that, right?

JLove: That's pretty crazy. And you feel that *Seinfeld* was just the younger version of *Curb Your Enthusiasm* in terms of Seinfeld being the victim?

Danny: Well, if you think about it not in conspiracy terms but a syndrome of this feeling of white victimization and feeling alienated, you would have thought that because Larry David created and produced every episode of *Seinfeld* that he would have got that out of his system. But it wasn't enough. He had to go make his own show with him in it because he's...he's walking around plagued by this syndrome of symptoms, which is: I am white, and I am in power, and I feel like a victim. I am white, and I have white privilege, and the world is against me. I am white, and I am in control of media in the form of two mega-hit shows, and no one listens to me. And that's a syndrome. Right?

JLove: Yeah. I think you need to name that syndrome.

Danny: Uhm...White Cluelessness Syndrome.

JLove: The power of media, right? Because, obviously, people are watching, and people love it. I wonder what the impact of the unconscious message is. I wonder how many people of color watch these shows. I think *Seinfeld* was pretty across the board successful, wasn't it?

Danny: *Seinfeld* was across the board successful, as is *Curb Your Enthusiasm* because, again, no matter what your background is, if you're white and you have this syndrome or even if you have symptoms of the syndrome, you're going to identify with Larry David or you're going to identify with Jerry Seinfeld because you're gonna be, like, "Yeah, why is all this stuff happening to me?" People of color, I think, embrace the show for a different reason. Like, "Look at this white guy go down," or "Look at this white guy fall on his face," or "Look at all the stupid shit that happens to this clueless white guy." And we can laugh at that. And, therefore, the show seems harmless. I mean *Seinfeld's* moniker was even: It's the show about nothing. But the reality is, it wasn't nothing that was happening in the episode. What was happening in the episode was that people of color were predominantly absent. And when people of color showed up, it was only to reinforce how alienated and disenfranchised Jerry Seinfeld was. I haven't brought this shit up since 1997 but, like, my own experience on the *Seinfeld* show reinforced that for me. When I showed up, they wanted me to do this clowny, minstrel character with, and I quote, "A funny Puerto Rican accent." And I explained to them I wasn't going to do that, and I remember Larry David coming to the set and trying to coax me into it. And I was, like, you have to understand who's watching this show and what you're saying if you present a person-of-color character that's a clown when Jerry gets to live in three dimensions. And Elaine gets to live in three dimensions. And Kramer gets to live in three dimensions. And George gets to live in three dimensions. But once every twenty-five episodes you have a non-white character or a non-Jewish character, and those characters are limited to only one dimension. I said, "It's destructive." Of course, they didn't even know what I was saying. It was like I was speaking fucking Swahili. And you know when I was performing in Australia, I remember these people came up to me, and they said, "Hey, we don't know what you're complaining about because we get all the shows, like *Seinfeld* and *Cops* and, you know, *In Living Color*. So we know all about the blacks and the Hispanics in the United States." And I was, like, "Really? You know all about them?" "Yeah, we know all about them. So what are you going on about?" And the subtext of what the Australians were saying to me—keep in mind *Cops* to this day is the most watched American television show in the world outside of the United States—confirms that these shows bolster the idea that racism does not really exist. That it's in our minds. And that white privilege certainly doesn't exist. It's not even a concept.

❧ *What If the Tea Party Was Black?* ❧

By *Jasiri X*

The inspiration behind bi-weekly Internet Hip-Hop news series, "This Week With Jasiri X" was, believe it or not, Fox news. The incredible spin and right wing bias that they put on so called "news" is ridiculous, but the final straw was their coverage of self professed "hockey mom" and VP presidential candidate Sarah Palin and, specifically, her teen daughter's pregnancy. Not only weren't the Palins vilified as bad parents, they were applauded by the Right for choosing to support their daughter's decision to have the baby. Can you imagine the reaction to one of Obama's daughters getting pregnant? The hypocritical outrage would have been deafening.

I saw the same bias with the rise of the Tea Party. Here was an armed group of angry anti-government protestors, but instead of being portrayed as un-American they were called patriotic. They caused me to raise the question, "What if the Tea Party was Black?" I think we all know if Black folks marched on the White House with guns, the response would not have been non-violent. So I decided to use my voice as an emcee activist to speak truth to power. Check the lyrics:

What if the Tea Party was black
Holding guns like the Black Panther Party was back
If Al was Rush Limbaugh and Jesse was Sean Hannity
And Tavis was Glenn Beck would they harm they families
If Sarah Palin was suddenly Sistah Souljah
Would they leave it with the votes or go and get the soldiers
Y'all know if the Tea Party was black
The government would have been had the army attack

What if Michael Baisden was on ya FM dial
For 3 hours every day calling the president foul
Would they say free speech or find evidence how
To charge him with treason like see he's un-American now
What if Minister Farrakhan prayed for the death
Of the commander in chief that he be laid to rest
Would they treat it as the gravest threat or never make an arrest
Even today he's still hated for less

What if President Obama would have lost the election
Quit his job so he could go talk to the left and
Bash the government for being off of direction
Fraught with deception
And told black people they want all of our weapons
And we want our own country and called for secession
Would he be arrested and tossed in corrections
For trying to foster aggression
Against the people's lawful selection
Our questions

What if the Tea Party was black
Holding guns like the Black Panther Party was back
If Al was Rush Limbaugh and Jesse was Sean Hannity

And Tavis was Glenn Beck would they harm they families
If Sarah Palin was suddenly Sistah Souljah
Would they leave it with the votes or go and get the soldiers
Y'all know if the Tea Party was black
The government would have been had the army attack

What if black people went on Facebook and made a page
That for the death if the president elect we prayed
Would the creators be tazed and thrown in a cage
We know the page wouldn't have been displayed all these days
What if Jeremiah Wright said that everybody white
Wasn't a real America would you feel scared of him
If he had a militia with pictures that depict the president as Hitler
They would kill and bury that
Wait
What if Cynthia McKinney lamented the winning of the new president
And hinted he wasn't really a true resident
With no proof or evidence
Would the media treat it like a huge press event
They would have attacked whatever group she represents
They would have called her a kook on precedent
And any network that gave her due preference
Would be the laughing stock of the news so our question is

What if the Tea Party was black
Holding guns like the Black Panther Party was back
If Al was Rush Limbaugh and Jesse was Sean Hannity
And Tavis was Glenn Beck would they harm they families
If Sarah Palin was suddenly Sistah Souljah
Would they leave it with the votes or go and get the soldiers
Y'all know if the Tea Party was black
The government would have been had the army attack

Dear John, the Power of the Lens

A love letter. That's what I've been asked to write. How do I do that? Where do I start? I do not love you. So maybe this should be a Dear John letter, a break-up letter, where I go back and look at our dysfunctional, interdependent, interconnected relationship, minus hatred or rose-colored lenses. Except that our history keeps us connected, and leave though I try, I keep running into you everywhere I go; damn. Okay, forget about the Dear John part. Let's just share. Me first.

My relationship with you has been rocky from the beginning. The intimate tongue of the lash and the kiss of the lynch made me wary of you all those years ago. In the beginning you always had your way, called the shots, laid down the law. You always demanded the missionary position, had to be on top. I had no choice. It was an abusive relationship. I always felt like I was struggling to breathe. It was fraught, tense, violent, scary. It went on for hundreds of years. Wasn't exactly a marriage—no white dress, no aisle, no flowers, no honeymoon. It was a relationship, though.

Change came, as it always does. I stopped working for you—at least in that capacity. I fought for you to recognize my humanity. Blood was shed so I could get a chance to be in a classroom, graduate, go to college, work for myself—or, indeed, you. And all these years later, here we are. What we have run from is our truths; our individual truths; yours and mine. Let's not run anymore. Walk with me. Isn't love truth? Some say the truth will set you free. Cliché? Maybe. Sometimes truth does other things. It binds you, cripples you, can paralyze you, even destroy you. I feel for you. I wonder how it must feel to know that your truth, that what you have and who you are, is a lie, wasn't achieved fairly. Breathe, no need to get defensive. Makes it hard to talk, right, really hard to speak any kind of truth. Another truth? You have watched me, scrutinized me, labeled me, categorized me, despised me, yearned for me, envied me, hated me, been scared of me—and then you voted for me. I vote for some truth between us.

Let the past be the past, you continually tell me. Okay. I can do that. First though, you need to hear how it affected us. You were lied to. When you described me as savage, less than, ignorant, unworthy—those were lies you told yourself and were told. Not just that I was less than, but that you were somehow better, more human, more noble. That, too, was your lie, your burden, your privilege, ultimately, your cancer. You carry that to this day. That's why you won't be part of something I'm part of. You insist on taking it over, invading it, razing it to the ground, re-writing it or re-telling it. The hero is always you; you either saved me or killed me. Or pitied me. You were hoodwinked, bamboozled. And now, you're suffering; the world that gave you so much is taking away those things that made you you; that gave you esteem, a sense of value. That's the danger of the single story. You can't always be the hero; you weren't. You were the villain, the criminal.

So now, it's time to just be. It's hard to swallow the resentment, the call to criticize, chastise, wail on you. I'm trying. Give me a minute. This is tough. Who might I have been with your path? Who might you have been with mine? We never got to walk in each other's shoes for a minute, much less a mile. So, no more single stories. No more versions of you where you rescue or save me. Our weird interdependent need has created cowards and built careers. Guilt has been the commodity that paved a lot of paths; truth was much harder to come by. We needed each other. Admit it. I know it's hard, but you did. Me too. Our versions of ourselves are connected due to our pasts. Were then. Still are. You need me. Still do. Like Ali, you think you're the greatest. It ain't bad, it just ain't true. Your version of me was your truth, your way of getting by. I survived us, our relationship. I got scars; you do too.

Now I watch you, read you, listen to you, and hear myself defined by you all over again. Whether it's the small screen, the big screen, the airwaves, the page—your version of me continues to provoke me, make me mad all over again. Now though, I challenge you. You voted for someone who looks like me, so no longer can a single story of your version of me dominate the lens. You gotta get up when I walk in, gotta call me Massa, or maybe just President. (Low blow, couldn't resist that one.) Look how far we've come, you say; some of us say that, too. And yet. And yet. Recent natural disasters remind me that your single story, your single version of who I am stays with you, in your brain, in your soul; you're fixated. You mean well. You don't mean any harm. That's what you say. But you cause harm. You do.

Your lens on my body has always been intrusive, zooming in, close up, nothing hidden, everything exposed. That lens didn't stop me from navigating around it, over it, underneath it to get to where I stand today. Here we are, you and me. I realize we have a strange interdependence. You became my fall-guy, my guarantee for blame; I continued to be who you perceived and portrayed me to be, someone you wanted, despised, feared, envied. Why? Why are you so attached to this single story of me? Why must you define me in these boxes and by these terms? Is that what your path did to you—robbed you of an ability to measure me beyond that single story?

Time to challenge you and do for me. So, my truth is this: there are no single stories—not yours, not mine. There is a power in the lens to shape, re-write, re-tell and re-package various truths. To whittle, mold, sand everything down into the single story. There are perspectives, versions, sides. You want absolutes; I can't give you those. That's what lies do, make things absolute, make them black and white. Truth is much harder, much grayer, more painful, but much more freeing. So, here we are, you and me. The power of the lens. No more single stories. What now?

Esther Armah

❖ ❖ ❖

10 Steps to Becoming an Ally[1]

Excerpted from *Love, Race, and Liberation: Til' the White Day is Done* Activity by Samantha Shapses Wertheim

Allies are members of the advantaged group who act against the oppression(s) from which they derive power, privilege, and acceptance.

Within the social manifestation of racism white people are the advantaged group, and People of Color: African-Americans, Asian Americans, Latinos, Native Americans, and Multiracial/Biracial people are the oppressed group.

10 Steps to Becoming an Ally: Ask participants for examples of someone being an ally to another person. Take a few examples, and then inform participants that we will now go through 10 steps to becoming an ally. These are only ten key points in ally development. They are not meant to be a complete list of all of the ways that can be an ally.

Being an ally is a responsibility that requires humility and integrity and should not be taken lightly. It is not about being a savior, nor does it require you to be an expert on someone else's experience. However, it does require that you believe oppression is wrong, whether it is happening directly to you or not, and that you are prepared to deal with the consequences of speaking up and/or acting against injustice.

- **Step One: Definitions of Diversity and Social Justice**

  Diversity is a complex interplay of multiple social identities and is-sues including gender, race, ethnicity, socioeconomic class, religion or spiritual affiliation, sexual orientation, national origin, age, physical, emotional & developmental ability, and language.

  Adams, Bell, and Griffin (1997) define social justice as both a pro-cess and a goal. "The goal of social justice is full and equal participa-tion of all groups in a society that is mutually shaped to meet their needs. Social justice includes a vision of society that is equitable and all members are physically and psychologically safe and secure."

  Diversity is who we are; social justice is what we do.

- **Step Two: Privilege**

  Learn what it means to have privilege based on your social identities and social location.

- **Step Three: Social Power**

  Continue or begin to explore how social power works in U.S. soci-ety and globally—who has it and who doesn't, and why.

- **Step Four: Oppression**

  Gain awareness of the levels and types of oppression: Individual, Cultural, and Institutional.

- **Step Five: Awareness**

  Learn your own history. (A People's History of the United States by Howard Zinn is a good place to start).

- **Step Six: White Guilt**

  Work through any guilt you might have about having privilege. While guilt is a natural response to learning about unearned privilege, it is quite damaging because it centers the story/process/group back on the privileged person, which is typically the opposite of what would be liberating for the group. So working through guilt and finding a proactive positive outlet is not only beneficial but a necessity in becoming an ally.

- **Step Seven: Finding Support**

  Find a group of friends, colleagues, and/or classmates who will keep you honest about your work as an ally, and make sure they have agreed to be your accountability person or people.

◈ **Step Eight: Research**

DO YOUR OWN RESEARCH. Do not expect other people to take the responsibility for educating you about their experience. Take classes, check out web sites, attend a lecture, step out of your comfort zone, and take the learning into your own hands.

◈ **Step Nine: Making Mistakes**

Don't be afraid to make mistakes. Hone your instincts, and be sincere in your efforts. Operating with integrity will take you much further than being fearful.

◈ **Step Ten: Listen**

Listen to other people's experiences—if people are willing to share with you listen with an open heart and an open mind—it is a gift to be treasured, even when it is hard to hear.

[1] Adapted from a presentation by Marcella Runell Hall ©2010

Are Skin-Whitening Commercials Racist?

In the past twenty years, America has witnessed the rise of the tanning salon. White women and girls (some men, too) are just dying to sport a "healthy" glow. But what about the already-tan populace? While white girls show off their bronzed bodies, brown girls in this country (and all over the world) are gettin' down with whitening soap, cream, face wash, and lotions. In India, skin lightening products account for about 60% of the skincare market, reports Sara Sidner of CNN. About 37% of the global skin lightening marker is accounted for by the Asia-Pacific region. Has the world turned on its head? White people wanna look tan, and tan people wanna look white. Everyone wants what they can't have…

Chapter 6

❧ *The Criminal (In)Justice System* ❧

They led me off the bus, and I was acutely aware of the coldness of my new surroundings, the place that I would call home for the next 16 years. As I was shuffled in with the other inmates, I began contemplating how I would maintain my sanity and stay alive. At that same moment, a fly perched itself proudly on my shoulder. With my hands and feet shackled with steel handcuffs, I remained powerless, unable to do the simplest of all tasks, like brushing off a fly. At that moment, I felt the little fly had conquered me, had conquered my manhood. And that, my friend, is the clearest way I can describe what it feels like to have your freedom taken from you. Pray for me.

-Jay Mason, former inmate, current artist,
  written in a letter to JLove

We can't have a book about racism and white privilege without talking about the criminal (in)justice system, including the Prison Industrial Complex (PIC). For those who view prisons as necessary but who have no connection to them personally (they've never have been to prison, nor had anyone they know or love go to prison), it may rarely cross their minds, this prison thing. They might not even see it as an important issue or a concern to address.

For others, the PIC has literally taken away their lives.

Some argue it is the single most destructive system in the country to black and brown communities. It has taken away the parents or caregivers of millions of children and abandoned their young ones in the foster care system, changing their lives forever. The Applied Research Center, which publishes *Colorlines*, conducted a year-long investigation in 2011 and found that, minimally, 5,100 children were placed in foster care, due to their parents being detained or deported.

According to Michelle Alexander, author of *The New Jim Crow*, here are a few facts that put some things into perspective:

- There are more African-Americans under correctional control to-day—in prison or jail, on probation or parole—than were enslaved in 1850, a decade before the Civil War began.

- As of 2004, more African-American men were disenfranchised (due to felon disenfranchisement laws) than in 1870, the year the Fifteenth Amendment was ratified, prohibiting laws that explicitly deny the right to vote on the basis of race.

- If you take into account both prisoners and those formerly incarcerated, a large majority of African-American men have been labeled felons for life. They can be denied the right to vote, automatically excluded from juries, and legally discriminated against in employment, housing, access to education, and public benefits—much as their grandparents and great-grandparents once were during the Jim Crow era.

Say what? Yes, startling facts. I brought in expert Eddie Ellis to help us really understand the PIC, its impact on our communities, and what can we do about it.

❧ Who Made this Mess and Why Can't We Clean it Up? ❧
By Eddie Ellis

In the United States today there are 2.5 million people in jails and prisons and five million more on parole and probation. The national rate of recidivism is around 65%. There is an obscenely disproportionate number of African-American, Latino, and poor people in the system, most coming from and returning to inner city neighborhoods upon completion of their sentences. The entire notion of "justice" is questioned in urban communities of color as police killings of black and brown youth continue to rise, while one in three black males and one in seven Latino males is either in prison, on parole, or on probation. The term "criminal justice" to describe the system is misleading, an oxymoron, perhaps better described as a "criminal punishment" system. Either way, the public is no safer today than it was three decades ago. Still, we pour billions of taxpayer dollars, year after year, in this failed, broken, costly system.

The cost of incarceration is so high that at state levels, spending on education, health, and housing budgets have to be reduced to accommodate a finite yet shrinking tax base. Prison programs designed to prepare people to return to society have largely been eliminated. Punishment and incapacitation still rule the day. Due to reductions in programs, education, and other socialization activities within the prisons over the past 15 years, people returning from prison find it exceedingly difficult to complete successful transitions into their respective communities. More and more jobs require higher levels of education, while communities face a shortage of affordable housing, all of which make the transition back into the community difficult. Additionally, under the pretense of "getting tough" on crime, numerous legal, civic, and social barriers have been erected that create disincentives for post release success. Finally, public perception, discriminatory practices, and institutional and personal bias exacerbate an already difficult situation.

Federal, state, and local governments presently are under tremendous fiscal and budgetary strains. Within that strain sacred cows, heretofore untouchable, are now up for consideration. New York State, for example, which increased its prison budget four-fold over a period of 25 years, now has been force to close several prisons as a cost-saving measure. Interestingly, the fiscal crisis has uncovered numerous wasteful practices that border on being criminal and that had both racial and political implications themselves.

While white rural communities in the northern and western areas of New York state were benefiting from mass incarceration, get tough legislation, and the healthy economy, protests and cries for cost effectiveness and racial justice from downstate and New York City went mostly unheard. Yet, when the stock market crashed and the economy tanked, ushering in a period of extended recession, the insanity of mass incarceration, expansion of the prison system, and "throw away the key" attitudes came under closer scrutiny. The expensive, wasteful, and illogical nature of current drug and prison public policy became exposed and challenged to change. Ultimately New York's governor, Andrew Cuomo, under unrelenting pressure from both advocates and opponents of prison closings, was forced to close five prisons as a cost-saving measure in his budget.

According to a January 2012 study compiled by the Vera Institute of Justice, state taxpayers pay, on average, 14 percent more on prisons than corrections department budgets reflect. The report, *The Price of Prisons: What Incarceration Costs Taxpayers*, found that among the 40 states that responded to a survey, the total fiscal year 2010 taxpayer cost of prisons was $38.8 billion, $5.4 billion more than in state corrections budgets for that year. When all costs are considered, the annual average taxpayer cost in these states was $31,166 per person incarcerated.

How Did We Get Into This Mess?

We must ask ourselves: What have been the clear and measurable benefits for communities of the current costly criminal punishment system? There are precious few. The claim of its impact on crime has been debated for years with little consensus among criminal punishment and justice professionals. And, the results of current programs have not convinced the public that prison, parole, probation, or community "corrections" are highly productive public safety measures. With the rate of recidivism sky high, such claims fly in the face of the facts. To understand it better, let's look at the thinking that has brought us to this point.

The origins of this mess can be traced to James Q. Wilson's *Thinking About Crime*, an article that appeared in Atlantic Magazine in 1975. In his article, Wilson outlined a series of ideas that called for increased and aggressive law enforcement, stricter laws, harsher and longer sentences, and the building of more prisons, thoughts that pleased conservatives and have shaped the nation's crime policies ever since. Wilson debunked "root-cause" anti-crime stratagems, traditionally espoused by mainline sociologists and psychologists, as not only ineffective but having contributed to the condition for more crime. The end result of Wilson's thinking was federal and state legislation, mostly enacted in the mid 1980s, that has misguided America's criminal punishment policies for more than twenty years.

> "The term 'criminal justice' system is misleading, an oxymoron, perhaps better described as a 'criminal punishment' system."

It is clear now, as a result of the enormous challenges presented by the large numbers of people emerging from prisons, that Wilsonian thinking and many of the policies he and others advocated are simply not working in the way that they were conceived. The unintended consequences, if they were "unintended," have become unbearable both fiscally and in terms of public safety. There are now hundreds of thousands of ill-prepared men and women returning to under-served urban communities from confinement annually. The public sees no measurable increase in public safety resulting from their confinement. The cost of confining such large numbers of people has skyrocketed and is now out of control. The thinking that gave us broken windows, zero tolerance, three strikes, super predators, and mandatory minimums and at the same time demanded a "tougher" approach to criminal and social problems, has brought us to an impending public health and safety crisis.

Still, many policy makers continue to attempt to infuse new life into policies and practices that rely on remedial services provided with a "law enforcement" approach to community reintegration. The central features of this approach are improved surveillance, restrictive curfews, extensive use of urine testing, and greater reliance on electronic monitoring. All of these are necessary, of course, but none are sufficient. Without identifying economic, social, and political assets and problems from a community perspective, then locating resources, leadership, and solutions within the community to address the fundamental problems, post-release success will remain elusive. Ironically, instead of changing or adding critical new concepts to these policies, they are basically left as they are, repackaged with different language, recycled under a different name—"*community corrections*"—and touted as "new" and more effective ways of crime containment, violence reduction, policing, supervising, and controlling people on parole or probation.

Where Do We Go From Here?

Much more expansive thinking is needed to break from traditional models and to establish ideas evolving from the conditions and needs of inner city urban communities and people who return to them from prisons. For these reasons, we must develop and promote new, community-based economic arrangements, constructed from community development and "entrepreneurial business models," to supplement existing therapeutic community and remedial service provision program models.

The new paradigm should be created from models that are wholly self-sufficient, seeking limited government or foundation support, raising capital through creating offerings, cost saving management strategies and alternative methods that operate upon labor intensive market-driven business rather than social service principles. Such models, to the greatest extent possible, have as their guiding principles three key objectives:

1. A triple bottom line: returning a profit while doing social good and enhancing public safety;

2. Greater reliance on community economic development initiatives to supplement treatment and social programs; and

3. Financial self-sustainability, through income/revenue generation, while providing employment and services to its client base.

To achieve this new paradigm requires a primary shift in our thinking such that new policies are developed along the following lines:

- A fundamental re-allocation of public spending that co-invests "correctional" dollars and other government and private funds in educational, business, housing, and healthcare infrastructure to strengthen the civil institutions of high incarceration neighborhoods instead of wasting resources on ill conceived "corrections/re-entry" programs that are poorly constructed, costly, and ineffective.

- A fundamental change in the mission of institutional "corrections" and parole/probation to establish a civic foothold that works against economic and political disenfranchisement, stigmatization, and exclusion. This redefined mission would have "correctional" institutions become service learning environments and move parole/probation functions towards enhanced public safety through community building, economic development, and service operations.

- A fundamental change in the character and scope of the community's responsibility for successful transition from prison to community that involves academic institutions, community development corporations, entrepreneurial enterprises, faith institutions, and other local entities as more effective transitional gateways than the traditional remedial programs and re-entry social services currently offered.

One of the most critical components in resettlement thinking is that government must establish opportunities, not obstacles, for people formerly incarcerated as they seek to make the transition from prison to community.

Any state or federal rule restricting people with convictions from obtaining housing, employment, public benefits, education, the franchise, or other elements of a law-abiding life should be individualized on a case-by-case basis and bear some rational relationship to the benefit denied in light of the criminal conviction.

Government policies and monies should be restructured to create economic and infra-structural development incentives for strengthening the capacity of under-resourced, high incarceration neighborhoods to keep their residents in the community and out of prison. Less reliance upon incarceration as a solution to socioeconomic and public health (read: drug problems) needs to be the order of the day. Instead of advocating for marginal, add-on "re-entry" services, which are the last to be funded, never funded at adequate levels, and the first to be eliminated, the bulk of existing resources must be targeted to achieve enduring reductions in recidivism and incarceration, especially among young people.

Decent jobs and housing have to be top priorities. People with criminal convictions must be viewed as potential community assets and encouraged to participate meaningfully in community building activities through responsible work and service to others. This means creating opportunities, not barriers, for civic participation.

Finally, to repair the harm caused by violence and deprivation, individual, community, and system level (institutional) transformations are necessary to restore public confidence, especially in urban communities, in the legitimacy of a "justice" system, perceived by people of color to provide them with precious little justice. Agencies at every level of government must reorganize resources, even in these times of fiscal deficits and the attending budget constraints, to support the challenges presented by the unprecedented numbers of people returning from prisons to urban minority communities.

"We must ask ourselves: What have been the clear and measurable benefits for communities of the current costly criminal punishment system?

There are precious few."

❧ *I Am Trayvon Martin* ❧

By *Kevin Powell*

I am Trayvon Martin.

So are you. And, so is any human being who has ever felt cornered in a dark and desolate alley between life and death. Add the grim reality of skin color in America, and you have the disastrous spectacle of 250lb George Zimmerman, 28, pursuing 140lb Trayvon, 17, until that man-child is screaming "Help!"—and then gasping for air after a bullet from Zimmerman's 9mm handgun had punctured his chest. A majority-white, gated community became on 26 February the makeshift mortuary for a black boy who will not get a chance to live, to go to college with his exceptional high school grades, or to make something of his life. Trayvon's fatal act: a mundane walk to the nearby convenience store to buy a can of iced tea and a bag of Skittles.

This is what racism, the American version of it, means to black boys like Trayvon and to black men like me. That we often don't stand a chance when it has been determined, oftentimes by a single individual acting as judge and jury, that we are criminals to be pursued, confronted, tackled, and, yes, subdued. To be shocked and awed into submission.

The police authorities in Sanford, Florida, where the shooting occurred, are apparently so mired in racial prejudice and denial that George Zimmerman, at this writing*, still has not been arrested nearly a month after Trayvon was killed—in spite of Zimmerman being told, on 911 police dispatch audio, not to follow Trayvon Martin.

In spite of Zimmerman being charged in 2005 with resisting arrest with violence and battery on a police officer. In spite of Zimmerman calling the police 46 times since January 2011. In spite of Zimmerman, according to neighbors, being fixated on bracketing young black males with criminality. In spite of Zimmerman being the subject of complaints from neighbors in his gated community, due to his aggressive tactics. In spite of the officer in charge of the crime scene also receiving criticism in 2010 when he initially failed to arrest a lieutenant's son who was videotaped attacking a homeless black man. In spite of Zimmerman violating major principles of the Neighborhood Watch manual (the manual states: "It should be emphasized to members that they do not possess police powers. And they shall not carry weapons or pursue vehicles.")

In spite of Zimmerman not being a member of a registered group, which police were not aware of at the time of the incident. And, in spite of the Sanford, Florida, police failing to test Zimmerman for drugs or alcohol. (A law enforcement expert told ABC that Zimmerman sounds intoxicated on the 911 tapes and that drug and alcohol testing is "standard procedure in most homicide investigations".)

Finally, what was a man like George Zimmerman doing with a gun in the first place? And, will Florida's very controversial "stand your ground" self-defense law prevent Zimmerman from ever being prosecuted, especially as he and his lawyers are claiming he was protecting himself from harm?

Finally, does any of the above truly matter if the shooter has white skin and the victim's is brown?

Racism remains the greatest cancer of American society and has been since the founding of this nation—by men who owned slaves. You cannot slaughter and push from the land Native Americans, enslave black people, harass and marginalize Asians, Latinos and Jews, and scapegoat immigrant white ethnics and Arabs through your long and tumultuous history and then wonder how the killing of Trayvon Martin could happen in the first place? The former is the context for the latter.

We, most of us, have been socialized to fear and demonize difference, the other. Trayvon's murder is of a piece with hysterical and overzealous anti-immigration policies and new voter ID laws that recall the days of segregation and harsh American racial apartheid. Left unchecked, as George Zimmerman has been left unchecked, and you perpetuate this ugly national tragedy.

American racism is not merely a distortion of human psychology that teaches the George Zimmermans of our nation to see Trayvon Martin as nothing more than a criminal; it is also the debilitating disease that allows us, on the one hand, to denounce the alleged atrocities of Kony in faraway Africa that we've seen in that ubiquitous viral video and on the other, to overlook the Trayvon Martins, just as we ignore the routine stop-and-frisk harassment of legions of black and Latino young males.

We are trapped in the stereotyping that saw my friend's son being told by his teacher in Fairfax County, Virginia, recently, as he recited a Langston Hughes poem, that he needed to read it "blacker". The stereotyping that allows us to cheer loudly for the majority-black college basketball teams during March Madness, yet won't permit us to pay attention to Trayvon Martin's parents, clearly shattered, pleading for some shred of justice.

The Justice Department's intervention is welcome, if belated. But it is American racism that constrains our leaders, like President Barack Obama and Attorney General Eric Holder, from speaking forcibly and publicly about this destructive cancer for fear of alienating "regular" folks. If the president could call on Sandra Fluke, considering the insult she'd received from Rush Limbaugh, we should be able to expect him to offer his condolences to Martin's parents for the grievous injury they have received.

For the sake of Trayvon Martin and the Trayvon Martins who never had this sort of mass outcry, something must be done. But if we choose to turn our ears and hearts away from his parents and his community, then Trayvon Martin's blood will be on the hands of this entire nation. Will we ignore that call for help, as Trayvon's went unheeded?[1]

"Racism remains the greatest cancer of American society and has been since the founding of this nation--by men who owned slaves."

❖ ❖ ❖

[1] Printed With Permission

Trayvon Martin Case Update as of May 2012

George Zimmerman is charged with second degree murder in the fatal shooting of unarmed 17 year old Trayvon Martin after 45 days of national protests, petitions, and media coverage. This is an important step toward justice not just for Trayvon Martin and his family but for all people who have been victims of racial profiling, racialized violence, and a historically based racist justice system. As a white woman and as a mother of two bi-racial boys, I will continue to stand up and speak out against racial injustice, always working toward liberation for all people. I believe, as many of my counterparts believe, our liberation and freedom are intertwined. Toward more peace and more justice.[2]

Antiracist Pledge:[3]

- ❖ I hold myself accountable for furthering racial justice in my sphere of influence.

- ❖ I stand for respect, dignity, and human rights for all individuals, regardless of race, ethnicity, gender, sexual orientation, socio-economic status, or creed.

- ❖ I will use my experience and any privilege or resources I have to transform the systems that support violence and oppression against any person or group.

- ❖ Through self-reflection, knowledge, and understanding I seek to build a community of hope and promise.

- ❖ From this day forward, I will increase my efforts to end all manifestations of racism.

[2] JLove's statement and update on the case

[3] Adapted in 2010 by JLove Calderón and Chelsea Gregory from the "Atlanta Pledge" by the Coalition to Remember the 1906 Race Riots

❧ *Anniversary Poem* ❧

By *Jennifer Cendaña Armas*

En route to camp
We tried perfecting el hymno de Zapatista
In the evenings, Tzotzil boys sang to us their songs of freedom
Muddied feet and boiling water for tea
The indigena looked just like me
Danced all night with the children New Year's Eve

My body home in Chiapas

Where land is stolen
Stripped by multinationals
Saved by environmentalists kicking families onto uninhabitable soil
A poverty unknown even in the worst of my time

The revolution is not a romantic notion in the mountains or basins
Fighting daily to show communal efforts don't have to fail even though it's
Harder without government subsidies and it's always
Westerners seem to have the debate whether armed
Struggle is needed by the oppressed

Survival blurs lines of presumed right and wrong
There is no romanticism in los caracoles

These words rough and stumbling:
After all these years
We still feel the effects of the first Kastilas

It's easy to forget

Grassroots freedom fighters are always
Terrorists, immoral savages
Whether they are or not
Stories flip
Government directives make people scared of their own people
Whether they should be or not

We become not our own
They become strangers and radicals
Second and third person references are big
Identities are absentia

But what government has been created without the bloodshed?
And everyone asks whether the Zapatistas will succeed

The need for food, water, school, and land always turns political
Yo trabajo sin reposo
Basic needs force our blood to strain and dissociate
Yo trabajo sin reposo
What government has been created without the bloodshed?
And everyone asks whether the Zapatistas will succeed

New York to Dallas
D.F. to Tuxtla Gutierrez
Bus it to San Cristóbal
Oventic
La Garrucha
years since body home in Chiapas

❖ ❖ ❖

A Love Letter

A love note to a world free from the burden of race and its micro- and macro-aggressions. I miss the freedom, the peace, and the ease that comes from being in the majority. I long for the time when I don't have to wonder if the cop who stops to question me or the woman on the train who clutches her purse, or the cashier who overlooks me when I'm next in line does so, not because of my race but because they are simply stupid, afraid, or rude.

Believe me, it makes a difference.

For four years, 1996–2000, I spent my summers in the Caribbean, teaching in Barbados, traveling and doing research in Grenada, Puerto Rico, the DR, Cuba, Trinidad and Jamaica. After each trip I found myself feeling unusually refreshed and unstressed with lightness in my step, music thumping in my head, and a profound sense of inner peace.

Of course, my sense of inner tranquility never lasted for long. Within a day or two I was back to feeling stressed, rushed, and too often irritable. The transformation was impossible to ignore. Part of it was simply my lifestyle. Rushing to appointments, drinking three cups of coffee a day, sleeping four hours a night, all added to my stress and made it necessary for me to walk around with Tums in my pocket to fight off the heartburn I experienced regularly.

But it was more than just my lifestyle and crazy work habits. I realized that I smiled more easily and more readily when I was in the Caribbean, and I laughed more, too. At first, I attributed the peace I felt to my lighter schedule and the slower pace of life. But as I thought about it, I realized that while there I drank coffee (and quite a bit of rum), maintained a full schedule, ate spicy food, and often partied 'til late at night, and yet, I still felt less stress when I was in the Caribbean.

What was it about being in the Caribbean for an extended period of time that left me feeling so chill, so relaxed, and so unburdened?

As I thought about it my mind quickly drifted to the small things: my interactions with the market women in St. Georges, asking for directions from some kids playing stickball on the streets of Habana Vieja, buying coconut water after a soccer game on the Savannah in Port of Spain. Each of these interactions was free of the suspicion and veiled hostility that too often accompanies even mundane conversations in the US.

I realized that I was at ease because I was no longer suffering from what Chester Pierce called MEES—mundane, extreme, environmental stress. That's the fancy term that he used to describe everyday racism. Mundane because it happens all of the time, most often through micro-aggressions—small slights, frowns, raised eyebrows, etc. Extreme because when a person is bombarded by these kinds of mini-assaults, it takes a toll and wears away at your sense of humanity and humor. Environmental because it's pervasive and almost impossible to escape if you live in the US. And, Stress because all of this induces a considerable amount of stress that we adapt to, but it takes a toll on our physical, spiritual, and mental health.

MEES isn't like straight-up, in-your-face racism, and it certainly can't be equated with cross burning, lynching, or any of the other gross assaults on our humanity that we endured in the past (and that some still must contend with). But that doesn't mean it's minor or shouldn't be taken seriously. Being bombarded by micro-aggressions, institutional racism, and police harassment (even when the cops happen to be Black or Latino) takes a toll on you. You only really appreciate it when the burden is lifted and you have the privilege of being yourself.

So this is my love letter to mi Caribe. It's not a love letter written out of naïveté or idealizing the grim realities of the islands. I know that many of my people in the Antilles suffer from underdevelopment, political corruption, hunger, disease, and violence. I know that while the Caribbean may be paradise for North Americans, more often than not it is a site of suffering for us.

Still, I appreciate the benefits of being in the majority and of being among my people with all of their flaws and hang-ups. It's often said that you only appreciate your health when you are sick. Because I live in a sick land, I really appreciate it when I can get a break away.

The Caribbean may not be paradise and the escape from white supremacy may only be an illusion, but I feel different when I'm there, and I love the difference.

Dr. Pedro Noguera

❖ ❖ ❖

Racial (In)Justice in the Age of Stop-and-Frisk

685,724 New Yorkers were stopped by the police in 2011[4]

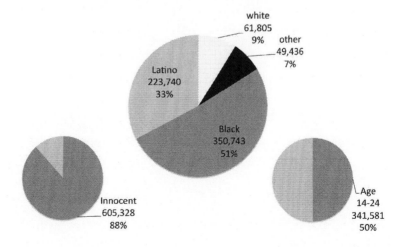

[4] New York Civil Liberties Union www.nyclu.org

❖ ❖ ❖

Males incarcerated age 18 or older[5]

white   1 in every **106**

Hispanic   1 in every **36**

Black   1 in every **15**

The Prison Industrial Complex

There are presently **80,000** inmates in the U.S. employed in commercial activity, some earning as little as **21 cents an hour.** The Federal Prison Industries (FPI), a program of the federal government, currently employs **21,000** inmates, an increase of **14 percent** in the last two years alone. FPI inmates make a wide variety of products—such as clothing, file cabinets, electronic equipment, and military helmets—which are sold to federal agencies and private companies. FPI sales are **$600 million** annually and rising, with over **$37 million** in profits. In addition, during the last 20 years, more than 30 states have passed laws permitting the use of convict labor by commercial enterprises. These programs now exist in 36 states. Prisoners now manufacture everything from blue jeans, to auto parts, to electronics, and furniture. Honda has paid inmates **$2 an hour** for doing the same work an auto worker would get paid **$20-$30 an hour** to do. Konica has used prisoners to repair copiers for less than **50 cents an hour.** Toys-R-Us used prisoners to restock shelves and Microsoft to pack and ship software. Clothing made in California and Oregon prisons competes so successfully with apparel made in Latin America and Asia that it is exported to other countries. (www.wsws.org)

---

[5] www.pewcenteronthestates.org

Chapter 7

❧ *Art and the Heart* ❧

Art has had a huge impact on historical political movements, from Capoeira—where slaves in Brazil pretended to dance but were really practicing a martial art used to free themselves from bondage—to spirituals, to jazz and blues, to b-boyin/b-girlin, to graffiti, and on and on. Today, more and more ARTivists are continuing this subversion and beautiful tradition, making change in the social and political discourse of this country by addressing, not only the minds of the people, but the hearts and souls, as only art can do. This chapter allows the reader to hear from several artists who are creating justice and healing through their visionary talent.

❖ ❖ ❖

By now you all know that Hip-Hop has helped me through some of the hardest times of my life and blessed me with an incredible global community. It was also my first political lens, the place I got information about what was really going on in the streets of our great country. Growing up, Public Enemy was a voice of particular importance for my consciousness raising. Today, it is Hip-Hop group dead prez, comprised of stic.man and M1.

I was introduced to M1 during a college tour we were a part of, along with Rosa Clemente and DJ Kuttin Kandi, talking power and politics. I wasn't sure he would talk to me; word was he hated white people. But, I didn't want to pass up the opportunity to share how much his music moved me.

The conversation surprised me. I learned this man stood strong for his community. He is as much an organizer and intellectual thinker as an emcee. And, no, he doesn't hate white people he hates white supremacy. Since then we have continued to develop a friendship and a working relationship that has lasted years.

I believe in the power M1 and stic.man bring through their music and their message. Their slogan, "revolutionary but gangsta," is appealing because the ability to keep it street makes politics and activism inviting and accessible for marginalized young people all over the world. To me, dead prez is the new Public Enemy, giving truth and knowledge to aid the fight against colonialism and white supremacy. Their passion for liberation is heard in every beat and lyric they spit. Who knows how many young people they inspire every day?

Curses and all, dead prez is the new vanguard of revolutionary rap. So turn off your radio!

❧ Penning Protest: Art, Power, and Race ❧

An Interview with *M1 conducted by JLove Calderón*

JLove: How do your politics and art tie together?

M1: They are one. You want to create a space to just make art for art's sake sometimes, but I'm not afforded that place, not really. Most of the time my art is based on the political perspective from where I sit, because I've declared myself a revolutionary, and I see the importance of this role. On top of that I love it.

JLove: So you believe that art can impact racism?

M1: Art *does* impact racism. All art is the cultural gauge for our political maturity. You can look at the art that comes out of us as the writing on the wall, as it were, for what's going on inside our heads. That's why it's so crucial for the powers that be, that the system monopolizes or co-opts Hip-Hop so that it won't say anything relevant or productive. We know that the music of Nina Simone or John Lennon or Peter Tosh—that whole crew—caught some larger vibration and fed the world. Music can definitely influence the idea of what real power, equal rights, and justice is, what happiness is, our standard of living. So what's important and what's not important is influenced by the music.

JLove: There is a perception out there in the world that you hate white people. What say you?

M1: I don't hate white people. I hate white supremacy, which is difficult to articulate, especially when it comes from this hole that's been dug, this pit that Black people have been thrown into. The task that I've always had is to separate white people from whiteness and white legacy. It's not easy.

Pretty much everything you hear out of that pit is mixed up with rage, anger, hatred. But then there is a voice of reason, a legitimate place we come from deep down inside this pit. When we're able to get to that voice and clearly articulate what it is that we want …we begin to question. Do we really want to rid the world of white people? Or do we want to be able to function regardless of whatever any white person does to us? That became the true question for me.

JLove: How do you feel racism impacts white people?

M1: White people wear racism like a coat that's warm but uncomfortable. They enjoy the spoils of the system that has provided them with their foundation but feel a certain kind of guilt behind it. At my shows white people say, "It wasn't me; it was my parents. Why should I have to pay the price for something that they did?" They're not seeing the divide between what they just said and the behaviors that brought them to where they are, standing in front of me. They're not seeing the larger system that they're operating in and how it's benefitting them—but they still know enough to feel a little guilty.

And some white people probably find much pride in white power—the traditional white power. I think there's a certain part of white America that wants to withdraw from America, who has this idea of patriotism and believes that the America of today is being run wrong by the white people who are in control. Who believes that the red, white, and blue have been stained by this kind of liberalism that has let people, like rapper 50 Cent, become popular and has let the Mexicans through the border. There's this purist faction of white people who want to see an even more pure brand of it. Which I believe they have the right to have.

JLove: What do you mean by that?

M1: I think the more people declare what they are actually in unity with, the quicker we're gonna get to the solution. I don't make any assumption that we can all of us move toward humanity unless people tell the truth about where they are. You have to declare your side for us to say, "Ok, now we can move forward."

There are those who will hold onto capitalism until the death of it, who would rather see themselves buried by it than move out of the way and let it fall down. And when we have a newer and better way, there are going to be people who disagree even with that. I don't believe in any kind of utopia. I think there will be a way that works better for everyone and that people will have to unite behind it, but I don't think it will be because everybody finally gets it and moves into harmony. There are people who will oppose, who gonna wanna be the greedy capitalists, even when that's not fashionable, and we are gonna have to fight that down and persecute so that they don't get up to their old tricks again. You know what I mean? But they will be trying to do it, and so I think it's important that they declare where they stand. You and I both have a right to be a revolutionary in America. Even though the U.S. is still tied to Great Britain today, the attempt to break certain kinds of ties with the mother country was a revolutionary act. I think you and I should both have the right to use the same tools to gain a new life for the people who believe in peace and freedom today. That's why I think racists should have the right to say, "I hate niggers."

JLove: What does being a revolutionary look like for you?

M1: It's a long-view look at humanity that sees change as inevitable and recognizes that sometimes we'll have to endure growing pains in that change. In order to be that revolutionary, we have to be as human as possible. We have to invite every kind of person to push the world forward because we have been taking steps back in humanity

> "I am offering an invitation for white people to come to humanity."

lately. We have been consuming and not producing. We have made decisions that have been to the detriment of life.

In order to push that the right way we have to unite with people around the world who are gonna do that. That's part of what it's gonna mean to be a revolutionary. A revolutionary, though, is informed by a revolutionary political education that comes from revolutionary organization. That might sound all kind of staunch, real kind of dogmatic, you know, but it's not.

JLove: Do you have to be part of an organization to be a revolutionary?

M1: Yeah, there's no lone revolutionaries. It's a "we" action. I can't have a personal revolution. I can come to some inner conclusions that are revolutionary but I can't have my own revolution.

JLove: Break that down; what do you mean?

M1: It means that if we can see capitalism as a bloodthirsty kind of guiltless, victim-consuming machine that goes on and on and is fueled by mass exploitation and only has the worst kind of intentions for the rest of humanity, then we are on the right track.

And we have to work together in our revolution. It was in African-centered organizations, based in the African community off the heels of the black revolution of the 60s, where I saw white people who can truly unite with black power. I had never seen it before. I will always remember the speech of the white girl who went up to Malcolm X and said, "What can I do for you?," and he said, "Nothing." I totally disagree. I think it was important for Malcolm to say that then, but there is much that the white community can do in order for us to have a revolutionary process in America. White people can talk to white people about revolution, because sometimes black people can't. I work close, hand-in-hand, 15-hour days, doing fundraisers in different intensive political education activities beside some white people who are as committed to liberation for African people in this country as much as I am, for the reason that it will benefit them just as much as me. I know that relationship is possible.

JLove: I would like to hear your thoughts on the criminal justice system and race. What are the implications for poor people and people of color in terms of what's happening with the high percentage rates of African-American and Latino males locked up?

M1: This is a system that makes up the law as it goes and makes it up for just a certain segment of our population. It's totally hypocritical. When something happens in the working class scenario, it's a felony, but when it happens in their world, it's not a crime.

My mother did 12 out of a 14-year felony sentence for having a package of crack delivered to her front door, and she'd never had a criminal record. If she'd been a white woman and the equivalent had happened with a derivative of crack cocaine in a different neighborhood, there would have been a much different kind of outcome.

The main goal is to criminalize a certain sector of the population. Crack was not invented in the 'hood. Everybody knows it. It wasn't invented by some 16-year old cat living in the projects who had a beaker and a lighter and a white lab coat listening to Hip-Hop. He didn't come up with that. The imposition of drugs is a tirade against our community and an undeclared war, if you will. Definitely, after our movement, the black power movement, was militarily defeated, you see the advent of heroin and crack cocaine in our community. This is not a coincidence, and you can see that when you look at the rate of people going into prisons, yet the drugs are still here. The reality is that we go away, and the drugs stay. So I think we clear about what I'm saying: it's about population control. But population control issues, I think, have a lot to do with the future of the government, the future of what the complexion of America is about. Population control isn't just inside the prison industrial complex or these undeclared wars on drugs or poverty or whatever. It's now, you know? Population control is gonna happen just because we're poor. We won't deserve the right to have a better kind of condition to live and grow in, therefore we can't afford the kind of food that we need, or the kind of vitamins that we need to grow, and so we become susceptible to, basically, things that are curable by all human standards. But because we won't have access to them, then millions of us will die just because of that. And that's real; I'm not spreading the panic at all.

JLove: If you could wake up tomorrow and it could be your kind of world, what would it look like?

M1: My world would envision freedom, and that freedom would be the kind of self-determination where we have to focus on the world's most pertinent issues en masse so that, if we give them that kind of focus, we can resolve the problems no matter what they are—whether they involve the ability to feed ourselves as a world community or the ability to use Mother Nature to forward technology, or whatever.

I think in a lot of ways we have to redistribute the wealth, and it's gonna be painful for people who have gotten used to living a certain way. I know I have 50 pairs of sneakers. I have two feet, but I have 50 pairs of sneakers.

That kind of excess in America is common. We pride ourselves on the race to have more sneakers or more things when all around the world there are people who haven't had shoes for a long time and could use them. We live in this comfort zone based on exploitation. The only way we able to do that is because we live in the empire that has created a deep hole somewhere else. We're gonna have to even the land out so we can all benefit. I think after that it will be the best kind of world to live in.

JLove: Do you really believe that we can do that?

M1: I've got to because if I didn't what would drive me forward? The thing is, scientifically, this can't carry on the way it's going very much longer.

JLove: Which aspect?

M1: Physically with the Earth. We are stripping it bare. Even economically, what we are attempting to do is rob Peter to pay Paul. Everybody's broke. Our system is a big sham to keep only a few people rich—and I mean only a few, very small amount of people rich. The rest of us suffer. That thing is going to weeble and wobble and fall down really soon, you know what I mean? I think we're seeing it.

So what do we replace it with? If we don't think creatively right now, some people will envision the same system re-cooked with them on top, benefiting. Some black people would do it: "Let's build it up again, but I'm gonna have it all this time." I see the flaw in that one. We know how that goes. Everybody's read George Orwell, so you know what time it is and we're not going there. So how do we create a government that's better for everybody?

I don't know. I don't know freedom. I've never had it. My attempt is to break free. I'm a rebel all the way to the bone, but even as much as I try to break free, the clothes that I'm wearing today, the English that I speak, they're from a colonial mentality. I'm using all the tools of colonialism to try to break free from colonialism. I'm living in 36 years of deep dish capitalism, bullshit up to my knees, elbows, eyes, so sometimes my ideas are fucked up because this is what I've been fed. There is a deep contradiction here, but in my highest aspiration I want to have nothing to do with it, and I would love to have a system that's totally beneficial. That's my idea. What's your idea?

Ariel Luckey is another creator who addresses racism head-on in his art. Using storytelling, spoken word, dance, acting, and Hip-Hop music, Ariel travels nationally with his shows that address personal and political transformation. This is one of my favorites; it is as much a poem as it is a history lesson. After you read it, pick 5-10 names he drops of people you don't know and do some research.

❧ *ID Check* ❧

By *Ariel Luckey* © *2009*

I am a blue-eyed devil, peckawood, and country cracker
Red neck, white trash, and urban wannabe rapper
I am the man
                    who's got the God complex
Pimping privilege from class, skin color, and sex
I am the president, the pope, and the cop on your block
I'm the banker buying stock in selling bullets and glocks

This is an ID check
Like a rope around your neck
Better know who you are
When death calls collect

This is an ID check
Like the border patrol
But this is not for your country
This is for your soul

I am the great great great grandchild of the Mayflower
Gave thanks to God for smallpox so I could take power
I'm the great great grandchild of broken treaties
Inheritor of racial slurs spoken freely
I'm the great grandchild of BIA and Homestead Act
I shot Wounded Knee, stabbed Crazy Horse in the back

I'm the grandchild of Jim Crow and burning crosses
I yelled for a lynching, then brought my children to watch it
I'm the child of GI Bill, white affirmative action
Got promotions and jobs reserved for Anglo-Saxons
I am the father of Katrina and government neglect
This is a race roll call
This is an ID check

I am President Andrew Johnson, I took your 40 acres away
I am William Simmons, I led the KKK
I am Senator Joe McCarthy, I blacklisted the nation
I am Governor Orval Faubus, I blocked integration
I am Roy Bryant and J.W. Milam
I murdered Emmett Till and then denied that I killed him
I'm Lawrence Brewer, John King, and Shawn Allen Berry
Dragged James Byrd to his death in a black cemetery
I am Michael Brown, I directed FEMA
I am Walter Reed, I prosecuted 6 from Jena
I am Bill O'Reilly, I spew hate everyday
I am George W. Bush, what else do I need to say

This is an ID check
Like airport security
The real terrorism
State of emergency

This is an ID check
Like the border patrol
But this is not for your country
This is for your soul

I'm a 12th generation illegal immigrant
My family sold our culture as an economic stimulant
I have stolen the language of West African griots
Sampled the stand up bass of standard jazz trios

I have eaten the heart beatin of the boogie down Bronx
Carved a new ivory tower out of elephant tusk ankhs
I appropriate your culture 'cause I sold my roots
Got my hair did in corn rows, sport Timberland boots
I wear a bindi on my forehead, Che's face on my chest
I wave sage and an eagle feather and call this space blessed
I got a Chinese character tattooed on my arm
Rock an Om necklace as a good luck charm
I am Wonder Bread, I am the Melting Pot
I buy my coolness at the mall cause that's what I've been taught
I'm a Pilgrim, a Cowboy, All-American athlete
I am Elvis, Kenny G, Vanilla Ice, and Backstreet

This is an ID check
This is a shattered mirror
This is the voice of whitey
This is the psyche of fear

This is an ID check
Like the border patrol
But this is not for your country
This is for your soul

I walk on red carpet sewn in maquiladoras
I pimp the stock market with the ruling class employers
I make a living from your dying, I am free trade
I'm the law that says IMF loan interest gets paid
I am middle-class white flight and suburbanization
I'm a yuppie drinking latte, Starbucks gentrification
I live in Sundown towns and feast on strange fruit
I get paid for every ghetto youth the army recruits
I am the air you breathe, the water you drink
I'm the hegemony underneath the way you think
I am white supremacy and patriotism

I am the private profits made from public prisons
I'm the cop in your head, I am COINTELPRO
I'm the non-profit industrial complex's cash flow
I am white collar crime and corporate subsidies
I spit dirty white lies, I'm Fox news publishing
I'm Cheney's Energy Task Force getting together
I'm the smoking gun, I am Enron's paper shredder
I'm a Blackwater mercenary paid by your taxes
I'm a federal bail out to Wall Street while the economy collapses
I am the stars and stripes, huh, united we stand
I'm the great white hope, I am superman

This is an ID check
Like 3 o'clock road block
This is psychotherapy
By electric shock

This is an ID check
Like the border patrol
But this is not for my country
This is for my soul

'cause
I am also Robert Carter, I freed 500 of my slaves
I'm Supreme Court Justice John Jay, I ruled against racist ways
I am Preacher John Woolman, I'm a Quaker Abolitionist
I'm Henry David Thoreau, I wrote Civil Disobedience
I am John Brown, I raided Harper's Ferry
I'm Ralph Waldo Emerson, a poet revolutionary
I am Mark Twain, I protested imperialism in the Philippines
I am Albert Einstein, I raised my voice against lynching
I am Myles Horton, I founded Highlander Center's popular education
I'm Abraham Joshua Heschel, Marching with Dr. King my feet were praying
I am Andrew Goodman and Michael Schwerner

I campaigned for justice in the Freedom Summer

I am Bill Ayers, I forecast the Weather Underground

I'm Jack Junebug Boykin, I led the Young Patriots in Chicago's Uptown

I am Howard Zinn, I wrote the People's History

I am Noam Chomsky, I drop knowledge on society

I am Paul Kivel, I wrote Uprooting Racism

I am Tim Wise, I speak truth across the nation

I'm the push for racial justice

I am freedom on the rise

I am the possibility

in my son's blue eyes

This is an ID check

like the border patrol

but this is not for our country

this is for our soul

Note:

While this poem is specifically about white men and the legacy of white male racism and resistance in the united states, I must acknowledge the contributions of white women antiracist activists, such as Virginia Durr, Anne Braden, Linda Evans, and Mab Segrest, among many others, who have played critical roles in the movements for racial justice.

—Ariel Luckey

❖ ❖ ❖

Chelsea Gregory and I share a history of white girls deeply rooted in multicultural communities. As such, when we "found" each other in the intersection of organizing, empowerment, and art, we hit it off immediately. Throughout the years we have worked hard to impact race and social change in communities across the nation; we have also worked hard internally, within our own friendship, to authentically address ways that we as white people, and more specifically white woman, relate, support, and hold each other accountable. The internal work is, indeed, as important as the external work. Without transforming the negative dynamics of our relationships, how can we affect change in others? It's called "doing the work" for a reason.

I am so proud of the work that Chelsea has done with the Jena 6 Project. Hear her story.

❧ *The Story of "The 6 Project"* ❧
By *Chelsea Gregory*

The power that art has to transform us as individuals, communities, and cultures does not cease to amaze me. Moving through the last decade as an artist, educator and cultural organizer, I have seen creativity inspire new ways of being and reconnect us to the clarity, compassion, and integrity that is our nature. My focus has been primarily in the realm of dance theatre because the physicality and intimacy of embodied performance is something so many of us are in need of. To quote playwright and activist Eve Ensler, "Maybe this is the purpose of art, and theater in particular—to experience what we experience, to see what's in front of us, to allow the truth in, with all its sorrow and brutality…We are there, for these moments together, joined by what we see and hear, made stronger, hopefully, by what opens us." Artists like Ensler, Augusto Boal, Anna Deavere Smith, Universes, Moisés Kaufman, and Sarah Jones have all effected social change by using theater toward this end, and The 6 Project was created in an effort to contribute to that legacy.

Racial justice is an issue that has been central to my life for as long as I can remember, and it is from this experience that The 6 Project grew. I was raised in Atlanta, GA, a city that has been an epicenter of the struggle for racial justice in this country. For the first half of my childhood we lived in a black neighborhood, and I remember the feeling of an invisible wall between us and our neighbors that no one quite knew how to get through. My family was in a position of relative socio-economic privilege, and I could see that many of my black peers did not have the same quality of life that I did. I was educated in the Atlanta Public Schools, which are predominantly black, but have "gifted" tracks in which most of the white students were placed. There were those that managed to socialize on both sides of the divide, but for the most part, school (and life) remained segregated. Racial tension was inflamed by conflict between students that, at times, was based almost entirely on skin color. I was confronted several times because of my race, and from early on I sensed that these pieces of the puzzle connected and that race and class privilege evoked at least some of the animosity I felt from black peers. It has taken years to find the language to begin to talk about it, but this experience has had a tremendous impact on my identity and sense of place in the world.

As a young adult I began to explore performance as a means to dialogue around these issues, and I saw the way theater could hold space for that through the work of Anna Deavere Smith, Sarah Jones, and Danny Hoch, as well as Dan Hoyle's *Tings Dey Happen*. When the Jena 6 Case became widely publicized, a group I was doing racial justice work with saw it as a great opportunity to expand these conversations, and The 6 Project was born. We had learned that young white men hung nooses in a tree on a Jena, Louisiana, high school lawn in response to a young black man's decision to sit under that tree at lunch. A series of racial conflicts unfolded over the next few months, and in the aftermath, 6 black students sat in jail charged with attempted murder for a schoolyard fight. The white students walked away unscathed, including those who had hung nooses, brandished shotguns, yelled slurs, and engaged in the conflict in various other ways. This story held many lessons, and I wanted to learn more and develop a project that would share that learning in a creative, accessible way. As I conducted research and interviews, connections to my own personal history began to emerge, so it became necessary to raise the stakes and put that on stage alongside the interview-based material. I was resistant to the idea at first, but director Tamilla Woodard, who helped develop the script, insisted on it, and I am so thankful she did. It was extremely painful to explore my own life in the context of white supremacy and privilege, and also clear that if I didn't, a piece of the conversation was missing.

My paternal grandfather—may he rest in peace—was an overt white supremacist originally from Birmingham, AL. He spoke highly of his friend Bull Connor, the Klan member and Birmingham Public Safety Commissioner notorious for using fire hoses and attack dogs against non-violent civil rights demonstrators. In the 1960s Birmingham was given the nickname "Bombingham" because of the frequency of Klan attacks on black homes, churches, and places of business. If my grandfather was directly involved in any of this, he never talked about it. Yet, it spoke volumes when he described Connor as a great man, and referred to the 1963 bombing of a black church that killed 4 little girls as an unfortunate accident. He met my paternal grandmother when he moved to Atlanta, and not long afterwards they followed the 2nd wave of white flight to Forsyth County, GA, because the number of African-American residents had surpassed the number of white residents in the Metro-Atlanta area. I first learned the story of Forsyth County when I did a reading of an early draft of The 6 Project in Atlanta, and an audience member mentioned it in the talkback. I did a bit more research after that reading, and came across a direct link between my own family history and what was happening in Jena, LA. That revelation became an integral part of the play:

When I was a kid I used to visit my grandparents just about every weekend just outside Forsyth County, Georgia, but it wasn't 'til 20 years after the fact that I learned what had happened there in 1987. By age 7 I'd probably noticed the contrast between my grandparents' neighborhood in Forsyth County and our neighborhood in Southwest Atlanta. Where they lived, there was not a black person for miles around. But what I didn't know was that in 1912 all of the African-American residents of Forsyth County were forced to leave and their land—including the cemeteries where their ancestors were buried—was "legally" handed over to white residents. The county became known for a sign that warned black people "don't let the sun go down on your head in Forsyth County." By 1987, not a single black person had lived there in 75 years.

So a white resident of Forsyth County organized a brotherhood march to reconcile the county's racist reputation. He backed out after threats from white supremacists, and Hosea Williams and a group of black activists from Atlanta picked up the baton. When they held the brotherhood march on Martin Luther King Day of 1987, they were attacked by local whites in an onslaught of racial slurs, rocks, and broken bottles. I was probably just a few miles away—fishing with grandpa or painting my fingernails with grandma. A new white supremacist organization called The Nationalist Movement was actually formed that day in response to the brotherhood march. It so happened that this was the very same organization I would encounter 20 years later in Jena, LA as they organized local white supremacist response to the Jena 6 case.

My grandparents had moved to Forsyth county because it was "safer," and they wouldn't have to worry about the "nigras," as my grandfather called African-American people, "raping and pillaging." The irony of that stays with me when I think of what has actually been perpetrated against African-American people in Forsyth County and throughout this country. My grandpa—may he rest in peace—passed away in late 2007 and left me some money in his will. It was just enough to cover a plane ticket to Atlanta and a rental car to get me to Jena to conduct interviews for this project. I knew he was mad at me for this 'cause he kept comin' to me in dreams, but I told him "you gotta trust me on this one grandpa—I'm tryna help you get your karma right."

Author and playwright James Baldwin once said that "white people in this country will have quite enough to do in learning how to accept and love themselves and each other, and when they have achieved this, [racism] will no longer exist—for it will no longer be needed." The 6 Project is an inquiry into the contemporary manifestations of white supremacy, and an invitation to reflect on why, as Baldwin notes, racism was "needed" in the first place. Why is it that my grandfather and those of us who embrace a sense of racial superiority, whether consciously or not, must perceive an inferior "other" in order to feel secure in the self?

There is a rich history of creative dialogue around this initiated by artists of color, but rarely do we see the topic addressed by white artists. The 6 Project is an attempt to open space for this, and to explore how we as white artists can create work that reflects on and raises awareness around the conversation of race. Actress and playwright Anna Deavere Smith says that, "As artists, we make culture… The animals know how to survive through

DNA. Humans know how to survive through watching and studying culture." History has shown us that the laws, policies and programs that address institutionalized racism are only as successful as our culture allows them to be. If people learn to survive as social and political beings by absorbing culture, it follows that we can use the arts to transform destructive patterns and nurture a commitment to racial justice in our communities.

Between 2007 and 2010, The 6 Project toured colleges, universities and community organizations in 12 cities throughout the US. Through workshops, performances, and community dialogues we were able to engage over 2,500 people in the conversation of race, and it felt especially timely, given that it was right before and after Barack Obama's election. Also in the course of the tour, the young men known as the Jena 6 were freed and able to move on with their lives, and 5 of them are now enrolled in college. It is not possible to say whether The 6 Project contributed directly to this outcome, but it was part of a massive effort on the part of the many activists, educators, and independent media sources that brought the visibility and resources needed to ensure justice for these young men.

In his book, *Theatre of the Oppressed*, Augusto Boal speaks of theater as "rehearsal for revolution," and revolution in this context can be seen as synonymous with evolution if we consider both the internal and external impacts of social change. I am excited to see how we will continue this rehearsal process, expanding the potential of theater and the arts in general to evoke real personal, political, and structural transformation.

Excerpts from "The 6 Project"

The Prologue is an excerpt of Lillian Smith's book *Killers of the Dream*, published in 1949. The remainder of the play is written from my point of view as writer/researcher where it says "CHELSEA," and all other text is taken verbatim from interviews conducted at and around a white supremacist rally in Jena, LA, on 1/21/07.

PROLOGUE

Lights fade up- CHELSEA is leaning against the back wall. As the Lillian Smith recording plays she looks at the audience for a long moment, takes in the text being spoken, and begins to move around the tree.

RECORDING: Even its children knew that the South was in trouble. No one had to tell them; no words said aloud...Some learned to screen out all except the soft and the soothing; others denied even as they saw plainly and heard. But all knew that under quiet words and warmth and laughter, under the slow ease and tender concern about small matters, there was a heavy burden on all of us and as heavy a refusal to confess it.

This haunted childhood belongs to every Southerner...We run away from it, but we come back like a hurt animal to its wound or a murderer to the scene of his sin. The human heart dares not to stay away too long from that which hurts it most. There is a return journey to anguish that few of us are released from making.

Scene 3- BILLY HUNTER'S SON/ BOBBIE CORNETT

BILLY HUNTER'S SON: (he is wiping down a table in the McDonald's) Ain't really been no different to me since the whole Jena 6 thang happened- I pretty much stay to myself. I was born here but when I was young they killed my daddy so I got sent to live in Texas…

CHELSEA: Billy Hunter was lynched at the Jena Fairgrounds in 1975- his son works the late shift at McDonald's. He was the first person I met when I got to Jena.

BILLY HUNTER'S SON: Them killin my daddy coulda turned me real mean if I let it. But I learned to stay focus on the positive—I try to stay outta the middle a thangs n jus keep my peace.

BOBBIE CORNETT: (sits down at table and spreads napkin over lap) Now I never even thought about anybody's race until this whole Jena 6 thang happened—and now I'm aware of it every single day!

CHELSEA: Bobbie Cornett—the wife of the former District Attorney— became a local celebrity after going on the Dr. Phil show and calling Al Sharpton a racist bully.

BOBBIE CORNETT: They said I called him a weasel and a bully, but I didn't— watch it online and you'll see—I called him a RACIST bully for using our town as a political platform. I never even thought about anybody's race 'til this whole incident happened. (*picks up MickeyD's coffee cup and drinks from it*) We had help in our home, but they were part of our family I don't think I ever even noticed a difference! I was never even aware that I was white! (*puts the cup back down*) But when I came back from Dr. Phil I said we've got to get some PR people in here 'cause we're just this sleepy little town—we never had to deal with anything like this.

BILLY HUNTER'S SON: (*he takes that in and then moves the coffee cup briskly out of his way so he can wipe down the table and continue his story*) It happened up at the fairgrounds—they set dawgs on 'im cause they wanted to see 'im run. He was runnin from the dawgs n when he turn around to see how close they was to 'im he knocked over a lil white girl on accident. That's when they stomped him to death.

BOBBIE CORNETT: I mean I recently found out that historically this town does have some racism. Somebody I thought sounded pretty reasonable said there was some racial strife in the past—I wasn't there, but he was so I'm just listenin to what he's sayin. It is what it is—you can't hide from the truth.

Scene 7- TRAVIS JENKS

CHELSEA: When the white supremacists began their march, I met the only white resident of Jena who had come out to protest—a 17 year old Jena High School student. Until the cops stopped him, he had followed the white supremacists in silence with a poster around his neck that quoted Dr. Martin Luther King- "Nothing in the world is more dangerous than sincere ignorance and conscientious stupidity."

TRAVIS JENKS: I'm white and I'm from Possum Point—that's like the big racial thing that no black people go down there—well I'm from down there and I say to hell with this! I'll admit when I was little, I was racist 'til I got to kindergarten I—I b'lieved evry black person was trash. An' Miss Faith—she works right over there in the Walmart—she's a black lady—she wus one of my kindergarten teachers n she taught me there's trash among every race not just the black—n' she brought me off racism that was—my whole deal I- I don't like racist people I don't like racism to be around me—n' that's why I'm here at the march today. Because when the black people marched they didn't say that, they said they wanted equal justice and now the whites over here sayin they want to own the country! That is wrong because if they wanna get technical with it the country dutn't belong to white people it never did- it belonged to Native Americans first it's their country. But they don't look at it like that- so I'm here to march against them to counter-protest because what they're doin is wrong. I believe in standin up for what I think is right so I'm gon stand up for it- even if I am the only one.

EPILOGUE

CHELSEA: There are nooses in the family tree
        Times when life has been taken
        Loved ones strung up for all to see
        For being too powerful
        Too beautiful too different
        Too much a reminder of
        How we love/hate
        Our history

        There are nooses in the family tree
        Times we accept atrocity
        If it's committed in our name
        I have seen us grinning, batting eyelashes, and gnashing teeth
        As we harvest strange fruit from centuries-old trees
        Young black men shot by cops at point blank range
        Or shipped off to prison—80 to life for a schoolyard fight
        Each time another life is taken we rebirth this beast
        Emancipation proclamation, Civil Rights Act, Black president-
        We still have yet to be released….
        What if we didn't cut down the tree anymore?
        What if we looked at the tree? And listened to the tree?
        And took good enough care of it that one day
        Its branches could outgrow the nooses?

❖ ❖ ❖

A Love Letter

Dear Father,

I want to share with you a story. It is a love story. Not the sweet, romantic, butterfly kiss kind of love, though that also makes good stories. This is a story of a love of people and of justice. Actually, it is several stories that make one.

When I was about 6 years old, your mother, you, and I were walking down to the Oakland Rose Garden to play catch among the flowers. I was laughing and running ahead when I fell and scraped my knee on the sidewalk. I promptly burst into tears. Grandma flashed red and scolded me. "Stop crying! You're a big boy now." "No, it's okay," you said, "it's okay to cry," and you hugged me close and brushed off my knee. In those simple words and the example you lived that demonstrated them, you taught me one of the most important things about being a healthy human being. It is essential to open my heart to life's wide range of emotion: to feel and express my pain and vulnerability and that of others. For a white man in this culture, this is revolutionary and takes daily practice.

Four years later, driving me to a doctor's appointment, you hand me a children's book to read in the car. "What is this?" I ask. The book looks like it's for toddlers. "Just read it," you say, "and tell me if you notice anything." It's about different things people do for a living. Some people are doctors. Others are carpenters. Still others bake bread.

"Okay, I read it." "What did you notice?" "Um, nothing." "What did you notice about the people?" "They were doing different things?" "Yeah, and what kind of people are they?" "I don't know, just normal people." "Look again." I scan through the book, trying to figure it out. "I don't know. What about the people?" "They're all white," you say calmly. And it slowly dawns on me, a steady brightening of awareness. I never thought about "reading" a book like that before. Even though many of my classmates speak Arabic, Spanish, Mandarin, Farsi, and Amharic at home; even though many of our neighbors come from countries all over the world; even though many of the doctors, carpenters, and bakers in my community are people of color; I still saw a book of only white people as so normal that I didn't even notice it. "That's part of how racism works," you say. "It makes people of color and their contributions invisible." And then we park the car and walk over to the doctor's office.

One afternoon you pick me up from high school and we head to the BART train station to ride under the Oakland hills to the suburbs beyond. We carry two boxes of colorful flyers that boldly pronounce the name of the grassroots group you have been organizing with: Angry White Men for Affirmative Action. Drawing attention to the long legacy of affirmative action programs that exclusively benefited white men, you, along with several hundred other progressive white men, have been campaigning against Proposition 209. Prop 209 would end all affirmative action programs, many which now benefit white women and people of color in the state of California. For two hours we stand outside a BART station, passing out flyers and talking to commuters about how affirmative action seeks to mitigate the many barriers to equal education still imposed by institutional racism and sexism. On the way home, we talk about the campaign, people's responses to the flyers, and the politics of being a white ally to people of color.

In small everyday ways and in larger breakthrough moments, you taught me to love people and justice. You taught me about compassion, critical thinking, and action. Your book, Uprooting Racism: How White People Can Work for Racial Justice, taught me a lot about being a white ally. But your example and your fatherhood taught me so much more.

Love,

Ariel

Dear Son,

I want to share with you a story. It is a love story. Not the sweet, romantic, butterfly kiss kind of love, though that also makes good stories. This is a story of a love of people and of justice. Actually, it is several stories that make one.

On the first day of school in fourth grade I sat next to a boy who had recently arrived from Ethiopia. He lived with his Mom and four other relatives in a two-bedroom apartment two blocks from my house. We quickly became best friends. We walked to and from school together every day. We played together after school and had sleepovers on the weekends. We developed a deep bond of friendship, and I grew to love him dearly. He could speak English well and had quickly adapted to life and culture in the States, but he had joined our school after they taught students basic reading skills, and he had dyslexia. He was a young black boy in an Oakland public school who didn't know how to read. While our teacher failed him and made him repeat the fourth grade, there was no one who took the time to actually teach him to read. Year after year he slipped through the cracks, and I learned that a young black man graduating high school with a fourth grade reading level was no big deal to the teachers and administrators in the school system. It was business as usual to them, but it angered me deeply. Love for my friend and my desire for him to have an equal opportunity to get an education sparked my commitment to racial justice.

Many years later, while facilitating a diversity training with climate change activists, focusing on how to build the organization's capacity to address racism internally and within the movement, I led the group through the Forum Theater process, developed by Brazilian actor Augusto Boal. Forum Theater uses theatrical techniques to walk a group of people through a collective strategizing session on how to solve a common problem. The first step is to create a short scene that demonstrates the problem. Then invite members of the audience to one by one enter the scene and "act out" potential solutions. After each solution is tried, the group reflects on its effectiveness and applicability in real life. We created a scene that depicted an interpersonal act of racism that no one interrupted. Instead of just talking about how we should all interrupt racism, participants have to actually get out of their seats and use their bodies and voices to practice interrupting racism.

Even in a supportive environment with a hypothetical theater exercise, this is not easy to do. Let alone in real life! The typical responses to interpersonal acts of racism are either to do nothing and feel bad about it or to lash out and attack the person who committed the act. Neither is effective. Doing this work and reflecting on my own life, I have found that challenging family members and others we love closely is even more difficult. Of course, this only makes it more important to do. A third possible response is assertive and challenging engagement grounded in love and compassion, one much more likely to result in dialogue and a movement towards racial justice. And like any skill set it takes intention, commitment, and practice to develop. It also takes love, sometimes tough love, for people, and for justice.

One evening a few months ago you and I were snuggling in bed while I read your bedtime story. Your Mama was out with a friend for dinner. As I finished the story we heard our front door open and someone come inside. You immediately bounced out of bed and ran into the living room to see who it was. "Who is it?" I called. You ran back to your room, "Mama and the brown guy." "The brown guy" is an old and close friend of ours, one you know well and love. "You silly," I say, "that's our friend." And I say his name. I know you know his name. And, you are noticing and articulating difference in skin color. At four years old you are already learning about race and our conversations are just beginning. As you grow up and grapple with who you are, your role in community, and your relationship to racism, I am here for you; to support and challenge you, and to be challenged by you; to help you learn about compassion, critical thinking, and action; to stand with you for racial justice and love.

Love,

Ariel

> "**P**eople should fear art, film, and theatre. This is where ideas happen. This is where somebody goes into a dark room and starts to watch something and their perspective can be completely questioned...the very seeds of activism are empathy and imagination."
>
> —Susan Sarandon

Chapter 8

❧ *Occupy Wall Street:*
Movement and Accountability ❧

> "*E*ach generation must, out of relative obscurity, dis-
> cover its mission, fulfill it, or betray it."
>
> --Frantz Fanon

So much has been said about the Occupy Movement. A different perspective from damn near everyone. Some love it, some hate it, and then
there are the myriad of debates between those continuums. Where I am
and what I believe in the swirling of conversations is: a global wave
of communities are energized and are in action. The impact continues
to deepen as people see the power and potential in Occupy. I find that
global energy positively needed. A way to empower all people across
race, class, religion, gender. A coming together of those who have less
and deserve more.

Yet there are many valid issues, concerns, and critiques of the Occupy
Movement, some of which you will read in this chapter. Every constructive
movement heeds the philosophy of Paolo Freire's See, Judge, Act, and then
Reflect.

Let's reflect together. DJ Kuttin Kandi starts us off in that reflection.

DJ Kuttin Kandi is an extraordinary individual who changes lives. She
is a brilliant activist, Hip-Hop legend, friend, sister, mother, daughter, who
routinely brings more peace and more justice to the global Hip-Hop community as well as the global justice movement. Her words, her artistry, her
spirit are a blessing to us all.

❖ ❖ ❖

❧ *Where is the Color in Occupy?* ❧

By *DJ Kuttin Kandi*

Building a radical anti-imperialist, anti-colonialist, anti-corporate globalization movement that is Antiracist, Anti-Sexist, Anti-Heterosexist, Anti-Homophobic, Anti-Transphobic, Anti-Oppressive, and Anti-Zionist.

In honor of Elizabeth Betita Martinez's original 1999 piece *Where Was the Color in Seattle?*

October 1, 2011

We are at a crossroads, a place where time is ticking for all of us. But let us be clear my friends. Folks, the movement has not "just begun." The Revolution has BEEN happening, long before you and me got here.

While you tune into television and watch larger movements growing across the country, while you peer out your window onto the streets of your downtown neighborhood, stare out from your offices watching people camping out, rallying with their fists up high and chanting while putting their lives at risk, while arrests are being made and police brutality is on the rise, people of color around the world are and have been risking their lives everyday.

People of color, working class communities, LGBTQGNCPOC (Lesbian, Gay, Bisexual, Transgender, Queer, Gender-Non-Conforming, People of Color), and other movements around the world have been rallying, chanting, marching, and resisting every day, for years and years, and generations and generations. It has never ended. I believe it hasn't ended, and it shouldn't end because in Martin Luther King's true words, "Until we're all free, none are free." Many of us continue resisting, not necessarily just because we want to but because we have no choice but to resist. We live the political life because our very lives depend on our own voices. We are saving our own lives every single day.

As I watch these current Occupy movements grow and as I anticipate Occupy coming soon to San Diego, I can't help but take a step back to reflect on the big question that people are already asking me, and without fail, are going to ask even more:

"Where is the COLOR?"

Now, when white folks ask me this question, it's usually because they honestly don't know. When I ask myself this question (and I do on the regular), it's not because I am clueless but more as a reflection of how much work we have left to do.

This question is NOT NEW.

In 1999, I came upon Elizabeth Betita Martinez's article, *Where Was The Color in Seattle?* in *Colorlines*. It was written in response to the World Trade Organization (WTO) shutdown in Seattle, and it woke me up to the real lack of knowledge white folks had on intersectionality, the existence of their "check-in privileges," and their lack of real ally-ship within the radical-activist-leftist movements. Particularly, many of the mainstream anti-war movements and current corporate globalization movements were missing these practices and self-reflection pieces.

But, one does not have to read Elizabeth's article to know this to be true. All you have to do is go to these larger demonstrations, and you can experience the racism. As people of color, many of us can see it, but many who are white don't see it because they don't experience it, nor do they live it. If it's not white folks being unaware of their privileges, it's white folks asking "Where are people of color?" or saying "We need to get people of color here."

Before I even address this question and this statement, let me go back to the time co-organizers and I took a contingent of high school students to some of the anti-war rallies during the GOP Convention back in NYC in 2004 or the following year when we took students to the huge anti-war rally in Washington, DC. As we marched through the streets, the students were proud that they were present at such large rallies. But all of the students and staff couldn't help but notice how no one looked like us. We were Black and Brown, we were students, teachers, parents, all of us as people of color standing out amongst the mostly white crowd. It was powerful that we were present, but it was also a reality check for all of us that many communities of color were not present.

About eight years later the same question—"Where are people of color?"—pops into my mind just as Occupy is about to begin here in San

Diego. Again, I find myself pondering this question not because I actually wonder where they are. I ask this question because I wonder how will we respond to Occupy. Will there be a response? *Will we participate? Do we even have the time? Do we even have the capacity?*

This brings me to the time in 2005 when one organization reached out to me and asked me to help "get people of color" to come out to their rally. At first, I thought to myself, "Okay, that makes sense; we are always working to have our communities present at many movements."

However, take a step back and reflect on this request: "Get people of color here."

Umm, yeah. IT'S DAMN RIGHT INSULTING.

This "get people of color" request sounds more like "join our movement," and it says to me that white folks are not respecting the historical legacy of people of color and our own fight for our liberation. When white people ask us, as POCs, to mobilize to a rally they organized rather than meeting with us at the table, this reveals how some white people seem not to care about recognizing our movements. It seems to ignore the fact that we, as POCs, have already been in multiple movement(s) in various communities for generations. The question and the invite may be "well-intentioned," but they are insults and imply that white folks have all the answers and that we need to learn from them. They also make the assumption that people of color are not already in our own current movements, already building resistance in the ways that we can, how we can, and when we can. Many of the more mainstream left movements may have some people of color present, but a huge majority of them are white attended and often white-led. And more importantly, the issues that these movements mostly focus on are issues that generally affect the white working class.

> "White folks, I'm sorry, but it's not allyship to ask us to put our own needs aside or to not even recognize that you're asking us to do so."

We all know that the economy has hit all of us hard. But what many folks still need to realize is that when the economy is down, it has a major impact on people of color communities, even more so than white communities. In 2011, FairEconomy.org released their yearly Dream Act report, and it stated, "Due to pre-existing wealth disparities, Blacks and Latinos depend on unemployment insurance in times of crisis more often than Whites." It also stated that "Blacks are 1.3 times as likely to work in public sector jobs than the general work force."

I really don't need to look at these statistics to know these to be true because I personally have lived the experience of struggling to make ends meet when my partner lost his job over a year ago. Currently, both of us are working part-time, while he's still receiving unemployment, which will soon run out. What makes things difficult for both of us is that neither of us have college degrees. Obviously, landing a job does not come easy for us. Right now, I have been blessed to be able to work at a university part-time; my partner has found a part-time job to help keep us afloat; and we still have a roof over our heads. We have family members to go to if we are in need. So, I recognize our privilege.

But, like many others, we are still struggling to just maintain. I cannot help but think about my struggles each time I organize, each time I step into a rally or a march. And I cannot help but think about the many others who are in the same struggle with even harder conditions than my own. I think about those who do not have the privilege or ability to take time off work to organize, attend a rally, and mobilize. Although there are many of us who may have the desire to march through the streets, with permits or not, right now some just simply cannot. They cannot take the risk of getting arrested or hurt, not because they may not be able to afford bail but because some have children or families to feed, or work to do in their own communities. It's just asking too much to expect to have us there.

Which brings me to another point—if many of us as people of color in smaller cities and conservative towns like San Diego join in protests that have a lot of risk of injury, police brutality, arrest, deportation, and even death, what will happen to our own movements if our numbers are diminished? We need to be around for our own movements. We cannot risk our own lives for movements that do not make people-of-color struggles their central focus. White folks, I'm sorry, but it's not allyship to ask us to put our own needs aside or to not even recognize that you're asking us to do so.

Furthermore, while many recognize the connection of oppressions happening in their communities to other oppressions, many still cannot afford the risk of being part of movements that have no long-term planning and where white folks do see our movements connected to theirs but don't support our everyday demonstrations.

If movements are short lived, we go back into our own communities, dealing with the repercussions and the harsh backlash. For example, if police brutality is affecting people now in these large white-dominated rallies, imagine how much harsher it will be amongst people of color and LGBT communities. While I recognize police brutality happens among white folks in large demonstrations, such as "Occupy," white folks need to realize that racial profiling still takes place and even more so during these demonstrations. It is an opportunity for racial criminalization, racial profiling, a.k.a. white supremacy, to be in action.

Don't get me wrong, I'm all for civil unrest, civil disobedience, and utilizing different models of protesting, and I've done plenty of it in the past. I agree that it would be good to be present at these mostly white-male-dominated demonstrations. I recognize the importance for our communities-of-color, who as it is are already underrepresented, to be present in these white-led and white-dominated spaces. We need to express our communities' concerns about the WTO, war, and capitalism and their impact on communities of color. We also need to make a statement that the movement BELONGS to no one particular group.

However, there need to be people of color in leadership, as well as there need to be privileges checked, as well as there needs to be an understanding that many are doing what they can in the ways that they can.

I say it again: People of color and LGBTQGNCPOC communities have BEEN rallying and chanting for many generations. And we still do today, everyday, all around the world. We've been doing sit-ins and civil disobedience, and we are literally fighting our own wars to save our own lives. Even if there may not be all of us taking up picket signs or chanting, there are many of us who are still doing something to contribute to the change we want to see in this world. I once heard Ethnic Studies Professor K. Wayne Yang from UC San Diego call this kind of work "deep organizing" work. Deep organizing is work that often goes unnoticed. It's behind the scenes, and it isn't accompanied by any hype. It isn't acknowledged. But yet, while white activists are fighting for fair wages and an end to capitalism, which mostly affects people of color of the working class, these activists are not recognizing the very people they are supposedly "fighting for"?

Well, I don't need anyone to fight for me or save me, nor do I need or want anyone to speak for me. So, when I do show up to Occupy and all these white-led spaces, I am going for myself, to represent and to claim space. I am going to follow in the journey of those who came before me, our ancestors who led a true freedom struggle and a true resistance. I am going to give voice to the explicit issues that transcend race, class, and gender. I am going to speak on how we are all too familiar with Occupy. As a Filipina-American who recognizes my homeland and my people's history of being occupied, I know that occupation is something I can never live by or stand for, even if it is to "reclaim"; especially on a land that does not belong to us.

Perhaps the real question that activists should ask—instead of asking us to do the work of mobilizing our people for white people and white-dominated movements—"How can we be antiracist, anti-sexist, anti-classist, anti-ableist, anti-homophobic, anti-transphobic, anti-heterosexist, anti-religious oppressive, anti-imperialist, anti-colonial, and anti-etc. activists committed to dismantling white supremacy, patriarchy, heterosexism, cisprivilege, and all other oppressions within ourselves and within our own movements?" That pretty much says it all.

The fact that white activists can't even figure out why they "can't get people of color to join" speaks to how disconnected they are to our communities. Having a few people of color friends in your circles does not mean you are connected to our communities or invested in our communities at all. The question should really be less about what people of color and LGBTQGNCPOC are doing and aren't doing and more about what white-straight-male-identified folks are doing and aren't doing.

Many white folks think that just by being around or being in the same room with people of color, this alone teaches them about white supremacy and that there's no need to go further. But that's the thing about multiculturalism and multiracialism—just because the diversity is there does not mean the environment is antiracist and anti-oppressive overall. Ending white supremacy and patriarchy takes a lot more than just diversity alone.

All activists, particularly white-straight-male-identified folks, need to continue to develop their understanding of how white supremacy and patriarchy operates in the activist movement. I am not trying to lump all white men into one category, nor am I saying only white men need to do this. We all have work to do. We ALL need to learn intersectionality, interconnections, and anti-oppressive practices to do the work. As we strive to topple corporate globalization, as we strive to end war, police brutality, the death penalty, or whatever injustice we are striving to end, we need to reflect on our own behaviors and actions and how we perpetuate all forms of oppression. We need to understand power, privilege, and oppression. We need to create spaces where we can check each other's privileges, be it white privilege, male privilege, class privilege, straight privilege, cisprivilege, sizism privilege, abilities privilege, and so on. If we fail to do this work, we are failing the movement. Instead, we will be creating more of a conquer-and-divide situation, something our oppressors already do. We would be actually doing that work for them: they wouldn't even have to infiltrate to do it because we will be dividing ourselves already.

This piece is written not to discourage folks from continuing to mobilize, organize, or attend current movements now. No, this piece is meant to encourage us all to do some self-reflection, to examine our own perpetuation of different forms of oppression, and to address the so-often asked question of "Where is the Color?" I know I will continue to attend and organize within white-led and white-dominated movements, despite how uncomfortable it may be, despite the possibility of being shut down or feeling shut down. This piece is a mere reflection on the work we need to do to get to a place where movements can be universal. It is imperative that there be more bridge building, and continued discussion needs to happen before we even get to rallies and actions. We need to connect the dots and open all communications. These are the solutions that are needed to create an anti-oppressive world among ourselves, among all movements. These are the ways we can ultimately defeat the imperialist machines and leaders of the world. After all, capitalism, imperialism, globalization, and colonization all rely on white supremacy in order to function. bell hooks defines capitalism as "white supremacy patriarchy." If we can just start with listening to one another and recognize how white supremacy and patriarchy take form in our own actions and behaviors, then we can actually move forward toward ending capitalism, imperialism, globalization, and all other oppressive systems.

"This 'get people of color' request sounds more like "join our movement," and it says to me that white folks are not respecting the historical legacy of people of color and our own fight for our liberation."

❖ ❖ ❖

❦ *Showing Up for Racial Justice* ❦
By *Z! Gonwa Haukeness*

Lately, when asked why I'm committed to racial justice as a white person, I have been talking about a middle and high school teacher that influenced me at my small, mostly white school in the middle of the cornfields of rural, Midwest Wisconsin. Mr. Connolly was a fiery and often funny history teacher that pushed me to look at race. One day he came into our Middle School class upset and said, "You are all racist and your parents are too!" Although I may not use this approach myself, what he was speaking to was institutionalized white supremacy, and he planted a seed deep within me. This incident, along with his encouraging my classmates and me to do projects about the Indigenous/Native history of the area and how it intertwined with our personal European ancestry, about Hmong people living as refugees in our neighboring town, and about the complexities of how the Irish became white and other similar projects, were helpful in my early understandings of race and racism.

When I went to college in Madison, Wisconsin, I was drawn to courses that delved into race and class in the U.S. Even with some decent lessons from Mr. Connolly, however, I was unprepared for what I learned about the undeniable genocide of indigenous people of the Americas, the horrors of slavery, the continued legacy of colonization and slavery in the prison industrial complex, the achievement gap, (im)migrant[1] scapegoating, redlining, land theft for mining, and the long list of systemic oppression that communities of color continue to face.

I got connected to a white antiracist group on campus, began building relationships with student-of-color organizations on campus, and continued my up-and-down journey of working for racial justice. A growing love for Hip-Hop music and culture gave me a deeper context for the shock, anger, confusion, and deep personal transformation that was taking place inside me, and highlighted a pulse of resistance ever-present in the oppression I was learning about. After graduating with a degree in Afro-American Studies, I became involved in community organizing with a community-based, white antiracist group called Groundwork and, later, a national organization called SURJ (Showing Up for Racial Justice) and have worked closely over the years with various racial justice organizations rooted in communities of color. It is the relationships that I have built with people in these organizations that keep me in the work for the long-haul.

Whatever your perception and understanding of the past four years, when Obama was elected president it was a time of great hope for many people. It was also a time of a rise in overt racism. It was at this juncture of possibility and ugliness that SURJ as we know it today was born. (It evolved out of a smaller organization called US for All of Us: No Room for Racism.) As a young organizer it was inspiring to see such a large number of white antiracist activists, educators, and organizers—many of whom I considered role models—coming together from across the country to make a unified front against the rise of the Tea Party, the spike in white nationalist groups, the pervasion of the notion of colorblindness, and the racism that was increasingly evident in the mainstream media.

In our early three years of organizing, SURJ has been a strong part of a vibrant and growing movement for racial justice. Part of the value and beauty of the organization is the way it connects local white antiracist organizations with other groups working for racial justice across the country, creating a framework for best practices to be shared, as well as information, challenges, lessons learned, and successes. Throughout our existence, we have continued a focus on building a base in white communities across the country with national ties.

In the Summer of 2010, we were able to demonstrate just what a network of white people showing up for racial justice can do. We quickly mobilized people across the country in resistance to SB1070—the proposed Arizona state bill that would be the first of a series of copycat state legislation to legalize racial profiling and further criminalize (im)migrant communities— by encouraging solidarity actions and coordinating volunteer organizers to go to Arizona. This added capacity, vision, and skills to the already strong (im)migrant rights movement in Arizona and in localities across the country.

Our resource sharing about issues, such as the rise in white nationalism and the Tea Party, the egregious SB1070 Copy Cat Bill in Alabama, the inspirational Georgia Prison Strike, the Uprising in Wisconsin, and most recently the Occupy Movement, has empowered antiracism activists across the country. Fifty organizations are now a part of SURJ, as well as more than a thousand individuals.

The Occupy Movement has been and continues to be a huge opportunity for engaging white people for racial justice. We have collaborated with Occupy Racism, a network similar to SURJ, to address racism throughout the Occupy Movement. People are fed up with the economic injustice that is permeating the lives of the 99% and are more and more willing and able to see that in order to fully liberate the 99% we must address racism and white privilege and work to build a vibrant multi-racial movement. Together we are a power to be reckoned with.

In the same vein, the statement below speaks to the importance of resisting the strategy of dividing people, who may in fact hold very similar interests, based solely on race.

---

[1] I choose to use the word (im)migrant because some people believe "we didn't cross the border, the border crossed us" referring to thousands of years of indigenous migration in the Americas. I want to maintain the right of human migration; many people identify with the term migrant rather than immigrant.

Statement of Commitment and Call to Action by SURJ

We long for a country that lifts all of us up, dares to care, offers love, generosity, and justice. We reject the racism that keeps us divided. We celebrate our interdependence and our capacity to love our neighbors as ourselves.

We are white people standing together for a community of caring. Racism is not just a thing of the past; it continues to be woven into all of our institutions and structures, privileging those of us who are white and creating inequities for people of color. Racism is used to confuse us, make us forget that our lives and futures are interconnected. We believe that racism, in all its forms, robs us all of our humanity.

We are white people standing against the racism we see, hear, and feel as the nation's right wing and some in the media whip up a backlash of fear about the leadership of President Obama, the first African-American President of the United States, and the agenda for change on which he was elected.

We see blatant racism showing up in hostile signs, words and actions at "tea parties," demonstrations, and town hall meetings; in the effort to stop school children from listening to the President, something school children have done since the dawn of radio; in public tolerance of ministers who openly pray for the President's death; in the scapegoating of immigrants; and in the organized attacks on people and groups working for urgently needed change. Far beyond legitimate disagreement over policies, these are old fear-and-smear tactics used by those who profit as we fight among ourselves.

The stresses of financial meltdown, unemployment, environmental crisis, and war make us an easy target for race-based fear-mongering. But this time we will not be fooled and we will not be divided. We understand how our lives are shaped by race, by class, by gender, by who we love and where we come from. We also honor our deep connections each to the other as we work together to solve pressing problems.

Our ability to transform this country into one that truly works for all of us – where we effectively address our serious economic and environmental problems — is made possible only in a racially just society. Let's work together to build what Rev. Martin Luther King, Jr. called "the Beloved Community."

For more about our current work and the future of SURJ visit: www.showingupforracialjustice.org.

❖ ❖ ❖

❧ Code of Ethics for Antiracist White Allies ❧
By JLove Calderón and Tim Wise
Sponsored by SURJ-Showing Up For Racial Justice

We are persons classified as white who oppose racism and the system of white supremacy. As such, we are committed to challenging the individual injustices and institutional inequities that exist as a result of racism and to speaking out whenever and wherever it exists. We are also committed to challenging our own biases, inculcated by a society that has trained all white people, including us, to one degree or another, to internalize notions of our own superiority.

As antiracist allies, we seek to work with people of color to create real multiracial democracy. We do not aspire to lead the struggle for racial justice and equity, but rather, to follow the lead of persons and communities of color and to work in solidarity with them, as a way to obtain this goal. We do not engage in the antiracist struggle on behalf of people of color, so as to "save" them or as an act of charity. We oppose and seek to eradicate white supremacy because it is an unjust system, and we believe in the moral obligation of all persons to resist injustice. Likewise, we believe not only that a system of white supremacy damages people of color but also that it compromises our humanity, weakens the democratic bonds of a healthy society, and ultimately poses great risks to us all. Because we believe white supremacy to be a contributing force to war, resource exploitation, and economic injustice, our desire to eradicate the mindset and system of white domination is fundamentally a matter of collective preservation. Though people of color are the direct targets of this system, we believe that white people are the collateral damage, and so for our own sake as well, we strive for a new way of living.

To do this with integrity we believe it will be helpful to operate with a code of ethics in mind, so as to remain as accountable as possible to people of color and to each other, as we challenge white supremacy. We know from experience how easy it can be to act with the best of intentions and yet ultimately do harm to the antiracist struggle by choosing tactics or methods that reinforce privilege and inequity, rather than diminish them, or by acting within the confines of an echo chamber of other antiracist white allies, while failing to ground our efforts in structures of accountability led by people of color.

In recent years, the number of white folks engaged in one form or another of public antiracist work or work around the subject of white privilege (as scholars, writers, activists, organizers and educators) has proliferated. Likewise, schools, non-profit organizations, and even some corporations have begun to look at matters of racism and white privilege within their institutions. As this work expands at many different levels, it is perhaps more necessary than ever that white people who are working to be strong, antiracist allies take a good look in the mirror, analyze and critique what we do as well as how we do it, and ask: How can we, as antiracist white allies, operate ethically and responsibly as we work toward helping to dismantle white supremacy?

To this end, we propose the following code of ethics for antiracist white allies. Though it is hardly an exclusive or exhaustive list, we believe it is a start toward a more responsible and responsive antiracist practice for white persons who wish to act in solidarity with people of color in the battle against racism. The code should not be viewed as a fixed or final document, let alone as a checklist or "rulebook" for responsible antiracists. It is merely a guidepost. We hope that it will lead to productive reflection, discussion, and even healthy debate among those who are engaged in the antiracist struggle.

Code of Ethics for Antiracist White Allies

1. *Acknowledge our racial privilege.*

   Self-reflection matters. So does public acknowledgement. Although there are many ways in which white people can be marginalized in this society (on the basis of gender, sex, sexuality, class, religion, disability, etc.), this truth does not eradicate our racial advantage relative to people of color. As white people, we can be oppressed in these other categories and still benefit from privileges extended to white people. Acknowledging racial privilege doesn't mean that we haven't worked hard or that there weren't barriers we had to overcome; it simply means that our racial identity helped us along the way. Indeed, racial privilege will even work in our favor as we speak out against racism. We will often be taken more seriously in this work precisely because we are white, and we should be clear on that point.

2. *Develop interpersonal connections and structures to help maintain antiracist accountability.*

   Accountability matters. When we engage in antiracist efforts, be they public or private, we should remember that it is people of color who are most affected by racism, and thus, they have the most to gain or lose as a result of how such work is done. With this in mind, we believe it is important to seek and obtain regular and ongoing feedback from people of color in our lives (friends and/or colleagues) as a way to better ground our efforts in structures of accountability. Although this kind of accountability may play out differently, depending on our specific job or profession, one general principle is that we should be in regular and ongoing contact with persons in the communities that are most impacted by racism and white supremacy—namely, people of color.

3. *Be prepared to alter our methods and practices when and if people of color give feedback or offer criticism about our current methods and practices.*

   Responsive listening matters. It's not enough to be in contact with people of color as we go about our work. We also need to be prepared to change what we're doing if and when people of color suggest there may be problems, practically or ethically, with our existing methods of challenging racism. Although accountability does not require that we agree with and respond affirmatively to every critique offered, if people of color are telling us over and over again that something is wrong with our current practices, accountability requires that we take it seriously and correct the practice. And, all such critiques should be seen as opportunities for personal reflection and growth.

4. *Listening to constructive feedback from other white people, too.*

Community matters. Particularly as we work to reach a broad base of white people, we need to listen to feedback from the people we are working with. White privilege tends to breed individualism, and this plays out in the form of white antiracists distancing ourselves from other white people and competition between antiracist whites to be the "most down." Listening to feedback from each other as white people helps to counter that tendency, and encourages us to collectivity.

5. *If we speak out about white privilege, racism, and/or white supremacy, whether in a public forum or in private discussions with friends, family, or colleagues, we should acknowledge that people of color have been talking about these subjects for a long time and yet have been routinely ignored in the process.*

Giving credit matters. Because many white people have tuned out or written off the observations of people of color, when another white person speaks about social and racial injustice it can be a huge "aha!" moment for the previously inattentive white listener. The speaker may be put on a pedestal. We should make sure people know that whatever wisdom we possess on the matter is only partially our own: it is also the collective wisdom of people of color, shared with us directly or indirectly. Likewise, beyond merely noting the general contribution of people of color to our own wisdom around matters of race, we should make the effort to specify those people of color and communities of color from whom we've learned. Encourage others to dig deeper into the subject matter by seeking out and reading/listening to the words/work of those people of color, so as to further their own knowledge base.

6. *Share access and resources with people of color whenever possible.*
Networking matters. As whites, we often enjoy access to various professional connections, resources, or networks from which people of color are typically excluded. The ability to act as a gatekeeper comes with the territory of privilege. The only question is, will we help open the gates wider or keep them closed? As allies, we should strive to share connections and resources with people of color whenever possible. So, for instance, we may have inroads for institutional funding or grant monies that could be obtained for people of color-led community organizations. We may have connections in media, educational institutions, or even the corporate world, which if shared with people of color could provide opportunities for those people of color to gain a platform for their own racial justice efforts.

7. *If you get paid to speak out about white privilege, racism, and/or white supremacy, or in some capacity make your living from challenging racism, donate a portion of your income to organizations led principally by people of color.*
Giving back matters. Although it is important to speak out about racism and to do other types of antiracism work (organizing, legal work, teaching, etc.) and necessary for people to be paid for the hard work they do, whites who do so still have to admit that we are able to reap at least some of the financial rewards we receive because of racism and white privilege. Because so much of our own understanding of race and racism comes from the collective wisdom of people of color, it is only proper that we should give back to those who have made our own "success" possible. Although there is no way to ascertain the real value of the shared and collective wisdom of people of color on the understanding that white allies have about racism, it seems fair to suggest that at least 10 percent of our honorariums, royalties, salaries, or other forms of income should be shared with people-of- color-led orga-

nizations with a commitment to racial and social justice. It would be especially helpful if at least some of that money goes to locally-based, grassroots organizations that often have a hard time getting funding from traditional sources.

8. *Get involved in a specific, people of color-led struggle for racial justice.*
Organizing matters. If we are not fighting against police brutality, against environmental dumping in communities of color, or for affirmative action, for immigrant rights, for access to health care, or for antiracist policies and practices within our own institutions and communities, what are we modeling? How are we learning? What informs our work? Can we be accountable to communities of color if we are not politically involved ourselves in some aspect of antiracist struggle?

9. *Stay connected to white folks, too.*
Base-building matters. In addition to our roles in active solidarity with people of color, white people involved in racial justice work also need to reach out to other white people to broaden the base of antiracist white people. Unless we do the latter, we fall short in our accountability. Accountability means showing up, not just with ourselves, but with more white people each time.

10. *Connect antiracism understanding to current political struggles, and provide suggestions or avenues for white people to get involved.*
Accessibility matters. We can connect the participants in our networks, classes, and trainings to opportunities for ongoing political work. We can bring current grassroots political struggles into our activism, education, and organizing by addressing the issues that people of color tell us most directly affect their lives. We can give tools and resources for getting involved in the issues the participants identify as most immediate for them, whether those be public policy issues such as immigration, affirmative action, welfare, or health care; or workplace, neighborhood, and community issues, such as jobs, education, violence, and toxic waste. After contact with us, people who we come into contact with should be able to connect directly and get involved with specific current struggles led by individuals and groups with a clear antiracist analysis.

The premise of this code is simple: White people have a moral and practical obligation to challenge racism in a responsible and responsive manner. To this end, we believe that the principles of self-reflection, accountability, responsive listening, building community, giving credit, resource sharing, giving back, organizing, base building, and accessibility are important starting points for whites who are engaged in any kind of efforts to eradicate racism and white supremacy. We hope that this code, devised as a set of suggestions and guideposts for white allies, will prompt constructive dialogue and discussion regarding how white allyship can best be developed and deployed for the purpose of building true multiracial democracy.

A note about how this code was created:

The initial code concept was created by JLove, who then joined with Tim. Together they wrote the first draft of the code. That draft was sent out to a multi-racial, intergenerational group of activists, organizers, educators, artists, and everyday people who care deeply about social and racial justice. Input was given, and the authors took key insights and common themes and incorporated them into the editing process. Another round of feedback was led by Paul Kivel. We thank everyone who took the time to bring their wisdom and expertise to the table for this accountability work.

❖❖❖

"Each and everyone of you has the power, the will, and the capacity to make a difference in the world you live in."

—Harry Belafonte

(Not Exactly Love) Letter[1]

... Since you quote bell hooks, a scholar-activist for whom I have high regard, should I take it that you desire to struggle to end structures for cultural domination in America—racial, class, and gender? I admire those, especially whites, who espouse such a view. I think that more than ever before what is needed today is critical and committed dialogue between and among individuals and groups who want to struggle to end white supremacy in this country and in the Lafayette area. This dialogue, however, needs to be an informed and intelligent one. Whites who want to engage in dialogue with black people need to discontinue calling on black people to explain rage, resentment, despair, anguish, and dread of being oppressed by America's historic (and present) culture of racism.

Whites need to familiarize themselves with the history, character, and meaning of the black experience and the devastating impact of white supremacy. Study the slave narratives of Linda Brent and Frederick Douglass; the speeches of the black abolitionists like Henry Highland Garnet; the life and times of anti-lynching crusader Ida Wells-Barnett; the scholarship of W. E. B. Du Bois; the life and times of Sojourner Truth, Mary Church Terrell, and Anna Julia Cooper; the literary work of such writers as Nella Larsen, Richard Wright, James Baldwin, Lorraine Hansberry, Ralph Ellison, John A. Williams, Toni Morrison, Ishmael Reed, Sherley Anne Williams, Alice Walker; the life's work of Booker T. Washington, Marcus Garvey, Paul Robeson, A. Philip Randolph, Roy Wilkins, Martin Luther King Jr., Malcolm X, Shirley Chisholm, and Adam Clayton, Jr.; the Harlem Renaissance the Civil Rights Movement, the Black Arts Movement, the Black Studies Movement, and the black feminist self-assertion.

Whites need to listen to, understand, and learn from the mournful yet uplifting sounds of black music: Mahalia Jackson's spirituals; Bessie Smith and Billy Holiday's blues; Charlie Parker, Miles Davis, and John Coltrane's jazz improvisations; Sarah Vaughn, Joe Williams, and Ella Fitzgerald's lyrical jazz; Sam Cooke, Marvin Gaye, Smokey Robinson, Aretha Franklin, and James Brown's soul music, along with the contemporary male and female rap artists who are expressing the rage, resentment, and anger of living in racist and postcapitalist America. Whites who want to engage black people in dialogue—whites who want to resist and transform America's racist culture—need to learn the meaning of blackness. In the process, they also will learn the meaning of whiteness in America. This is a tall order, isn't it? Annihilating wars, enslavement, segregation, and racism also have been major white undertakings.

Whites initiated and implemented annihilating wars against Native Americans and the terrorist enslavement of captured Africans. Whites initiated, implemented, and now maintain a violent and vicious system of racist culture in America. It is they who must end antiblack racism. If whites decide to no longer practice antiblack racism in all of its dimensions, it would end immediately. Therefore, it is my judgment that whites need to initiate serious, critical, intelligent, and committed dialogue about the struggle against America's longest evil and hatred. And because of the long nightmare of white supremacy and antiblack racism, whites should not expect substantial numbers of black people in this area (or any place else in America) to trust them. Why should black people trust white people's sincerity? There is no concrete basis for it!

...I am trying mightily not to be completely cynical about the possibilities of overturning antiblack racism (along with the cultural domination of other people of color) in this nation and in this community. However, I see the growing antiblack racism today as comparable to that same dynamic in the 1890s, which witnessed lynching and culminated in the 1896 Plessey v. Ferguson Supreme Court decision. More and more, I am wondering if legal scholar Derrick Bell isn't correct when he says in his book, Faces at the Bottom of the Well: The Permanence of Racism (1992), that: "racism lies at the center, not the periphery; in the permanent, not in the fleeting; in the real lives of black and white people, not in the sentimental caverns of the mind"(p.198). But on the next page, Bell also says:

> [I]t is not a matter of choosing between the pragmatic recognition that racism is permanent no matter what we do, or an idealism based on the long-held dreams of attaining a society free of racism. Rather, it is a question of both, and both the recognition of the futility of action—where action is more civil rights strategies destined to fail—and the unalterable conviction that something must be done, that action must be taken (p.199).

What I find disconcerting... is the unrelenting denial by most whites that ordinary and everyday racist cultural practices exist here—at schools, businesses, Purdue University, or other institutions. Ironically, this is a conscious and knowledgeable way of being unconscious and unknowledgeable about antiblack racism. It negates whites' responsibility to act against white supremacist thought and behavior. ...

The struggle against cultural domination and antiblack racism is the greatest challenge facing America. It is an internal dynamic that demands attention now. Otherwise, this nation will continue to side down the slippery slope of moral nihilism and social anarchy.

Floyd W. Hayes, III, Ph.D.
Senior Lecturer, Department of Political Science
Coordinator of Programs and Undergraduate Studies
Center for Africana Studies, The Johns Hopkins University

"With the value of the dollar declining

maybe

the value of people will be on the rise"

--Kahlil Almustafa
From Auction Block to Oval Office

Chapter 9

❧ *Ending Racism:*
No One is Free Until We Are All Free ❧

Here we are. The final chapter. The journey of the book is coming to an end.

The work I have committed to has stayed the same for most of my life. What has changed drastically are the strategies I employ to do that work. I mentioned before that I moved from re-traumatizing white people into white guilt to my AHA circular methodology of Acknowledge, Heal, Act. In this chapter, our journey is officially in the ACT phase.

Many fellow white racial justice organizers tire of the perpetual "paralysis of analysis" we are so well known for: All talk, no action. My challenge to each of you (and to me) is to commit to being in action around our principles and values and to diving deeply into the wells of our own discomfort for the sake of justice.

Yes, you will make mistakes. I have made many and continue to do so. But it is better to act than to do nothing at all. For every mis-take, there is a learning opportunity waiting for you. Mis-takes form the totality of who we are. If I had never engaged in a self-destructive lifestyle I would be incapable of being a clear-sighted and credible empowerment coach for young women. Had I not lost people I loved to the prison industrial complex, I would not understand the devastation of torn families and voices lost, and I would not be such a passionate advocate for justice. Had I not been in such a dire financial position that I resorted to crime in order to eat, I might not understand the root causes and connections between poverty, race, and the criminal (in)justice system.

Everything happens for a reason. How are you uniquely poised to make a significant difference and lay claim to your most powerful legacy? You are reading this book because you have the opportunity and ability to do things differently and to make a positive impact in the world for peace and justice. It starts with belief and follows with actions.

The two voices you are going to hear from are wisdom-filled voices. Collectively, Margery Freeman and Cameron Levin have been on the front lines of racial justice work for more than four decades, gathering, integrating, and spreading the wisdom that goes along with all that experience. That's a lot of wisdom! They have supplied me with knowledge and new models that ignite the fire inside me. As we close this part of the journey, I hope they are able to inspire you, as well. As Margery once told me during hard times, "There's all kinds of smart."

What kind of smart are you?

❧ *AntiRacism Organizing for the Long Haul[1]* ❧

By *Margery Freeman*

Nearly thirty years ago, I attended my first "Undoing Racism™/Community Organizing" workshop, sponsored by the People's Institute for Survival and Beyond.[2] I was already in my 40s, an experienced activist, educator, and recognized child advocate.

The workshop caught me flat-footed: I was pissed off! How could I have not seen the evidence of racism that now seemed so stark? Not only was I angry, but I also was humiliated: Here I was, highly educated, well-traveled, steeped in radical politics; I, a veteran marcher for peace, civil rights, women's rights, learning that I had been utterly blinded by white supremacy.

Soon after that introduction to an antiracist analysis, I learned that there were thousands of White people just like me. For generations, Well-Meaning White People have tried to fix the racial inequities of this society. Only we were working on the wrong goal. We thought our goal was to Fix People of Color. As I continued my antiracist journey, I realized that the real goal was to fix ourselves and transform the institutions that have been created to serve us. This goal requires very different strategies. Mostly it requires a lot of self-reflection and self-analysis.

I was lucky: I lived in New Orleans, surrounded by some of the most effective community organizers in the country. From people like Ron Chisom, Barbara Major, Angela Winfrey, Diana Dunn, Kimberley Richards, and David Billings, I learned that as a middle-class white woman, my organizing job was to bring an antiracist "lens" to the work I was already doing as a school teacher, a child advocate, and in adult literacy. That was a new message to me: For years, I had been throwing stones at "the man"—criticizing "the system" for what it was doing to "them." With growing clarity about my role in this race-constructed society, I began to look critically at my own behavior: Why, for example, did I assume I should set the agenda for staff meetings? And if I regularly had the "last word" in a discussion, whether with students or colleagues, didn't that reinforce my role as "the expert" (despite my denial, "But I didn't intend that!")? If I was always the expert, how could others develop their own leadership capacities?

I began to work collectively with both White people and People of Color to analyze the power dynamics of our workplaces, our community organizations. I became more acutely conscious of my role as a White activist in organizing social justice efforts. I struggled over what it means to follow the leadership of People of Color—those most oppressed by racism—in building an antiracist movement. At the same time, I became a trainer with The People's Institute, applying its principles and analysis in my life with my family; and bringing my everyday experiences to the "Undoing Racism™/ Community Organizing" workshops.

So How Do We Begin—And Sustain—Organizing To End Racism?

In conversations about racism, one of the first things I learned is that we need to be present for the discussion. The People's Institute understands this, so we have created a set of guidelines that help White people and People of Color have a genuine conversation about race and racism without fighting or leaving! I've come to realize that a family conversation, a workplace strategy session, a neighborhood discussion can be more effective when we:

- ❖ **Listen** with **respect**. Since all of us have experience and opinions about racism, listening with respect is difficult! We ordinarily spend much of our time arguing with the speaker or formulating a response. Yet, to listen with respect—especially when the subject is racism—is the first way we can be present to one another.

- ❖ **Participate** and **stay the whole time**. Many of us who work in the "helping professions" enter a community without asking permission, participating in its life only if we feel like it and leaving after our program or research grant ends. Yet when we sit on a family's stoop, visit without an agenda, buy our coffee at the corner store, and stay long enough to watch the children grow up, we are more likely to be heard, trusted, respected.

❧ *Struggle together—sit with our discomforts—recognize there's no quick fix!* The irony of discovering racism is that I brought my same internalized racial superiority to fighting racism that I had brought to fixing People of Color! The disequilibrium of a new world view, combined with impatience to fix these new [to me] problems of racism, made it hard for me to recognize that my first task—perhaps my most difficult task—was to do nothing! To sit with the discomfort of not knowing, not understanding, not having the experience and tools to fix the problem before me.

❧ *Stay focused on racism in the U.S.* Well, of course, you say. Yet, this way of being present is perhaps the hardest for White people to do. Since our internalized sense of superiority tells us that we're supposed to be the experts in all subjects, we become discomfited when the topic is racism. How can I be the leading voice on racism when I'm not the expert? So—we change the subject. We make "oppression" the topic. We raise other "isms"—after all, aren't sexism, homophobia, ableism, ageism oppressing millions of people worldwide? Yet somehow, as we become active against oppressions, racism often falls off our list. Look at the history of reform movements in the U.S.: Nearly every one of them has been weakened or destroyed by racism, whether the labor movement, populist movement, women's movement—you name it. Only the Civil Rights Movement, led by African-Americans and other People of Color, was able to sustain a multiracial approach for a while. Without an analysis of racism race continually divides us. That's racism's purpose. So if we're going undo racism, we have to stay focused on racism, even if we're not the experts on how to do it.

Many of us who live with identities that cause us hardship (being gay in a straight culture, being a woman in a patriarchy, being fat in a thin-is-best world, being old when youth has currency) want to believe that racism is just like any other "ism." We've been acculturated to see things in dichotomous (right/wrong, good/bad) terms, so we think that focusing on racism somehow makes other oppressions "less important." What I have found is that in this race-constructed society, bringing an antiracist lens to all anti-oppression work enables us to build and sustain effective coalitions and partnerships. We're not in an Oppression Olympics, after all. We're trying to create a just and equitable world.

"What Can We Do?"

That question is the most common one I hear as I do my antiracist organizing. To answer that question, I come back, again and again, to principles that guide the work of The People's Institute. I want to use these principles as a framework for my story, "Antiracist Organizing for the Long Haul."

Undoing Racism™

Organizers/educators with The People's Institute believe that racism is a dehumanizing ideology that is the single most critical barrier to building effective coalitions for social change. Since racism has been consciously and systematically constructed, we believe it can be undone as people understand what it is, where it comes from, how it functions, and why it is perpetuated.

Undoing Racism™ requires collective action. As David Billings, my husband, mentor and long-time antiracist historian and trainer, says, "The only thing that trumps racism is organizing!" Working to undo racism is counter-cultural: It can isolate us from those we love and can jeopardize our work or professional lives. To sustain ourselves as antiracist activists we must build trusting relationships where we can bring our whole selves. We must be able to laugh, be silly, cry, eat, get angry, share our confusions, celebrate together. We must see our work as multigenerational—my children's children's children will benefit from my work. Most of all, we must understand ourselves as organizers. Racism has been done, and therefore, it can be undone. It is man-made, not God-ordained. Its purpose is to keep us apart. So as antiracist organizers, our job is to bring men, women, children together across racial lines, building a bigger and bigger base of people who have clarity and commitment to undo this massive injustice called racism.

Understanding History

I love history! I majored in history, then taught American history in junior and senior high school. I was a progressive teacher: I had read educational reformers like Paulo Freire, Jonathan Kozol, and Herbert Kohl, so I knew that history needs to be culturally inclusive and reflect the stories of all peoples. I was enthusiastic!

However I didn't really know anything about U.S. history. When I began to realize all that I didn't know, I became furious. Again, that sense of embarrassment that I had gone to school for nineteen years and didn't know most U.S. history!

So understanding history means a lot of un-learning and re-learning. What's wonderful about being guided by this principle is that there are hundreds of books to help us. Some were written decades ago, only we didn't know about them, like W.E.B. Du Bois' *Souls of Black Folks* (1903), Ashley Montagu's *Man's Most Dangerous Myth: The Fallacy of Race* (1942), or Lillian Smith's *Killers of the Dream* (1947). Others are contemporary, like Michelle Alexander's *The New Jim Crow* (2010).

Reading history and watching documentaries with an antiracist lens deepens our understanding and makes us thirst for more. We begin to explore our family histories, not to find antiracist heroes/sheroes (we probably won't) or to bemoan their racist ways. My people were doctors and preachers—many were medical missionaries in India and China. With my antiracist lens, I now see how they/we were caught up in the web of ignorance and lies of white supremacy. Yet, as I peel back the layers of racism, I also find hope in their everyday acts of courage and kindness. I learn to love them all over again. As the great African-American theologian Vincent Harding wrote, there is Hope in History.

Celebrating Culture

Storytelling helps us recognize one another's humanity. Yet in a culture dominated by white supremacy, our "American" myth of "rugged individualism," of "making it on my own," separates us from our history, from our ethnic roots, from one another. Oppressed communities know that celebrating culture is essential to their survival. Treated as a "them" by the dominant culture, People of Color hold fast to the "we" of their lives, telling and singing stories of steadfastness and resilience in the face of hate and rejection. Singing and storytelling sustain liberation struggles. During the Civil Rights Movement, when violence seemed to lurk around every corner and people with power were indifferent or hostile to the demands for justice in Black communities, people sought strength and courage in daily churches and community gatherings. As the freedom movement expanded to cotton, lettuce, strawberry, and tomato fields, campus coffee houses, Native American councils, urban sweatshops, and jailhouses, songs and stories sustained the people struggling to determine their own lives and future.

Many White people have lost the connection with the "we" of our ethnic roots and the struggles of our ancestors. So we substitute accounts of our individual achievement; we brag about our wealth, our possessions, our status. The only trouble with these conversations is that they do not connect us with our own humanity. They alienate us from those who don't have as big a house, as fast a car, as important a job.

When I realized how important stories are to struggling communities, I resolved that at the adult literacy program where I worked we would begin staff meetings with cultural sharing. After an hour or so of sharing—maybe a recipe, a poem, a picture, a reminiscence—I then would say (because I set the agenda), "OK, now let's get to work." It took me years to realize that the stories were the work! I was so task-oriented, so caught-up in being in charge, that I had made "cultural sharing" a task on a list of "to do's," not fully realizing how this time of storytelling enriched our relationships, sharpened our sense of one another's humanity, made our work more effective.

In 2004, when David and I moved to New York City after 35 years in New Orleans, I had really internalized the value of cultural sharing. The group of organizers who had asked us to relocate to New York to help with antiracist movement-building there decided to have a "welcome David and Margery" party. We had a wonderful time, with people bringing all sorts of food and drink. As the party was coming to a close, someone said, "This was such fun! And, we didn't even have an agenda!" I said to the group, "Well, in New Orleans I learned that nothing really happens without food. Why don't we have regular monthly potlucks?" The group was doubtful. "New Yorkers wouldn't do that," one person said. "We're too busy." "Why don't we try?" I responded. And thus were born the AntiRacist Potlucks that have taken place every month for nearly seven years! No agenda, no "meeting," no one in charge. Just people coming together to share a meal and to get to know one another.

Networking

Seems so obvious, doesn't it? Everyone does it (the white "good ol' boy" network is the most notorious example). Yet many of us overlook the sheer necessity of networking in dealing with racism. We must take it seriously if we're going to build a strong antiracist community. An antiracist network is different from traditional networks. It's multiracial, strengthened by commonly-held principles, bound by beliefs forged in mutual goals. It's like a family: We may not always agree, we may not even like one another, but we recognize each other, even when we meet for the first time. There's an assumption of trust in our antiracist networking, even when we fall down on the job.

Networking came home to me in a profound way when New Orleans was besieged by floodwaters, following hurricane Katrina. Not only was the People's Institute office under 9 feet of water, but the homes of most of its staff, volunteers, and board members were destroyed. Our director, Ron Chisom, couldn't find his mother for three weeks and then had to deal with her untimely death shortly thereafter. We found ourselves dispersed in cities and towns across the country. Yet within days, the antiracist network became a lifeline, not only to connect loved ones, but to begin organizing on behalf of the tens of thousands of displaced people wanting to return home and begin rebuilding. From New York to Seattle, from Minneapolis to Houston, our network went into action, ensuring that people living in isolated hamlets and strange neighborhoods would know they were connected and supported. We raised money and found housing, clothing, schooling for hundreds, mobilized thousands to speak out about their situations, educated the larger community about the injustices of "recovery," bringing evidence of human rights violations before the United Nations. In the words of Jim Dunn, a co-founder of the People's Institute, we built a "net" that "works." Networking is the life-blood of antiracist organizing. For years, the People's Institute would bring hundreds of organizers together for 3-4 days of celebration, training and renewal. As people came from all across the U.S., Puerto Rico, South Africa, Ireland, Japan, and beyond, we would be nourished by old friendships and excited by new ones, feeling Jim Dunn's words, "A Whole Lot of People Is Strong!"

Addressing Internalized Racial Oppression

No challenges are greater to antiracist organizing than what we bring to the work ourselves! For White people, these challenges are especially daunting because we do not often recognize our own Internalized Racial

Superiority (IRS). The People's Institute defines Internalized Racial Oppression as a multigenerational process of disempowerment (Internalized Racial Inferiority for People of Color) or entitlement (Internalized Racial Superiority for White people). White people receive and internalize a system of power and privilege given to us in a race-constructed society that has designated Whites as the superior race. IRS manifests itself in behaviors, such as denial/tolerance of racism, hyper-individualism, lack of historical/political consciousness, blame/avoidance, compartmentalization/professional specialization, and a belief in White people's singular ability and right to set or change the rules to ensure that we remain in power.

For antiracist White people, IRS is especially tricky. It trips us up again and again, despite (or perhaps because of) our sophisticated understanding of it. I'll never forget one time when I was participating in a bi-racial project, exploring how to build anti-bias early childhood systems. The group of six White women and six Black women had been very careful in our first weeks together, setting forth ground rules for how we were going to be present with one another. It turned out that when we pledged to "listen with respect," I must have had my fingers crossed behind my back. One day, one of the Black participants shared her experiences and views concerning sexuality. As I listened to what she said, I became filled with my own sense of self-righteousness ("How could she feel that way!"). I announced to the group that she was wrong. I waited for her to apologize for her thoughts.

The group might have ceased functioning at that point. ("White folks are always going to be White Folks," one of the other African-American women told me later she had thought to herself.) Fortunately for us all, after a few weeks of silence (I was still waiting for an apology), the Black woman, who had taken it upon herself to speak her truth in a circle she believed would be respectful, asked the group facilitator to bring us together. When we met, the proverbial scales fell from my eyes. It became clear to me that I had been participating in the group with the silent caveat: "I will listen with respect as long as you do not do or say anything I disagree with." Internalized Racial Superiority.

Ron Chisom, co-founder and current Executive Director of The People's Institute, and an important mentor of mine, once asked me, "Margery, what do White people bring to the multiracial table?" After a pause, he answered his own question: "You bring the rules."

This country has taught White people for generations that we are the rule-makers, the standard-bearers. Even after decades of antiracist organizing, I still try to set the rules.

Reshaping Gatekeeping and Maintaining Accountability

Internalized Racial Superiority is supported, day in and day out, by the institutions in which we live and work. In this racialized society, every system and institution is designed to make me feel comfortable in my whiteness. I once heard antiracist leader Daniel Buford quote Dr. Wade Nobles, professor emeritus in the Department of Africana Studies at San Francisco State, "For white people, living in this culture is like a fish living in water. You don't understand the nature of 'wet.'"

All of us who live and work with these institutions are gatekeepers—White people as well as People of Color. We are hired, ordained, certified, or sanctioned to maintain the status quo and to represent those institutional interests and their worldview. Those of us who are social change activists frequently work in oppressed communities where we interpret, define, count, measure, and speak for oppressed people with or without their permission in exchange for certification, resources, access, gratification, or power.

White social reformers have justified our gatekeeping role for centuries. We've called it "White Man's Burden," "Manifest Destiny," doing God's will, American exceptionalism, gentrification. What has been consistent throughout our history is that Internalized Racial Superiority has shaped our good intentions. IRS gets in the way of our being accountable to the people we seek to serve: As demonstrated by my experience with the anti-bias early childhood group, I listen to and respect people as long as they speak and act the way I think they should. When I have worked hard—really hard—to create programs and services that I think will help people and when 'those people' don't act right—don't come to my meetings, don't follow my suggestions, don't do what I think they should do—well, my accountability to them disappears. My relationship with them was built on their being fixable! This is what I call conditional accountability. As long as we keep trying to "fix" poor people (and all People of Color) we think they're broken. And there's no reason we should account to broken people.

So what is authentic, antiracist gatekeeping? Being an antiracist gate-keeper first means that I turn the mirror around and look at myself, at my people, my history. I become an expert on how my institutions (yes, the ones that nurtured me, pay me, allow me to purchase/rent a home, give me my standing in the community) have dealt with poor people and People of Color. I analyze each of the organizations I am part of. What is its purpose? How does it function? Who has power and who doesn't? What about the neighborhood where I live—who lived here before me? Who wasn't al-lowed to live here? Why did the earlier residents leave? What is the effect I have on it, with my "cultural capital" as a White person?

If I work with people who live in oppressed communities, my goal as an antiracist gatekeeper is to help them gain a sense of their own power and to be self-determined. Every activity and program I think is important begins and ends with the question, "Is this going to strengthen this person or this group?" If the answer is no, I don't do it, no matter how important the "is-sue" may be to me.

Being an antiracist gatekeeper means I work and live with other White people. I build full and genuine relationships in my family and community and workplace, not distancing myself from other White people because I am so much more "developed" as an antiracist. Such arrogance is neither humane nor effective.

Always, antiracist gatekeepers are present with others, listening with respect to people we work with, spending time with them, participating in conversations and activities that are mutually important to us. As our rela-tionships fill with trust, we are more likely to be listened to when we bring our stories about undoing racism into the conversation.

A few years ago I took a job with the New Orleans YMCA, known in the Black community as the "white Y," because of the history of legal segregation in the South (that shows up as everyday discrimination in the North). These "separate but equal" facilities resulted in "colored" YMCAs and "white" YMCAs, just as there were (and still are) Black and White churches and schools. Of course by the mid-1990s, the New Orleans Y had Black members and Black staff, though most of its senior management and board were still White.

I had been hired to run the adult literacy branch of the Y, known for years as "Operation Mainstream." Volunteer tutors were the central focus of the branch. As an antiracist gatekeeper, my challenge was to help transform the program so that the adult students became the focus of accountability for our work. We held community meetings throughout the city, asking people what they thought we should do. One of the first responses was to change the name! "When you have an 'operation,'" one person explained in criticizing our name, "you're either fighting an enemy or fixing sick people." Another man said, "Have you thought about what happens to our community when our people come to your mainstream?" We changed the name.

One of our meetings was held with Resident Council members of a housing development where I had been working over the years. "I've taken a job with the Y's adult literacy program," I told the Resident Council members. "What do you think?" "We want it!" they answered. "But we need you to set up your classes here in the neighborhood, instead of at the Y."

Well, in a volunteer-centered program, our job had been to keep the tutors happy. Most were White and would not come to the projects. What to do? "Are there residents here who would like to become literacy tutors?" I asked. "Of course!" was the reply. Within a year, indigenous literacy organizers were plying the courtyards and byways of several housing developments, recruiting neighbors for their classes. Books gained currency; reading clubs sprouted up.

We turned the program inside out, making students the policymakers and community residents the teachers. Participants gained a sense of their own power, motivated to become more effective readers and teachers so they could get better jobs and help their children with schoolwork.

Another Word about Accountability

Ironically, White people who called ourselves antiracist quarrel continually about the idea of accountability. I think that's because we still can't let go of the idea of being the experts. ("I'm right!" No, I'M right!") We squabble among ourselves, sort of like cats in the children's story "Millions of Cats," who fought about who was prettiest. The trouble with this quarreling is just like the trouble with fighting about who is prettiest: All the cats (but one) died. Our quarrels are taking place as millions of people are locked up, locked out, locked in—desperate and dying—because of the racist nature of the United States.

So what is antiracist accountability? Here's a story about an experience that helped me get clear about it: The story began when residents of the St. Thomas Housing Development in New Orleans called together the dozens of organizations, churches, schools, and health and human service institutions that had set up programs and services for them. The St. Thomas Resident Council had done its research: It had discovered that the St. Thomas residents were a major economic force for these institutions, whose staff salaries, research findings, dissertation results, and program statistics all depended on having access to them.

As we gathered, the St. Thomas Housing Development leadership made a proposal: In exchange for the privilege of being allowed into their community, the institutions and organizations would agree to follow the community's leadership. Shocking! Revolutionary!

But, it worked. A consortium was organized: All decisions affecting the community were democratically decided, except that the resident votes were weighted so they had twice the value of the other institutional votes. The Resident Council had veto power over actions that impacted the residents. Even philanthropic organizations who wanted to provide money for programs were required to agree to this power arrangement. Every one of the consortium members was also required to take a workshop about racism so that they would have a common language and understanding.

Consortium members signed a "Statement of Accountability," that said in part:

> Persons and organizations enter and work in the community upon request and after consultation with organized, indigenous leadership. No intermediaries, be they a local church, a non-profit group, or any other type of organization or institution, have the right to enter for work in the community based on outside determinants or "needs" factors. This method of operation runs counter to the principle of self-determination. The Consortium deems itself accountable specifically to the organized, independently-directed, low-income and indigenous poor of the area and the elders of the larger community whom residents designate to speak with them. [3]

I have found that antiracist accountability expands: From its basic premise of being accountable to the leadership of those most affected by racism, it leads us to being accountable to other antiracists, both White and People of Color. Within a trusted community, accountability becomes a way of life.

Developing Leadership

The final and perhaps most important principle taught by The People's Institute is Leadership Development. No matter how good we are at what we do, sustaining the work over years and generations means that new antiracist organizers need to be intentionally and systematically developed within local communities and organizations.

About 15 years ago, the People's Institute initiated a Youth Agenda, recognizing that young people needed opportunities to find their voices and to assume their rightful roles as antiracist leaders. Inspired by the Freedom Schools of the Civil Rights Movement, we recruited youth to participate in summer-long programs, modeled after those 1964 citizenship schools. Within a few years, People's Institute Freedom Schools were established in six or seven other locations across the country plus one in South Africa. The curriculum was simple: Engage youth (ages 8-18) in hands-on activities to bring alive the antiracist principles taught by the People's Institute.

Many Freedom School participants become antiracist organizers. One White young woman in New Orleans, for example, challenged her U.S. history teacher in high school about the racist text the class was using. Put down by the teacher for meddling in "his" business, she and her (also antiracist) mother brought their case to the principal, who agreed that using Howard Zinn's *People's History of the United States* was an appropriate book for the class to read. In Seattle, young people organized a one-day strike to demand a more inclusive social studies curriculum. Asian/Pacific Island, Native American, African-American, and Latino students and parents, supported by White students and teachers, held a "Teach In" that same day, bringing their stories and experiences to one another. The Board of Education voted to broaden the curriculum.

White antiracist leaders have a particular set of challenges: Because of the power dynamics of a White supremacist culture, we find it difficult to follow the lead of People of Color for many reasons, not least of which is that we have internalized the messages of this race-constructed society. People of Color know the risk of giving honest criticism to White people (if we get mad we can get back). And, White people are so conditioned to seeing People of Color in subordinate roles that we don't know how to take direction from them. We often mistake the opinion of a good Black friend for "how *they* feel/think," which not only may be misleading or wrong, but collectivizing People of Color in one person is racist in its own right. Our interracial relationships are often so fragile that we hesitate to give positive criticism to our Latino friend or our Black co-worker, fearing we will be called racist. Yet when our relationships are genuine, honest conversation nurtures mutual accountability.

White people's leadership in the antiracist movement is important. Racism has been created by and for White people, so we are crucial participants in ending it. At a People's Institute national gathering in 1996, Ron Chisom and Jim Dunn called the handful of White participants together. They asked us: "Why don't White people speak out against racism when there are no People of Color around?" We took up the challenge. We organized ourselves and called our group "European Dissent," since we dissented from the privileged status this nation has given us as people of European Descent. We spent a long time getting to know one another, listening to one another's stories. Over time, we took public stands against racism, writing letters to newspapers, picketing Klan events, working in political campaigns, sponsoring book-signing events for antiracist writers. We mentored other White antiracist groups, always with the message that David Billings taught us: "Antiracism is a verb—it means organizing." Today, White antiracists are organizing throughout the U.S.[4]

Everyday Antiracism—a Way Of Life

Sometimes I'm asked, often by a Person of Color, "Why do you do this, Margery? Don't you have a good life with things as they are?" That's an important question for each of us to answer for ourselves. For me, being antiracist means building a legacy to leave my children and grandchildren. I want them to take heart from the sense of hope that fuels my persistence in this work. The North African saint, Augustine, is said to have replied to one of his followers when asked why he felt hope in the face of so much evil in the world, "Hope has twin daughters: One is Anger about the way things are; the other is Courage to make change."

Anger is what propelled me into antiracist organizing. As a college student over 50 years ago, I was prohibited by my parents from going South to be part of the Civil Rights Movement. Outraged by their "liberal racism," I became a radical activist, blaming my people for all the injustice in the world. Years later, as I learned to love my family all over again in new ways, I recognized that they had taught me a great deal about courage. What humility I felt when I read the countless letters my mother wrote to politicians, school boards, and newspapers, arguing for a more just society! Yes, her life as a social worker was constrained by her missionary worldview; but aren't my own work and worldview constrained by White Supremacist views I've absorbed over the years? Everyday racism entraps us all. As we struggle to undo racism, in ourselves and in others we recognize and affirm each one's humanity.

I believe our hope for the future lies in breaking the silence that stops White people from speaking out about racism. Speaking out even when no People of Color are around. Speaking out when we're doing dishes with our dad or daughter. Speaking out at work, over a beer, in school. Everyday antiracism is thinking, talking, feeling, and acting in the full knowledge of our collective White identity. Our hope is in our collective outrage that propels our collective courage to act.

---

[1] I am grateful to the many organizers of The People's Institute for Survival and Beyond for much of my understanding of undoing racism.™ To learn more about The People's Institute, visit www.pisab.org.

[2] The People's Institute for Survival and Beyond (PISAB) is a national, multiracial, anti-racist collective of organizers and educators dedicated to building a movement for social transformation. Its aim is to end racism and other forms of oppression. Started in 1980 by two African-American organizers, Dr. James Norman Dunn and Ronald Chisom, PISAB today works with over 50 organizers/trainers across the country and in Puerto Rico and is recognized as one of the foremost antiracist organizations in the country. Through its "Undoing Racism™/Community Organizing" workshops, it has impacted well over half a million people across the country and worldwide.

[3] ACCOUNTABILITY STATEMENT of the St. Thomas/Irish Channel Consortium, New Orleans, Louisiana, adopted on November 19, 1992. Use with attribution only. For full text of Accountability Statement, contact Margery Freeman.

[4] In 2010, Crandall, Dostie & Douglass Books, Inc. a White antiracist publishing house in Roselle, New Jersey, published *Accountability and White Anti-racist Organizing: Stories from Our Work.*

❧ *A Different Way of Being White* ❧

By *Cameron Levin*

When Susan B. Goldberg and I sat down in her living room in the summer of 2002 to start to develop a new kind of radical white identity, there was electricity in the air. We explored, we theorized, we disagreed for hours and hours, and then the idea took form in the shape of words. *Radical White Identity.* As we spoke the phrase for the first time, it was an exhilarating moment. In fact, I have rarely felt as free as I did on that July morning. But, I have begun the story at the end.

Let's go back to what compelled us to create a positive racial identity for white people. Many said it was preposterous that Susan and I should lay claim to creating a whole subculture. And yet one has to ask, how does any subculture, culture, or racial identity begin? They are socially constructed realities that we all accept, and then we hold these "frames" in our mind to see and interpret the world through and to serve as a lens that provides meaning and context for what we are experiencing.

I grew up in a white, middle-class neighborhood in Woodland Hills in the San Fernando valley in Los Angeles, California, in the late 1970s and 1980s, not realizing I was white until I was 21 years old. You might ask how this is possible. Most of the people in my community were white, and my parents were liberal, teaching us to treat everyone fairly, and they never said explicitly racist things about people of color. I had a neighbor and close friend who was from India, and I knew he was a different color than I was and that at his house we at different foods, but I never saw myself as white or him as being not white. This all changed when I was 21, and I had the opportunity to work at a summer program called Brotherhood Sisterhood Camp (BSC), sponsored by the National Conference for Community and Justice. This is where I discovered my white racial identity, and I did not like it one bit.

In one particularly challenging activity we were broken up into racial caucuses and instructed to ask our racial group to list stereotypes of the other racial groups. Each group did the same, and then we brought the two groups together. Each group got to ask the other who said what stereotype, and then the person who said it stood up and had to listen to how hearing the stereotype affected this person. These types of experiences were often painful for everyone involved and made a deep impression upon my spirit. I knew I would never allow myself to consciously stereotype again. I now had a personal connection to the impact of racism, and I knew I was going to be an ally—the best one I could. It was this camp, along with a youth organizing group called Los Angeles Student Coalition and a youth leadership development organization Children of War, that served as the foundation from which I grew into the 20-plus year community organizer I am today.

BSC camp provided a foundation that allowed me to have a clear understanding of the importance of my racial identity and its impact on everything. The camp model fell short, though, by offering us the dominant white racial identity and failing to offer a viable alternative. As a Jew, I knew I could escape full responsibility for my white privilege by claiming that I am a white Jew. However, this did not sit right with me. I had to take full responsibility for the implications and realities that white privilege plays in shaping my opportunities for moving through and living in the United States.

What is wrong with the dominant white identity, you might ask? Because of the long history of racial domination in this country, white people have been instilled with a sense of entitlement and privilege that is very oppressive to folks of color, not to mention very unhealthy for white folks. This racial identity includes an awareness of being the oppressor, the contradictions of both benefitting from white privilege and feeling guilty about it, and an overall unconsciousness about systemic white supremacy. So the dominant white racial identity was no solution.

I now had to set out to find an alternative. Initially I found myself taking on the persona of *race traitor*, which encourages treason to the white race by resisting anything that comes from the dominant white culture. Death to whiteness—this had a certain appeal.

At the core of being a white, antiracist person is an identity rooted in guilt and shame. To prove my "downness" I had to prove to people of color and other antiracist white folks that I could join in attacking and judging both other white people and myself. Some people of color play a role in this kind of behavior when they expect and encourage white people to put down and make fun of other white people, and one skill I had to cultivate quickly working within communities of color and with people of color-led organizations was to talk shit about other white folks. The subtle message was that being down was demonstrated by my ability to be critical about other white organizers. This skill was valued and necessary proof that I was antiracist. White people are the only group of folks that are expected to bring other white people into the struggle by teaching them to hate themselves, to be ashamed of themselves, and to be immobilized with guilt.

I found myself keeping other white people away from me by looking for their signs of racism and using those signs as proof that they were not down and therefore could not be my allies. That's a great way to turn off the vast majority of white folks who may consider themselves to be antiracist but who can never relate to white antiracists.

Eventually, I realized that, regardless of how I defined myself, I could not change how society and those I interact with perceive me—I would always be treated as a white man. So, being a race traitor seemed pointless and self-hating. Therefore, I had to find a way to embrace my racial identity and turn it into a source of power for justice. As long as I can understand that justice means my liberation, I too, can be fully human. White people need a positive racial identity as much as any other racial group. We need an identity built on our communal commitment to the liberation of both people of color and white people from the white supremacist system. If white people cannot have a positive racial identity that helps us achieve our own humanity, then we can never really be whole people.

I have constantly worked to uncover how white privilege is operating in my daily actions so that I can walk in the world with what I call an "awareness of whiteness." When most of us go out into the world we are aware of many things that influence how we behave in society. Take traffic laws, for instance. When we drive, we follow the speed limit and stop at the red light. I found it so much harder to see the invisible air of white privilege I was always breathing. Finally, after paying a lot of attention to it, I developed an awareness that became integrated into my overall awareness, and it was easier to spot stuff when it happened in real time and sometimes stop myself before I acted out on white privilege unconsciously. Seeing as I was often the only white person in the room in many of my jobs as an organizer and social worker, I had many opportunities to act out my unaware white privilege. I was often criticized, rightly, for how much space I would take up in meetings. I had to learn to practice an awareness of how much I spoke, which I did through making marks on a note pad; then I could focus on not being the first person to speak. Eventually I got the hang of it, so it became a more natural practice, but even after 20 years I still always need to maintain an awareness because my unconscious state is to act out that privilege and be the first to speak every time.

As I developed as a white antiracist community organizer, I began to find parallels with bell hooks' analysis of patriarchy and its impact on men. I realized white people, too, were impacted by a society based on white supremacy. White people do get white privilege, and we pay a price. This realization allowed me to see that white people have a stake in a society based on equity and fairness for all groups of people. With a stake in the game, we have even more to fight for.

I started looking into history of the 1960s, 1930s, early 1900s and the Abolitionist movements, and I discovered for the first time a history of white people just like me. Courageous white people, like John Brown, the abolitionist who sought to ignite a slave rebellion thru his armed raid on the U.S. Arsenal at Harper's Ferry; and Myles Horton, founder of Highlander Research and Education Center in Tennessee, which was used as a strategic center for black and white civil rights workers in the 1950s and 1960s. From before the founding of this country, white people have been part of the resistance to the white supremacist system. Today, conscious white people stand on the shoulders of the John Browns and the Myles Hortons and countless unnamed individuals who came before us. It is with my self-respect as a conscious white antiracist—one of thousands in this country—that I can sit at the table with people of color and be accountable for any racism I will perpetuate, while at the same time working for systemic change and learning together how to bring about the change we are working towards.

To realize that we white antiracist folks today stand on the shoulders of those who came before us, we have to see them and to reclaim our history of resistance to white supremacy. I can only see these white sisters and brothers when I see it is our whiteness that unites us and our courage to struggle for racial justice that holds us together, linking us from then to now. Now, I can sit down in Susan's living room and begin a wonderful journey to create a radical white identity to help build a radical white culture/community of resistance called AWARE-LA (Alliance of White Antiracists Everywhere).

During my time doing racial justice work, I have also been a community organizer working with social justice groups in communities of color across Los Angeles. This experience has been amazing, and I have learned a great many things over the past 23 years. To me, personally, the most valuable was that I could make a meaningful and useful contribution in working with communities of color, as long as I did it with integrity and strong self-awareness. And, I have to be working in my own community of white folks and do the heavy lifting that needs to be done there, too. Once I had a positive white racial identity, I was ready to live as a radical white person who would work to build antiracist bases in white communities and to build our ability to join in alliances with communities of color across the U.S. to work for racial, social, gender, economic, environmental, and electoral justice.

If we are going to be successful we must realize that in today's reality words, like racism, have lost their meaning because right wing groups have been working to erode and confuse these ideas—and that's been going on since long before the Tea Party and Glen Beck. I see words like racism as too blunt and ineffective for beginning any type of meaningful dialogue in this "post racial" society. We need to find creative ways to reclaim the ground of racial justice and the disproportionate share of the economic crisis falling on the working poor of all races, especially the Latin and the black community. Calling someone a "racist" when we are really more likely trying to describe the unconscious racism of our white allies and potential allies isn't helpful because when you call someone a racist you seem to be suggesting they are tied to the KKK. Most white people—and people of color—who enact racism are not doing it intentionally or with hate in their hearts, and so using the term is like using a sledge hammer when you need tweezers. In my experience, moving white folks to look at their white privilege has to come from a loving and humble place, and to succeed at working with white folks I have to do it with genuine love in my heart. I have to greet every white person I meet as an ally or a potential ally until they prove otherwise. This is the same thing someone once did for me, and it's what allowed me to become who I am today.

❧ *Radically White* ❧

By *Susan B. Goldberg & Cameron Levin*

....Whites need to acknowledge and work through the negative historical implications of "whiteness" and create for ourselves a transformed identity as White people committed to equality and social
change. Our goal is neither to deify nor denigrate whiteness but to
diffuse its destructive power. To teach my White students and my
own children that they are "not White" is to do them a disservice. To
teach them that there are different ways of being White and that they
have a choice as White people to become champions of justice and
social healing, is to provide them a positive direction for growth and
to grant them the dignity of their being. [1]

With these words, Gary Howard captures the challenge for white[2] people who struggle to stand against racism. Our goal is to "teach different
ways of being white" by offering the idea of a Radical White Identity. This
identity offers white people a racial and cultural identity that directly addresses the history of white dominance in this country. We center our work
in racial identity development, and from this foundation we build a clear
analysis and practice for creating radical white culture. Our aim is to create
an alternative to the dominant white culture through building a community
of white antiracist people who represent a sub-culture of whiteness and to
offer a form of white identity that is explicitly antiracist and allows white
people to acknowledge and embrace our histories and cultures. Through
this evolving cultural/racial identity we will create our antiracist practice,
our racial identity model, and our role in the process of furthering radical
social transformation.

Guilt is a Place to Visit, Not a Place to Live

We are continuously struck by the power and legacy of white dominance
and racism in every aspect of United States culture and history. It is a legacy
that continues to fester and bleed because truths are not told, reparations are
not made, and racism continues to be a vital tool, shaping our nation's history and present day realities. The historical examples of racism from many
different peoples in this land are overwhelming and endless. We believe that
until the legacy of the system of white dominance is fully addressed, all

people living in the United States will be unable to move forward with our humanity intact.

We hope to facilitate change in white people, both those conscious and unconscious of racism. We address this community because it is our community. We have struggled with the painful realities of racism all around us and have searched for the most effective way to be involved in a movement for change. In our personal journey to come to terms with the realities of racism we have been told time and again by our friends of color that a critical piece of the work is to engage white communities in creating change.

Our framework is rooted in our belief in the importance of a racial identity model for white people. We recognize that racial identity is a social construct, and yet we cannot deny that racial identity is meaningful as it impacts and shapes every person's experience in this country. In our time spent working against racism, we have often come across overly simplistic analyses of racism. Some of these include:

1. Seeing racism as the problem itself rather than as a tool of a greater system
2. Seeing white people's experience as monolithic and creating a group identity solely based on racism
3. Seeing white people as having no real stake in changing the system
4. Failing to offer any alternative antiracist white racial identity

We believe that too many antiracist models for white people are constructed out of guilt. We recognize that feelings of guilt, as one begins to fully realize the extent of the realities of racism, are an important part of a heartfelt process of conscious development. Guilt is a place to visit, not a place to live. When guilt becomes the operating force of white people involved in antiracist work, their work and relationships are negatively impacted. Some examples of this are placing people of color on an unrealistic pedestal and a disassociation from whiteness and white people. Disassociation from whiteness can lead to cultural tourism, rejection and judgment of white people, and the inability to fully embrace all parts of oneself. White people driven by guilt (consciously or unconsciously) are limited in their ability to be effective allies in multi-racial movements and in building radical white communities of resistance.

Old View of Race

In a traditional liberal analysis, racism is seen as the source of racial oppression. This means that in the liberal model there are two roles: oppressor and oppressed. This model tells white people that they are only in the role of oppressor and have no common bonds with people of color and no stake in changing a racist system.

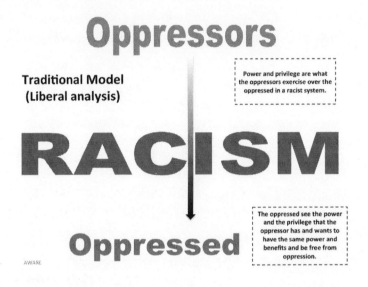

Oppressors

**Traditional Model
(Liberal analysis)**

Power and privilege are what the oppressors exercise over the oppressed in a racist system.

RAC|SM

The oppressed see the power and the privilege that the oppressor has and wants to have the same power and benefits and be free from oppression.

Oppressed

AWARE

New Views on Race

We see racism as a tool of the larger system of white dominance. The white ruling elite has power and class interests in keeping white people and people of color divided. For example, one of the very early formations of racism in law and custom in our country was motivated by the desire to break any potential bonds between poor European indentured servants and enslaved Africans. When the system is hidden, it obscures the role of the white ruling elite, the complexity of the differences among white people, and the power of white people and people of color uniting to create a road to fundamental change. With an understanding of the system of white dominance, a white person can also see that ending the system's control allows for the fullness of their humanity, because in denying the humanity of another we also deny our own.

White Supremacy System

RACISM

Racism is a TOOL of white supremacy. Racism is systemic but it is not the larger oppressive system of White Supremacy operating in US.

Forging a New Way of Being White

With this way of thinking we can begin to create an alternative racial identity for white people. All human beings must develop and sustain a healthy self-identity in order to thrive. This is particularly important for people who commit to a life struggling against the injustices of the system of white dominance. It is important for white people who challenge and fight the injustices of racism to have an honest sense of self without hiding or dismissing any of their realities. We've witnessed that white people who have developed this holistic radical white identity can sustain the struggle against racism; they are able to challenge, connect, and bring more white people into the struggle and to create and maintain honest relationships with people of color.

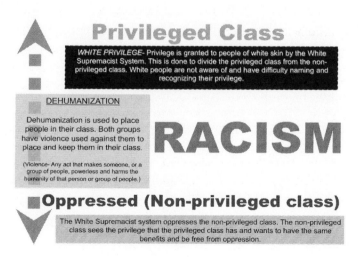

Privileged Class

WHITE PRIVILEGE- Privilege is granted to people of white skin by the White Supremacist System. This is done to divide the privileged class from the non-privileged class. White people are not aware of and have difficulty naming and recognizing their privilege.

DEHUMANIZATION

Dehumanization is used to place people in their class. Both groups have violence used against them to place and keep them in their class.

(Violence- Any act that makes someone, or a group of people, powerless and harms the humanity of that person or group of people.)

RACISM

Oppressed (Non-privileged class)

The White Supremacist system oppresses the non-privileged class. The non-privileged class sees the privilege that the privileged class has and wants to have the same benefits and be free from oppression.

The liberation movements of the 1960s are examples of the power of radical racial identities to transform communities. During this movement era, many communities of color developed radical racial identities, such as the Black Power, Asian American, and Chicano identities. These identities challenged the dominant, socially constructed, oppressive identities that had been forced on them by a system of white dominance. These racial identities stressed reconnecting with one's stolen cultural roots, resisting the system of white dominance through political and social struggle, and creating an identity based on self-expression and creation of culture. These identities offered people of color a way to resist the system of white dominance, take control of their communities, and claim their own culture.

RADICAL WHITE IDENTITY

4. PRACTICE FOR LIBERATION

Active resistance to White Supremacy by:

- Ongoing practice of decoding white privilege and racism.

- Connecting with other white anti-racists and building radical white community.

- Form alliances with people of color to work in solidarity for racial, economic, social, and environmental justice.

- Actively work to undermine white supremacy in ourselves, our communities and the world.

3. UNDERSTAND SOCIAL POSITION

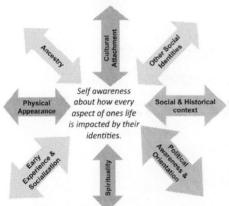

Self awareness about how every aspect of ones life is impacted by their identities.

Continually reflecting on and naming the realities of WHITE SKIN PRIVILEGE in every aspect of our lives.

2. HISTORY

White Anti-Racist people's history of resistance

1. ROOTS

Understands how one's connection or lack of connection to their ethnic Identity or heritage was the price of assimilation and it shapes one's racial identity

Radical White Identity model is based on three assumptions. 1st: White people have a stake in ending the White Supremacist System. 2nd: White people need to shed White Supremacist Culture to be fully human. And 3rd: When white people take up antiracist work, we are true allies in the struggle to end the system of white dominance. With these assumptions, we found a basis for creating a radical white identity.

Culture is an integral part of racial identity. It is our culture(s) that allows us to define who we are, our values, and what makes us distinct and unique from one another. Some elements of an alternative white culture include redefining social relationships, the creation of art that embraces a new vision of whiteness, and the participation in rituals of celebration and community.

Breaking It Down: Components of the Radical White Identity Model

The development of the radical white identity is an ongoing process based on the following core pieces:

1. Understanding white privilege

2. Ethnic/religious/cultural roots

3. Multiple identities

4. History of multiracial struggle and white antiracist resistance

5. White antiracist practice

Understanding White Privilege - All white people raised in this society are granted fundamental privilege in all institutions and aspects of U.S. culture. This white skin privilege is granted differently based on one's socioeconomic class, gender, sexual orientation, physical ability, and age. The white privilege we receive shapes our whole lives and how we experience our racial selves. White culture and racial identity are made invisible to white people. We are like fish that do not know we are swimming in water—it is everywhere, and yet we do not know how to see it or name it. It is difficult to understand how our actions and behaviors, which are not intentionally racist in many cases, can be oppressive to people of color. Through uncovering "cultural norms" of white privilege, we can begin to change and modify them so we are not acting out our ignorant racism, cultural racism, or institutional systems of white dominance. It is important to be continuously engaged in a process of uncovering how white skin privilege shapes who we are and how we relate to the world around us. We also need to explore how we can use privilege to undermine the larger system of white dominance. In our work we have found that for many white people, the process of uncovering our privilege is a challenging and transformative process. For many, this is the beginning of a journey to awareness and fundamental change.

Ethnic/Religious/Cultural Roots - As white people we have tremendous privilege, but it has not been without a price. When we came to this country we were not "white." We were Irish, Jewish, Russian, Italian, etc. Our ethnic identity was our primary identity, and it linked us to our community and culture. The dominant white racial identity was created through the process of assimilation. This meant people from European countries would be allowed access in this country as long as they left their customs, traditions, cultural practices, and social norms behind and assimilated to become (white) "Americans."

When European immigrants came to the United States there was immediate pressure to change their cultural practices and act "American." There were many "educational" services offered by churches and charity organizations that "taught" these immigrants how to leave behind their identities. More blatant measures were expressed in stories in newspapers and magazines, like the New York Times, Harpers, Atlantic Monthly, and other publications. In 1877, the New York Tribune identified the Irish as "a race with more wholesome and probably unreasonable terror of law than any other...Is there no other way [besides violence] to civilize them? This editorialist wanted to know."[3]

In her book, *Learning to Be White*, Thandeka writes that in the 1870s the Chicago Times "characterized the city's Slavic inhabitants as descendants of Scythians, "eaters of raw animal food, fond of drinking blood of their enemies... Let us whip these Slavic wolves back to the European dens from which they issue, or in some way exterminate them." [11] One of the primary ways of becoming "American" and erasing one's ethnic culture was to become a consumer. European immigrants were told to act "American" by becoming consumers of "basic necessities." Immigrants were actively discouraged from their own cultural practices, such as making clothes or home remedies—these were to be replaced with consumable goods and services. The market, butcher, and tailor were all offered to replace our ability to provide for ourselves.

Today, most white people think of themselves as having no real culture. We look at communities of color and see culture lacking in our own lives. These feelings leave a void in white people that causes us to develop oppressive solutions for filling this void. Sometimes white people appropriate the cultures of people of color. For example, white people embrace Native

American spiritual practice without reflection or consideration, or we deny any sense of racial identity, focusing on everyone being a colorless human or part of an indistinct colorful rainbow.

It is up to each individual to decide how we want to connect to our ethnic roots. But, all white people need to understand the history of assimilation into the dominant white race. It is important to understand that the primary way to assimilate people is to sever them from their ethnic and cultural roots and that this process has a profound impact on the humanity of a community.

Multiple Identities - Our whiteness always exists in relationship to other aspects of our identity. It is tempting to oversimplify for the sake of clarity when exploring our white identity. However, when we do this we are not telling the whole story. While we must strive to understand our whiteness, we have to be aware of all the different identities that make up who we are. One's class, gender, sexual orientation, and age all interact with racial identity and white privilege. When we see our overlapping identities, we can recognize the interlocking nature of oppressions and privilege. A poor white lesbian living in the South is very different from a CEO who runs a Fortune 500 company. Both of these people are white and share racial privilege, yet society treats them very differently because of the realities of their other identities. Ultimately, all systems of oppression are constructed around supremacy of one group exercising power over another. We must challenge and understand the interlocking nature of how our identities interact and shape one another.

What's missing from US social justice history?

- The original Rainbow Coalition
- Poor whites who were allying themselves with slaves
- The creation of white racial identity through the legal system in the US
- Anne Braden
- Maroon Societies of resistance
- The first group of people attacked by the KKK
- The history of multiracial struggles and white people resisting and working to end racism and white supremacy in the US.

History of Multi-Racial Struggle & Radical White Antiracists Resistance-
For any culture to exist it must have a history. Radical white people have a
history of resistance to white supremacy dating back to the founding of this
country. Millions of white people have stood against racism and white supremacy throughout our 400-year existence, but the history of white people
actively resisting the systems of white dominance has been covered over
and lost.

We never read in a standard high school history text about how a white
ruling class elite imposed a system of white dominance not only on people
of color, but on white people, too. We also do not learn the history of how
some white people have actively resisted racism, becoming potential role
models for those who have followed in their footsteps. We never learn about
multiracial efforts to come together to fight white supremacy. These individuals and groups serve as role models and are shining examples of resistance
and sources of inspiration—but only if we are aware of them. The history
of resistance in this country also includes countless examples of effective
multiracial coalitions. In the mid 1960s in Chicago, for example, the Black
Panther Party formed the original Rainbow Coalition with the Young Lords
(Puerto Rican youth group) and the Young Patriots, a group of white working-class radical youth who organized in white communities in Chicago.[5]

White Antiracist Practice - At the core of our model is a white antiracist
practice that grows from a holistic foundation. As white people we need to
develop a conscious practice that provides meaningful tools to stand against
systemic racism and that teaches how to participate in a multi-racial society
in ways that do not perpetuate oppression. An antiracist practice involves
actively working to build alliances with other white people against racism
in our homes, schools, workplaces, and communities. We need to continuously practice the skills and tools for challenging personal and interpersonal
racism and engaging in cross-cultural communication. In addition, we need
to work collectively with people of color and white allies to think critically
and work collectively towards a radical systemic change that addresses the
root systems of supremacy.

A Never Ending Journey

The work of struggling against racism is life-long. The work of deepening one's clarity about her/his role in the struggle is also life-long. In or-

der to sustain this journey, conscious white people need to have a process of understanding, challenging, growing, and developing a healthy radical white identity. This is an identity that is not about arriving at a fixed destination but rather one that shifts and changes with time, knowledge, experience, and history. This is an identity that owns the multiple truths of white people's experiences, the racial skin privileges, the history of resistance to white supremacy, and a role in the process of social transformation.

Radical white identity is about the practice of antiracist work and the practice of building and sustaining authentic relationships. It is important that white people develop the skills to engage with people of color in truly respectful and accountable ways. It is also important that white people develop the skills to connect and build community with other white people, continuously growing the ranks of conscious white people ready to work for racial justice. A racial identity based on the inherent valuable and complex humanity of each person involved will lay the foundation for this important work. "The work of dismantling systematic racism and building new institutions that are not based on white power and privilege needs to be infused with a deep love for and among all of us who are working together. Antiracism work can quickly become warped if it involves white people who fundamentally do not love themselves."[6] We hope that our model will help in some way to develop and sustain white people who are able to contribute fully to the incredible task of radical racial transformation and ultimately the abolition of all systems of oppression.

We would like to thank everyone who contributed to the writing of this piece. We would like to make a special mention of the members of AWARE in Los Angeles. Thank you.

[1] p. 17, Howard, Gary: *We Can't Teach What We Don't Know:* White Teachers, Multicultural Schools

[2] For the purpose of this article we will use the term "white" to describe a socially constructed racial group made up of European Americans living in the United States.

[3] P. 49, Jacobson, Matthew Frye, Whiteness of a Different Color, Cambridge: Harvard University Press; 1998.

[4] P. 67 Thandeka, Learning To Be White, New York: Continuum Publishing Group; 2001.

[6] (http://en.wikipedia.org/wiki/Rainbow_Coalition_%28Fred_Hampton%29)

[6] Tobin Shearer, "White spaces:" The Other Side Online, (March-April 2002, Vol. 38, No. 2.)

A Love Poem

a call for compassion during the dissolution.
a plea for love while we learn our lessons.

i find a sense of alchemical process in the machinations of movement.
come again.

is it possible to transform truly, finally, from one identity to another?

faith, magic, revolution, love—words which feel similar when we live them. when we somehow and impossibly will them into being, into our very beings.

after we burn away the gross and hype, what left? essence?
soul?

the scientific search for a philosopher's stone, across our various cultural histories, depended on turning the black to white. achieving one element from another. vessels were crafted, instruments drawn up and space made for the work. detail, trial, repetition. a poet would find this rhythm mesmerizing, reflective. also allegorical, as our lives are always in transition, often fragile and secretly as destructive as they are creative.

we aim to create a better world, but where the open spaces to unpack the ugly, the history, the guilt and shame, the horror and silence, all we have accumulated through our privilege and pain, our karma and memory? are our bodies and minds, then, the vessels for the changes requisite? what tools do we bring to a new day?

there isn't enough space to hold all the evil man has done. there isn't enough time to get into it. and obviously our bodies and minds have carried the experiments on our senses through, notice how sick we are.

inherited by every generation, language corrupted. now we each decide daily what weight, what meaning, is given words, colors, ideas. now we understand we need to burn through the white. we were taught ideas (which are things, which shape the world) that took us away from each other and from our selves. we are studying, gearing for the next. we do not know what is on the other side of transformation. in america we have never not known a white day. yet.

a love letter to your soul, on a journey towards a light never binary alone.

i wish for all we need to transform from one position to another. all the while dropping the weight, always where it belongs, not picking up what doesn't belong to us. not other's pain, this we hope to alleviate by right action. not other's projections, these scatter if we see clearly.

a love letter to your soul, because we fail at loving kindness toward others when we have not mustered it for our selves.
we are students and teachers at once.

balm for your wounds as you slay your specific demons.

am so sorry for the misdirected blows.
am so thankful for the needed ones.

a letter to imagination, the only nation any of us born in.

love to courage, the only armor for the soul.

Suheir Hammad

> "If you have come to help me you are wasting your time. But if you recognize that your liberation and mine are bound up together, we can walk together."
>
> --Lila Watson

Contributors' Biographies

Esther Armah is a radio & TV host, playwright, and award-winning journalist. In New York she hosts Wake Up Call, WBAI 99.5FM's morning show, and was a commentator and guest host on GRIT-tv with Laura Flanders. Esther has written extensively on African Diaspora, how emotionality shapes personal & institutional politics, and cultural issues for The Guardian, Essence magazine, and West Africa magazine. Themes of her written work are reflected in Armah's stage plays: Can I Be Me?, Forgive Me?, Entitled!, and SAVIOUR? Esther is the creator and moderator of 'Emotional Justice Unplugged': a multi platform, multi-media, critical conversation series in New York. Her upcoming book is: 'Emotional Justice: A Kiss Goodbye to Struggle'. Follow her on Twitter @estherarmah.

Jennifer Cendaña Armas is a performer, writer, and educator from New York City dedicated to telling stories of Diaspora through multilingual text, movement, and music. This commitment is rooted in growing up in Queens immigrant barrios and the desire to represent all the racial and ethnic lineages that make up her Filipino culture. She performs and facilitates workshops globally in schools, prisons, and community centers and is a resident teaching artist at Brooklyn Academy of Music. Follow her at www.junipersupadupa.com or on Twitter @juniperposts.

Arnette Ball grew up in Brooklyn's Fort Greene Project until she was 21. She created and ran a clerical training program for welfare mothers, was a performer and co-founder of The Back Alley Theater, and was active in the Civil Rights Movement. She married Leonard Carson Ball, who was active in the civil rights movement. Their son, Jared was born when she was 38. The marriage failed soon after and she raised Jared as a single working parent. She retired from a position as Judicial Administrative Assistant to a D.C. Superior Court judge. Now, at 78, she does nothing much but love her grandchildren.

Dr. Jared A. Ball is the father of two brilliant and adorable daughters, Maisi and Marley, fortunate husband of Nelisbeth Y. Ball, and Associate Professor of Communication Studies at Morgan State University. Research interests include the interaction between colonialism, mass media theory. Ball is also editor and producer of a radio column for BlackAgendaReport.com, producer and host of Washington, DC's Pacifica Radio's "Super Funky Soul Power Hour", and founder and producer of FreeMix Radio: The Original Mixtape Radio Show, an emancipatory journalistic political mixtape. He is the author of I MiX What I Like: A MiXtape Manifesto (AK Press). For more information, please go to www.IMiXWhatILike.org.

Héctor Calderón has been a respected leader at El Puente, a community-based, holistic learning and development organization in Brooklyn, for over 20 years, and is a co-founder of El Puente Academy for Peace and Justice; his leadership has made the Academy one of the highest achieving schools New York. He is the recipient of EL DIARIO's "EL" award, recognizing influential Latinos in the tri-state area. Héctor is a member of the founding Cohort of New Leaders for New Schools. He has lectured at a range of educational forums, including Maxine Greene's Center for Social Imagination; Harvard School of Education; and the PEW Forum on Education, and has been featured in The Village Voice, The Source, and "Human Rights and Wrongs" on PBS.

Jeff Chang has written extensively on race, culture, politics, the arts, and music. His first book, Can't Stop Won't Stop, garnered honors, including the American Book Award and the Asian American Literary Award. He has also edited an anthology entitled, Total Chaos: The Art & Aesthetics of Hip-Hop, (2007), and was named a USA Ford Fellow in Literature and a winner of the North Star News Prize. Jeff was a founding editor of *Colorlines* magazine, and a Senior Editor/ Director at Russell Simmons's 360hiphop.com. He began writing for URB and The Bomb Hip-Hop magazines, and has written for the San Francisco Chronicle, Vibe, The Nation, and Mother Jones, among many others.

Richard Chavolla Originally from Phoenix, Arizona, Richard is a long-time educator and advocate for educational equity and opportunities, working at numerous and varied institutions, including the American Council on Education, Yale University, Arizona State University, and the Maricopa Community Colleges. He was Director of the Center for Multicultural Education and Programs at New York University from 2007-2011. Most recently he has worked as an educational consultant and community organizer/advocate.

Chris Crass works to build powerful working class-based, feminist, multiracial movements for collective liberation. Throughout the 1990s, he was an organizer with Food Not Bombs, an economic justice anti-poverty group strengthening the direct action-based anti-capitalist Left. In the 2000s, he was an organizer with the Catalyst Project, which combines political education and organizing to develop and support antiracist politics, leadership, and organization in white communities and builds dynamic multiracial alliances locally and nationally. He lives in Knoxville, Tennessee, with his partner and their son, River.

Edwin (Eddie) Ellis is president of the Center for NuLeadership on Urban Solutions, an independent criminal justice think tank where he is a Research Fellow with the Dubois- Bunche Institute for Economic and Public Policy. He has lectured in the US, Belguim (Brussels), and South Africa, among others. He was a member of Governor Eliot Spitzer's Transition Team and has served as consultant to President Bush's Domestic Policy Advisor, NY State Black and Puerto Rican Legislative Caucus, and the Vera Institute of Justice. Mr. Ellis is host/executive producer of New York City's WBAI-FM's "On the Count: The Prison and Criminal Justice Report". Email him at eellis@centerfornuleadership.org or eddiellis1@aol.com.

Margery Freeman has been an educator and organizer for 40 years. Her experience includes public school teaching, early childhood education and child advocacy, and adult literacy education. Margery roots her work in the principles and practices learned through her 28-year relationship with The People's Institute for Survival and Beyond, a multi-racial, antiracist organization that promotes organizing for social change. She is a core trainer/organizer with the People's Institute, leading "Undoing Racism"™ workshops across the country.

Susan B. Goldberg is an artist and facilitator of change. She has been deeply involved in naming and challenging the dominant paradigm of race, gender, culture, body, and child-raising in this country. She encourages folks who are involved in the lives of children to check out Echo Parenting and Education (formerly The Center for Nonviolent Education and Parenting). She lives with her family in the beautiful city of Los Angeles.

Dr. Perry Greene is Associate Provost for Faculty Affairs at Adelphi University, holding the rank of Associate Professor. Dr. Greene's research interests are in the areas of teacher preparation, social justice, diversity, and the education of urban youth. Published articles include "Embracing Urban Youth Culture in the Context of Education (Urban Review) and "Teaching Race: Making the Invisible Concrete" (*Teaching Race in the 21ˢᵗ Century*). He has presented on these issues at professional conferences.

Chelsea Gregory is an artist and cultural organizer working through dance, theater, and poetry. Her work has been presented at venues such as LaMama ETC, Chicago Hip-Hop Theater Festival, and Eve Ensler and Jane Fonda's co-production, *We Got Issues*. Dance performances include ASE Dance Theatre Collective and the Atlanta Ballet and her choreography has been seen with Cornerstone Theater Company's Summer Institute. Her solo piece, *The 6 Project*, explores how race and cultural identity shape our viewpoints, and has toured over 10 US cities.

Marcella Runell Hall is a scholar and author holding a doctorate in Social Justice Education. Hall has worked as a freelance writer for the *New York Times* Learning Network and *VIBE* magazine; co-edited award winning books: *The Hip-Hop Education Guidebook* (2007), *Conscious Women Rock the Page: Using Hip-Hop Fiction to Incite Social Change* (2008); and authored a children's book, *The Ten Most Influential Hip-Hop Artists* (2008). She currently serves as Director of the Center for Spiritual Life at New York University and holds a Clinical Faculty appointment in the Silver School of Social Work.

She lives in Brooklyn with her husband, David Hall, and their daughter, Aaliyah Zoe. For more info, go to www.marcellarhall.com.

Suheir Hammad is a Palestinian-American poet, author, and political activist who was born in October, 1973, in Amman, Jordan, to Palestinian refugee parents and immigrated with her family to Brooklyn, New York City, when she was five years old.

Z! Gonwa Haukeness does white racial justice organizing with Ground work White Antiracist Collective and Showing Up for Racial Justice, and housing and homelessness organizing with Operation Welcome Home and Take Back The Land-Madison. Z!'s central work is rooted in addressing racism as part of dismantling interlocking systems of oppression while working to create a world based on interlocking our liberation. Z! does this work with love for justice and community. Transgender, queer, and white with a middle-class upbringing, Z! is rooted in their experiences of privilege and oppression, while honoring legacies of visionary resistance guiding their work.

Dr. Floyd W. Hayes, III, is a Senior Lecturer in the Department of Political Science and Coordinator of Programs and Undergraduate Studies in the Center for Africana Studies at Johns Hopkins University. He has taught at a number of universities, including Purdue University, Cornell University, and Swarthmore College. Dr. Hayes's teaching and research interests include urban politics and public policy, educational policymaking and politics, and jazz and politics. He is the editor of A Turbulent Voyage: Readings in African-American Studies. He is working on a book, entitled *Domination and Resentment: The Desperate Vision of Richard Wright*.

Jeff Hitchcock is Executive Director of the Center for the Study of White American Culture (www.euroamerican.org). He belongs to the People's Institute Northeast Leadership Collective, the AntiRacist Alliance-North Jersey, and the Newark-based People's Organization for Progress.

Danny Hoch is an actor, playwright, and director whose plays have garnered many awards, including a Guggenheim Fellowship, 2 OBIE's, an NEA Solo Theatre Fellowship, 2 Sundance Fellowships, the

CalArts/Alpert Award In Theatre, and a Tennessee Williams Fellowship. His plays have toured 50 U.S. cities and 15 countries.

Baba Israel was raised in New York by parents who were core members of the Living Theatre. He has toured the world, performing with artists such as Outkast, Ron Carter, and Bill Cosby. Directorial work includes Project 2050 (New World Theatre) and Sharpening SAWDS. He was co-founder and Artistic Director of Playback NYC Theatre Company, which brought theatre to under-represented communities. He became Artistic Director/CEO of Contact, a UK theatre with young people at its core in 2009. babaisrael.com

Jonny 5 (Jamie Laurie) is an emcee with the band Flobots and a founder of the non-profit organization Flobots.org. His first public performance was at a school talent show in 1996, which he did not win. His best-known song, "Handlebars" went platinum in 2008. Between those years, he received a degree in Africana Studies from Brown University, worked as an Americorps VISTA, lived in Japan and Argentina, and constantly sought out opportunities to integrate music and social change. In 2010 he posted a new "Rhyme of the Day" to YouTube every day. He enjoys studying new languages and amateur composting, and normally does not speak in the third person.

DJ Kuttin Kandi (Candice L. Custodio-Tan) born and raised Queens, NY, is widely regarded as legendary and one of the most accomplished female DJ's in the world. She is also known as a Writer, Poet, Mentor, Hip-Hop Advocate, Activist, Feminist and Community Organizer. She is a member of DJ team champions 5th Platoon, Founder and DJ for the all female Hip-Hop group Anomolies, Cofounder of the famed NY monthly open mic nights "Guerrilla Words" and CoFounder of the coalition R.E.A.C.Hip-Hop (Representing Education, Activism & Community through Hip-Hop.) Djing for nearly 15 years, Kandi competed in over 20 DJ competitions such as ITF and Vibe. She is the NY Source Magazine DJ Champion and has been the only female DJ to make it to the DMC USA FINALs. Kandi now resides in Chula Vista, CA and currently works at the Women's Center at the University of California, San Diego (UCSD).

Talib Kweli is a Brooklyn, New York native. He is one of the most critically acclaimed, if not commercially, successful rappers in the music industry today. For over 15 years, Kweli has been a staple in the every growing world of Hip-Hop music. He is world renown not only as a solo artist but, for his work with Mos Def as the duo "Black Star" (1998). In 2000 Kweli released "Train of Thought" with his production partner Hi-Tek; together they form the group Reflection Eternal a virtuoso Hip-Hop duo that continues to wow audiences and critics alike. After years of recording for major labels, Kweli now has the chance to record for his own independent venture Blacksmith Music. With this control he is able to invoke the true meaning of MC, Master of Ceremonies by delivering his music straight to his audience as well as being a CEO. Hence his new moniker the "MCEO". Kweli brings incredible power to his live shows and feeds off the spontaneous
energy of the crowd. This summer his 7th solo release titled "Prisoner of Conscious" will be released on Blacksmith Music.

Cameron Levin has been a community organizer for 23 years. He has worked with over 35 social justice groups in Los Angeles as a freelance organizer for the past 11 years on issues ranging from environmental justice to immigrant worker rights. In 2003 he co-founded AWARE-LA (Alliance of White Antiracist Everywhere), an organization dedicated to building antiracist white bases in white communities to form alliances with people of color in the struggles for justice. Through AWARE-LA, the radical white identity model, along with a model to apply community organizing in white communities, were developed. Email him at struggle@earthlink.net.

Ariel Luckey, born and raised in Oakland, California, is a son, brother, and father whose community and performance work dances in the crossroads of education, art, and activism. Named a "Visionary" by Utne Reader, Ariel performs his Hip-Hop theater solo show, Free Land, in theaters, classrooms, and conferences across the country. He recently published his first book, a collection of poetry and lyrics, entitled Searching For White Folk Soul.

M1 of dead prez, aka Mutulu Olugabala, as one half of the fully automatic rap duo dead prez, M1 and his partner, stic.man, have been hitting hard with albums, like *Let's Get Free* and most recently *Revolutionary but Gangsta Grillz* with DJ DRAMA. He is president of the Brooklyn Chapter of the National Peoples Democratic Uhuru Movement and an activist with Malcolm X Grassroots Movement. He has traveled to the Gaza Strip, Senegal, Greece, Italy, and Zimbabwe, spreading messages of internationalism and solidarity amongst African and indigenous through the globe. He has become one of the leading political voices in Hip-Hop culture and activism.

Peggy McIntosh, Ph.D., is founder and co-director of the National SEED Project on Inclusive Curriculum (Seeking Educational Equity and Diversity). She is Associate Director of the Wellesley Center for Women at Wellesley College. Recent articles: "White Privilege: An Account to Spend" and "White People Facing Race: Uncovering Myths that Keep Racism in Place", both by the Saint Paul Foundation (2009); and "Foreword" in Karen Weekes's *Privilege and Prejudice: Twenty Years with the Invisible Knapsack.*

Inga Muscio is an antiracist, feminist author, and one of the most personally engaging public speakers of our generation. She is the author of *Cunt: A Declaration of Independence* (Seal Press, 1998) and *Autobiography of a Blue-Eyed Devil: My Life and Times in Racist and Imperialist Society* (2005). As an author and agent for social change, Muscio continues to deliver challenging and socially-defiant work in her own uniquely humorous and disarming writing style.

Dr. Pedro Noguera is the Peter L. Agnew Professor of Education in the Steinhardt School of Culture, Education, and Development at New York University. He also serves as the Director of the Metropolitan Center for Urban Education and the Co-Director of the Institute for the Study of Globalization and Education in Metropolitan Settings (IGEMS). He is the author of several groundbreaking books and has published over 150 research articles, monographs, and reports on topics, such as urban school reform, conditions that promote student achievement, youth violence, and race and ethnic relations in American society.

Kevin Powell is an activist, public speaker, and the author or editor of 11 books, including his newest title, *Barack Obama, Ronald Reagan,* *and The Ghost of Dr. King: Blogs and Essays*. Email him at kevin@ kevinpowell.net, or follow him on twitter @kevin_powell.

Sofia Quintero Self-proclaimed Ivy League homegirl is the president of Sister Outsider entertainment. She is the author of several novels across genres, including feminist Hip-Hop noir (written as Black Artemis) and the award-winning young adult novel, *Efrain's Secret*. Sofia wrote and co-produced the short film *Corporate Dawgz*, a co-medic ode to White people who "get" it. To learn more about Sofia and her work, visit blackartemis.com; follow her on Twitter, or like her Facebook page at https://www.facebook.com/pages/Sofia-Quintero-aka-Black-Artemis

Sonia Sanchez Poet. Mother. Professor. Lecturer on Black Culture and Literature, Women's Liberation, Peace, and Racial Justice. Sonia Sanchez is the author of over 20 books and recipient of prestigious awards, including a National Endowment for the Arts, the Community Service Award from the National Black Caucus of State Legislators, American Book Award for *Homegirls and Handgrenades*, and the Peace and Freedom Award from Women International League for Peace and Freedom. She is featured in "Freedom Sisters," an exhibition created by the Cincinnati Museum Center and Smithsonian Institution Traveling Exhibition Sites. In 2011, Philadelphia Mayor Michael Nutter selected Sanchez as Philadelphia's first Poet Laureate, calling her "the longtime conscience of the city."

April R. Silver is a social entrepreneur, activist, and writer/editor based in New York. The former talk show host of *My Two Cents* (Centric TV) is also editor of *"Be A Father to Your Child: Real Talk from Black Men on Family, Love, and Fatherhood." Black Voices* cited the anthology as "...groundbreaking..." *Foreword* said that Silver turned "her first book into a must-read for anyone involved in the black community."A graduate of Howard University, she co-led the historic 1989 student protest. While in college, Silver was also the founding president of *The Cultural Initiative* – the nation's first hip hop conference which birthed the hip hop education movement. Since, she has also established, co-founded, and/or financed several *arts and activism*® projects, including *HipHop Speaks!* with Kevin

Powell and *PoetrySpeaks!* for the NY Chapter of the GRAMMYS® (where she served as a Governor). April's writings have been published in the NY *Daily News, Brainwashed: Challenging the Myth of Black Inferiority, Put Your Dreams First*, allhiphop.com, and other outlets. Silver has been covered by *Ebony, Essence, Ms., CNN, Time, Newsweek, The Washington Post*, and many other national and international outlets.

Tim Wise is among the nation's most prominent white antiracist educators, writers, and activists. He is the author of five books on race and racism and lectures across the United States about institutional racism, white privilege, and the ongoing struggle for justice and equity.

Jasiri X, emcee and community activist is the creative force behind the internet news series, "This Week with Jasiri X," which has garnered critical acclaim. From "What if the Tea Party was Black?" to "A Song for Trayvon", Jasiri uses Hip-Hop to provide social commentary. Guest appearances include *BET Rap City, Free Speech TV,* and *Russia Today.* He recently became the first Hip-Hop artist to receive the August Wilson Center for African-American Culture Fellowship. A founding member of the anti-violence group, One Hood, Jasiri started the New Media Academy to teach young African-American boys how to analyze and create media for themselves. He is currently working on his album, *Ascension*, with acclaimed producer Rel!g!on.

Index

Acknowledgements

Dedication: The book is dedicated to a very special young woman who left before her time and who is deeply missed: Kibibi Dillon.

A Note About the Title: A big thank you to Rosa Clemente who called me one day and said, "I have the perfect title for your book!" Rosa thank you for being such a profoundly loving (mostly tough-loving lol) my ride or die sista, warrior, my friend.

As well, artivist Ariel Luckey coined the term "occupying privilege" for a workshop series he developed and graciously allowed me to use the title for the book. Thanks, family!

❖ ❖ ❖

A special thank you to my angel editor, Nan Gatewood Satter, who spent hours and hours with me in pursuit of a solid body of work. When she heard that 100% of the proceeds were being donated to racial justice organizations, she made a major contribution by donating much of her time. Her generosity, and that of her husband, Andy Satter, speaks volumes.

Super big hugs to Agnieszka "Nikki" Orzel at Phoenix Studios who created the book cover and all the interior design—the amount of hours we spent going over this—she deserves a medal!!

My brilliant copyeditor Rachel Briggs—always appreciate and respect the Grammar Goddess!

Thank you to all the contributors who have spent their valuable time, energy, and insight to this book. I am truly humbled and honored to share space with you all.

My family: My husband is my light—a continuing inspiration after 15 years of love-n-life—looking forward to spending eternity with you! My beautiful children, Gabriel Amani and Camilo Mandela—your light shines from within, and brightens the world with love. To my beautiful Mom, thank you for always being there for me! To my amazingly creative and supportive Dad, can't wait until "all of a sudden." Peter and Shannon, John and Joahna, Millie and Natasha—thank you for your continued love and support. Eternal thanks to my father in-law, Héctor, Sr., who religiously takes care of my kids while I work and more importantly, shows them how to be independent and kind young men. Love to Nina, Jose, Carmen, Kiko, Alma, and Ana Calderón.

My friends and community: Asia-One, Jen Armas, Rosa Clemente, Justice, Heidi Marshall, Johnny Sanchez, Wanda Vazquez, Marcella Runell Hall and family, Suheir Hammad, Julia Grob, Kahlil Almustafa, Kelly Tsai, Sofia Quintero, Adeeba Rana, Lah Tere, Marti Champion, Anda Seale and family, Joanna Spears and family, Kim Peters, Vania Gallegos, Lalania Carrillo, Faatma, Inga, Iraida and family, Jasiri X, Kuttin Kandi and Rob, Amaryllis Dejesus Moleski, Ben Snyder, Rha Goddess, Queen Godis, Ashara, Ietef, Dana Balacki, Mo Beasley, Byron Hurt, Chelsea Gregory, B-Fresh, Cathy Appleton, Dan Charnas, Cristina Veran, DJ Chela, Dominic Colon, Peter Miranda, Frances and Luis and my entire El Puente community, my We Got Issues Tribe, April R. Silver and The Akila Worksongs Family, Thysha Shabazz, Shaun Neblitt, Esther Armah, Fritz, Rebel Diaz, Lathan Hodge, Marc Ecko, Katie, Kazi, KET, the Museum of Hip-Hop, Jonny 5 and the Flobots, MARE 139, Piper Anderson, Rafael Planten, Sacha Jenkins, Marlo Taylor, Toofly, Josh and Tresa Thomases, Adam Mansbach, Kevin Powell, Jacquelyn Alutto, Ami Desai, Jeff Campbell, Jay Mason, Dennis Wakabyashi, Sam and Brandy Barnes and family, my new SURJ family of white people showing up for racial justice, my wonderful intern Analie Javier, El Puente Academy's Ana Lazala and our young women's group, the Fly Girl Fest movement, my hair stylist who always looks out for me Andrea, Angeliq and Brooklyn, Annetta Marion—my TV visionary!, Ari Issler, Baba, Dawn and baby, Brooke Emery, Caits Meissner, Todd Hunter, Felicia and Speak Out community, my wonderful lawyer Suzanne, Terrence and The Prodigal Son.

Love Letters excerpted from *Love, Race, and Liberation; 'Til the White Day is Done* (edited by Marcella Runell Hall and JLove Calderón): A heartfelt thanks to our Love Letter writers for showing how love, vulnerability, and speaking your personal truths are key ingredients of courage.

This book is one initiative of the multi-media project '*Til the White Day is Done*. Many people have generously written, been interviewed, filmed, and otherwise supported the project. A special thanks to all those who have been instrumental in the journey of creating progressive, socially conscious, educational materials to inspire a more just world, especially: Dr. Jared Ball and his mother Arnette Ball, John Carluccio, Todd Chandler, Jeff Chang, Dr. Perry Greene, Chelsea Gregory, Baba Israel, Corey Kupfer, Talib Kweli, Cameron Levin, Miguel Luciano, Danny Hoch, M1, Victoria Sanders, Inga Muscio, Terrence Nance, Tim Wise, Adeeba Rana, Andy Ross, Sonia Sanchez, MC Serch, April R. Silver, Spacecraft, Kelly Tsai, Ariel Luckey, Paul Kivel, and Venus.

The Project: *'Til the White Day is Done* is a multi-media project focusing on racism and white privilege involving a multi-dimensional and interactive experience through the arts, education, and entertainment. It includes this book, the curriculum guide, Love, Race, and Liberation, edited by JLove Calderón & Marcella Runell Hall, a full length documentary *White in America*, created and produced by JLove Calderón, and a national town hall style tour.

And to everyone who came before us,
                thank you for your courage and commitment.

Occupy Denver Music Video 'The 99th Problem'

Features Jonny 5 of Flobots, Bravo One, Aja Black, T Minus Katlyn, Dyalekt

Dyalekt (Diamond Boiz)

We are the 99, but we aint being heard/
So we took to the streets, let freedom speak
they dismissed our concerns/
Used the corporate media to say that we're confused/
While the rich folks were amused,
they sent in the boys in blue/
Like we aint know you would cross our path
Like you always have, try to push us back/
I'm Apache man, I would know about that/
Now everybody pissed you aint even gotta ask/
Our country says all is being done/
But we gotta 99 problems and the rich aint one-Cmon!

Bravo One (One Eyed Kings)

We are the 99 percenters, you either riding with us/
Or you dividing us, death to the corporate lobbyists/
Death to the politics that's keeping us impoverished/
These politicians dipping in our wallets just to pocket it/
Can I get a witness? Children living sick as shit/
Big businesses ballin' like they shooting the "Big Pimpin'" vid/
We living it, in a world colonized by dollar signs/
Bottom line, we taking it back, together we occupy...

Aja Black (The ReMINDers)

Credit cards maxed out-Light bill, overdue
Loan payments backed up
whats this country coming to
When a momma cant afford no medicine

to bring down her babies fever
We not looking for help from the president
cause he aint gonna do ish either
How can we save for future we still paying for our past
Up to the neck in loans and debt and the waters rising fast
We standin' strong up in these streets in solidarity as proof
We gonna occupy the system and the nation and the booth!

Mane Rok (ManeLine/En Stereo)

Yeah it's socialism-what we've gave to the rich//
Like a wrecked relationship it's what made us all bitch//
Sick & tired from not being covered-American Dreaming//
Believin' we 're equal but the equation aint even//
I percent holds 99 in the palm of their hands//
99 raises their fist-Obama be damned//
We've hoped for change since they broke the chains
now we know the game//
American Revolution Part 2-Here we go again!!

T Minus Katlyn (Wheel Chair Sports Camp)

we're here to peacefully occupy
the already occupied land
poverty lost to find chance,
sovereignty crossed from our hands
to nominees bossed to sign scams,
a wall designed to block out natives &
pirates, but welcomed rich rapists with silence
disparities, american parodies, dismissed equality
made our dreams rarities with lacking corporate policies
this is way bigger than any proposed pension plans
leaderless with demands far greater than most attention spans

(cont.next pg)

Jonny 5

The whole world is watching
the whole world is listening - wait the
whole world has switched off the screen and is participating!
the revolution will be simulcast
as the vinyl scratches the 99
I'll slap you with some vital stats
1 people

1 planet fragile as a china glass
0 corporate charters that claim their bottom line is that
it's time to act
dial it past 11 like spinal tap
amplify our movement into a survival pact

Made in the
USA
Monee, IL